THE POPULAR DICTIONARY *of* BIBLE PROPHECY

RON RHODES

HARVEST HOUSE PUBLISHERS
EUGENE, OREGON

Cover by Dugan Design Group, Bloomington, Minnesota

THE POPULAR DICTIONARY OF BIBLE PROPHECY

Published by Harvest House Publishers
Eugene, Oregon 97402

ISBN 978-1-61664-156-6

Printed in the United States of America

To my wife, Kerri

Acknowledgments

I want to express my continued appreciation to my friends at Harvest House Publishers for their ongoing commitment to publishing books that help Christians to both understand and apply the Word of God to their lives. I especially single out Harvest House's president, Bob Hawkins, Jr., for his unbending commitment to the defense of the truth.

Also, as always, I thank my wife Kerri for the countless ways she blesses me every day with random acts of kindness. She is truly a pearl of Christ.

Finally, a big hug to my son David and daughter Kylie, now college students, who daily give my wife and I unceasing reason to praise God for the wonderful gift that they are to us.

Introduction

The study of prophecy or the end times is known in theological circles as *eschatology.* This term is derived from two Greek words: *eschatos,* meaning "last" or "last things," and *logos,* meaning "study of." *Eschatology* is the study of last things, or study of the end times.

Eschatology can logically be broken down into two primary fields of study. *Personal eschatology* concerns such things as death, the future judgment, heaven, and hell. (These are matters related to each person.) *General eschatology* concerns more general matters, such as the rapture, the Tribulation, the second coming of Christ, the millennial kingdom, and the eternal state. For your benefit, this dictionary contains common terms related to both personal and general eschatology.

A

24 Elders

See *Elders, 24.*

666

In Revelation 13:18, the number 666 is used in reference to the Antichrist: "If anyone has insight, let him calculate the number of the beast, for it is man's number. His number is 666."

Bible interpreters have offered many suggestions as to the meaning of 666 through the centuries. A popular theory is that inasmuch as the number 7 is a number of perfection, and the number 777 is a number reflecting the perfect Trinity, perhaps 666 points to a being who aspires to perfect deity (like the Trinity), but never attains it. (In reality, the Antichrist is ultimately just a man, though influenced—and possibly indwelt—by Satan.)

Others have suggested that perhaps the number refers to a specific man—such as the Roman emperor Nero. It is suggested that if Nero's name is translated into the Hebrew language, the numerical value of its letters is 666. Of course, all this is highly speculative.

The truth is, Scripture doesn't clearly define what is meant by 666. Hence, interpreting this verse involves some guesswork.

A

1948

See *Israel, Rebirth of.*
See *Regathering of Jews to Homeland, Necessity of.*

144,000

In Revelation 7:4, we read, "Then I heard the number of those who were sealed: 144,000 from all the tribes of Israel." Some modern Christians have taken this as metaphorically referring to the church. However, the context indicates the verse is referring to 144,000 Jewish men—twelve thousand from each tribe—who live during the future Tribulation period (see Revelation 14:4). The very fact that specific tribes are mentioned in this context along with specific numbers for those tribes (twelve) removes all possibility that this is a figure of speech. Nowhere else in the Bible does a reference to the twelve tribes of Israel mean anything but the twelve tribes of Israel. Indeed, the word "tribe" is never used of anything but a literal ethnic group in Scripture.

The backdrop to a proper understanding of the 144,000 during the Tribulation is that God had originally chosen the Jews to be His witnesses, their appointed task being to share the good news of God with all other people around the world (see Isaiah 42:6; 43:10). The Jews were to be God's *representatives* to the Gentile peoples. The Jews failed at this task, especially since they did not even recognize Jesus as the divine Messiah, but nevertheless this was their calling. During the future Tribulation, these 144,000 Jews—who become believers in Jesus the divine Messiah—will finally fulfill this mandate from God, as they will be His witnesses all around the world.

Some have wondered why the Old Testament tribes of Dan and Ephraim are omitted from this list of Jewish tribes. The Old Testament has some twenty variant lists of tribes. Hence, no list of the twelve tribes of Israel must be identical. Most scholars today agree that the reason Dan's tribe was omitted was because that tribe was guilty of idolatry on many occasions and, as a result, was largely obliterated (Leviticus

24:11; Judges 18:1,30). To engage in unrepentant idolatry is to be cut off from God's blessing. The tribe of Ephraim—like the tribe of Dan—was also involved in idolatry and paganized worship (Judges 17; Hosea 4:17). Hence, both tribes were omitted from Revelation 7.

Others have wondered why the tribe of Levi was included in the list of Jewish tribes rather than maintaining its special status as a priestly tribe under the Mosaic Law. It is probable that the tribe of Levi is included here because the priestly functions of the tribe of Levi ceased with the coming of Christ—the ultimate High Priest. Indeed, the Levitical priesthood was fulfilled in the person of Christ (Hebrews 7–10). Because there was no further need for the services of the tribe of Levi as priests, there was no further reason for keeping this tribe distinct and separate from the others; hence, they were properly included in the tribal listing in the book of Revelation.

200 Million

In Revelation 9:16 (ASV) we read of a large army in which "the number of the armies of the horsemen was twice ten thousand times ten thousand" (which is 200 million). Through the years there have been many who have assumed this must refer to the army of China, since China has long claimed to be able to mount an army of 200 million. Contextually, however, this does not seem to make sense. These 200 million are said to be led by four fallen angels (Revelation 9:14-15). Besides, the description of these "mounted troops" appears to be anything but human in verse 17. Apparently, these are demonic spirits who—under the leadership of four fallen angels—bring about mass murder among humans (see verses 15 and 18).

Abaddon

The term Abaddon, from the Hebrew word *Abaddon,* meaning "destruction" (see Job 26:6; 28:22; 31:12; Psalm 88:11; Proverbs 15:11; 27:20), is used in several senses in the Bible. In some contexts it can refer to the abode of the dead or the grave—a place of destruction. It can also refer to death, the grave, and general ruin. In Revelation 9:11, however, the term refers to a destroyer angel who reigns over the abyss—the world of the dead known as the "bottomless pit" (Revelation 9:1 NASB).

Abomination of Desolation

In the book of Daniel (see 9:27; 11:31; 12:11), the term "abomination that causes desolation" conveys a sense of outrage or horror at the witnessing of a barbaric act of idolatry within God's holy temple. Such acts utterly profane and desecrate the temple.

In Daniel 11:31, we read of the Antichrist, "His armed forces will rise up to desecrate the temple fortress and will abolish the daily sacrifice. Then they will set up the abomination that causes desolation." We find further clarity on this "abomination that causes desolation" in the New Testament. This abomination will take place at the midpoint during the future Tribulation period when the Antichrist—the "man of lawlessness" (2 Thessalonians 2:4)—sets up an image of himself inside the Jewish temple (see Daniel 9:27; Matthew 24:15). This amounts to the Antichrist enthroning himself in the place of deity, displaying himself as God (compare with Isaiah 14:13-14 and Ezekiel 28:2-9). This blasphemous act will utterly desecrate the temple, making it abominable, and therefore desolate. The Antichrist—the world dictator—will then demand that the world worship and pay idolatrous homage to him. Any who refuse will be persecuted and even martyred. The false prophet, who is the Antichrist's lieutenant, will see to this.

An abomination took place on a lesser scale in 168 B.C. At that time, Antiochus Epiphanes erected an altar to Zeus in the temple at Jerusalem and sacrificed a pig, an unclean animal, on it. Antiochus Epiphanes was thus a prototype of the future Antichrist.

We should note that some Bible expositors—particularly of the amillennial and preterist persuasions—see the abomination of desolation spoken of in Matthew 24:15 as being fulfilled when Titus and his

Roman warriors overran Jerusalem and destroyed the Jewish temple. However, Paul's prophetic discussion of this event in 2 Thessalonians 2 would seem to demand that this "abomination" occur in reference to the Antichrist during the future Tribulation. More specifically, the Antichrist will seek to take God's place in the temple and make people bow down and worship him (2 Thessalonians 2:3-4).

Abrahamic Covenant

A very famous covenant is God's covenant with Abraham (Genesis 12:1-3; 15:18-21), which was later reaffirmed with Isaac (17:21) and Jacob (35:10-12). In this covenant, God promised to make Abraham's descendants His own special people. More specifically, God promised Abraham:

1. I will make you a great nation.
2. I will bless you.
3. I will make your name great.
4. You will be a blessing.
5. I will bless those who bless you.
6. I will curse those who curse you.
7. All peoples on earth will be blessed through you.
8. I will give you the land of Canaan.

These covenant promises were "unconditional" in nature. As a backdrop, there were two kinds of covenants in biblical days: conditional and unconditional. A conditional covenant is a covenant with an "if" attached. This type of covenant demanded that the people meet certain obligations or conditions before God was obligated to fulfill that which was promised. If God's people failed in meeting the conditions, God was not obligated in any way to fulfill the promise.

As opposed to this, an unconditional covenant depended on no such conditions for its fulfillment. There were no "ifs" attached. That which was promised was sovereignly given to the recipient of the covenant apart from any merit (or lack thereof) on the part of the recipient. Some scholars refer to this type of covenant as a "unilateral covenant," or "one-sided covenant," or "divine commitment covenant."

The covenant God made with Abraham was unconditional in nature. It is characterized by God's "I will," indicating that God was determined to do just as He promised.

Abraham's Bosom

Bible expositors have held to different interpretations of Abraham's bosom through the years. There are two primary views:

The Hades view. According to this view, there were two compartments in Hades (the realm of the dead)—one for the saved and another for the unsaved. They were separated by a "great chasm" which no man could pass (Luke 16:26). The section for the saved was called "Abraham's bosom" (see verse 23 NASB). The section for the unsaved was called "Torments."

This view holds that when Christ, as the "firstfruits" of the resurrection (1 Corinthians 15:20), ascended, He led these Old Testament saints from Abraham's bosom into heaven with Him for the first time. It is believed that Ephesians 4:8 may relate to this Christ-led transfer: "When he ascended on high, he led captives in his train and gave gifts to men." It is also believed that Revelation 1:18 may relate to this event, since Christ is portrayed as the One who holds "the keys of death and Hades." Christ is said to have "unlocked" Hades for the righteous dead (Old Testament believers) and taken them to heaven.

The heaven view. Contrary to the Hades view, this view (my view) holds that the souls of Old Testament believers went directly to heaven the moment they died. For example, the psalmist believed he would be directly in the presence of God upon the moment of death, finding pleasure and fullness of joy in His presence (Psalm 16:10-11). Moreover, God took Enoch to be with Himself in heaven (Genesis 5:24;

see also Hebrews 11:5), and Elijah was caught up into heaven when he departed (2 Kings 2:1).

We also note David's assurance of going to heaven upon the moment of death. In the classic Psalm 23, David reflected: "Surely goodness and love will follow me all the days of my life, and *I will dwell in the house of the LORD forever*" (verse 6, emphasis added). David's hope was the same as that of the apostle Paul: to be "away from the body and at home with the Lord" (2 Corinthians 5:8).

In keeping with this, when Moses and Elijah (who had long departed earthly life) appeared to Christ on the Mount of Transfiguration, they apparently appeared directly from heaven (Matthew 17:3). It seems clear that their habitat had not been some intermediate compartment of Hades.

In this view, Abraham's bosom (Luke 16:23) is considered a metaphorical description of heaven. It is the place to which Abraham went, which apparently is equated with the "kingdom of heaven" (see Matthew 8:11). Abraham's bosom is a figurative phrase for paradise, or the presence of God.

Finally, this view holds that when Christ "led captivity captive" (Ephesians 4:8 NKJV), He was not leading friends into heaven, but rather bringing foes into bondage. It is a reference to His conquering the forces of evil. After all, Christians could never be considered "captives" in Abraham's bosom. We get to heaven by our own free choice (see Matthew 23:37; 2 Peter 3:9). Hence, while a number of highly respected theologians have held to the Hades view, I believe the heaven view is most consistent with Scripture.

Abyss

The abyss is the abode of imprisoned demons or disobedient spirits (Revelation 9:1-21), and is the place to which Jesus sent demons when He expelled them from people, a place which they clearly dreaded to go to (Luke 8:31). In the NASB, this term is translated two times as "the bottomless pit" (Revelation 9:1,2) and five times as "the abyss" (Luke 8:31; Romans 10:7; Revelation 9:11; 11:12; 17:8; 20:1,3). It is portrayed as a well-like domain from which smoke ascends (Revelation 9:2).

Scripture reveals that during the future Tribulation, myriads of these imprisoned demons will be let loose to promote apostasy and rebellion against God. However, at the second coming of Christ, Satan will be cast into the abyss where he will remain imprisoned during Christ's thousand-year millennial kingdom (Revelation 20:1-3). Descending into the abyss is presented in Scripture as a noted contrast to ascending into heaven.

Advent

The term *advent* means "coming" or "arrival." The *First Advent* thus refers to the first coming of Christ. This coming was with a view to providing salvation through His death on the cross. The *Second Advent* refers to the second coming of Christ. This is a coming in glory in the end times, after which He will set up His millennial kingdom.

Age to Come

The term *age to come* refers to the future millennial kingdom over which Christ will rule (Revelation 20:3). This is in contrast to *the present age,* which refers to the present Church Age.

Ages of Time

Scripture is not absolutely clear about the relationship between time and eternity. Some prefer to think of eternity as time—a succession of moments—without beginning or ending. However, there are indications in Scripture that time itself may be a created reality, a reality that began when God created the universe.

The book of Hebrews contains some hints regarding the relationship between time and eternity. Hebrews 1:2 tells us that the Father "has spoken to us by his Son, whom he appointed heir of all things, and through whom he made *the universe*" (emphasis added). The last part of this verse is rendered more literally from the Greek, "through whom he made *the ages.*" Likewise, Hebrews 11:3 tells us that "by faith we understand that *the universe* was formed at God's command" (emphasis added). This is more literally from the Greek, "By faith we understand that *the ages* were formed at God's command."

Scholars have grappled with what may be meant here by the term *ages.* It may refer not just to vast periods of time as mere time, but also to all that transpires in them. It may refer to the whole created universe of space and time. In keeping with this, church father and philosopher Augustine (A.D. 354–430) held that the universe was not created in time, but that time itself was created *along with* the universe. Put another way, the world was created *with* time rather than *in* time.

In view of the above, we may conclude that when the apostle John said "In the beginning was the Word, and the Word was with God, and the Word was God" (John 1:1), the phrase *in the beginning* has specific reference to the beginning of time when the universe was created. When the time-space universe came into being, Christ the divine Word was already existing in a loving, intimate relationship with the Father and the Holy Spirit.

Allegory

Whether a person takes prophetic passages literally or allegorically will largely determine what theological system he adheres to. For example, amillennialism takes an allegorical approach to verses that deal with the millennium, and concludes that when Christ comes, eternity will begin with no prior thousand-year (millennial) reign on earth. Amillennialists generally interpret the "thousand-year" reign of Christ metaphorically and say it refers to Christ's present (spiritual) rule from heaven.

Likewise, the postmillennial view allegorizes such verses, and teaches that through the church's progressive influence, the world will be "Christianized" before Christ returns. Immediately following this return, eternity will begin (with no literal thousand-year kingdom). Of course, a practical problem for postmillennialism is that the world seems to be getting worse and worse instead of being "Christianized."

Against allegorical interpretation, a literal and plain reading of Scripture leads effortlessly to premillennialism. A basic rule of thumb for interpreting the Bible is this: When the literal sense of Scripture makes good sense, seek no other sense. In view of this basic rule, I see no reason to allegorize Bible prophecies relating to the millennium. The Bible plainly teaches a literal 1000-year kingdom over which Christ will rule on the earth (Revelation 20:4,6).

This is not to deny that allegorical language *sometimes* appears in Scripture. Paul, for example, used an allegory and labeled it as such (Galatians 4:24). But even such allegorical statements communicate a literal truth that can be understood. Moreover, one should note that by specifically indicating within the text the presence of an "allegory" (Galatians 4:24), the Bible thereby indicates that the ordinary meaning of Scripture is to be a literal one.

Evangelical scholars have noted that every once in a while it may be difficult to determine when a passage should not be taken literally. Certain guidelines are helpful in making this determination. Briefly put, a text should be taken figuratively: 1) when it is obviously figurative, as when Jesus said He was a "door" (John 10:9 NASB); 2) when the text itself authorizes the figurative sense, as when Paul said he was using an allegory (Galatians 4:24); or 3) when a literal interpretation would contradict other truths inside or outside the Bible, as when the Bible speaks of the "four corners of the earth" (Revelation 7:1). In short, to repeat the dictum, "When the literal sense makes good sense, seek no other sense."

In regard to biblical prophecy, it is good to be reminded that the prophecies that have already been fulfilled in Scripture—particularly Old Testament messianic prophecies that refer to the first coming of Jesus Christ—have been fulfilled quite literally. This gives us great confidence to expect that prophecies not yet fulfilled will also end up being fulfilled literally.

Alpha and Omega

In Revelation 22:12-13, Christ the divine King says: "Behold, I am coming soon! My reward is with me, and I will give to everyone according to what he has done. I am the Alpha and the Omega, the First and the Last, the Beginning and the End" (see also Revelation 1:8).

These final words in the book of Revelation were intended to be a comfort and encouragement to Christians as they await the coming of their King. Christ assures His followers that He is coming soon and that He will bring rewards with Him.

To the modern ear, the claim to be the Alpha and the Omega may seem strange. But for the ancient Jew, Christ was describing Himself in a way they would have readily understood. Though the letters *alpha* and *omega* are the first and last letters of the Greek alphabet, John recorded the book of Revelation for Jewish readers who were also familiar with the Hebrew language and alphabet. And therein lies the significance of Christ's claim. In Jewish thinking, a reference to the first and last letters of an alphabet (*aleph* and *tav* in Hebrew) was regarded as including all the intermediate letters, and came to represent *totality* or *entirety.*

It is with this idea in mind that the Jews in their ancient commentaries on the Old Testament said that Adam transgressed the whole law from *aleph* to *tav.* Abraham, by contrast, observed the whole law from *aleph* to *tav.* The Jews also believed that when God brings blessing upon Israel, He does so abundantly, from *aleph* to *tav.*

When used of God (or Christ), the first and last letters express eternality and omnipotence. Christ's claim to be the Alpha and the Omega is an affirmation that He is the all-powerful One of eternity past and eternity future. He is the eternal God who has always existed in the past and who will always exist in the future.

It is highly revealing that the qualifying phrase *the First and the*

Last is used of God in the Old Testament. Isaiah 44:6, for example, records God as saying: "I am the first and I am the last; apart from me there is no God." Again, in Isaiah 48:12, God said: "I am he; I am the first and I am the last," and God said this right after His pronouncement that "I will not yield my glory to another" (verse 11b). Christ's use of this title was undoubtedly intended to be taken as a claim to equality with God. And it is precisely this that was to bring comfort and encouragement to Christ's followers. Christ wanted them to be absolutely assured that He is the all-powerful Sovereign who will be victorious.

Already—Not Yet

At the first coming of Jesus Christ, the kingdom of God invaded this world of sin, darkness, and rebellion. Because Jesus the King had arrived, the kingdom—God's "reign" or "rule"—had arrived, but it had *not yet* arrived in its entirety or fullness. This points to a future dimension of God's kingdom (see Matthew 6:10; 25:34; 26:29; Luke 19:11-27). The "already" aspect of God's kingdom relates to the first coming of Christ, while the "not yet" aspect relates to the second coming.

America in Biblical Prophecy

Various theories have been suggested through the years regarding whether or not America is mentioned in biblical prophecy. Many have been speculative and farfetched. Others take a more reasoned approach. Following are some of the primary theories:

America Is Only Indirectly Mentioned in Bible Prophecy. While there are no verses in the Bible that mention America by name, there are quite a number of theories regarding indirect references to America in Bible prophecy. For example:

One of the "nations." This theory says that while there are no direct references to the United States in Bible prophecy, there are a number of general prophetic references to "the nations" in the Tribulation that may apply to the United States. These passages might include Haggai 2:6-7, Isaiah 66:18-20, and Zechariah 12:2-3. Such general passages, however, do not tell us anything specific about the role of the United States in the end times.

Cooperation with Europe. Another theory is that even though the United States is not specifically mentioned in biblical prophecy, perhaps the United States will, in the end times, be in general cooperation with Europe—the revived Roman Empire headed by a powerful leader (the Antichrist). Since many U.S. citizens have come from Europe, it would be natural, some say, for the U.S. to become an ally of this Roman power in the end times.

The Babylon of Revelation 17–18. Some interpreters have seen parallels between Babylon the Great in the book of Revelation and the United States (or, more narrowly, New York City). After all, both Babylon and the United States are dominant, both are immoral, both are excessively rich, and both think they are invulnerable. However, this scenario is not given credence by most serious Bible interpreters. Such a view involves more *eisegesis* (reading a meaning into the text of Scripture) than *exegesis* (drawing the meaning out of the text of Scripture).

The land "divided by rivers" (Isaiah 18:1-7). Some interpreters claim that the United States is the fulfillment of Isaiah 18:1-7 since it is divided by the Mississippi River. The passage also makes reference to the nation being feared because of its military conquests, something believed to fit how many people around the world view the U.S. The obvious problem with this view is that the nation is explicitly identified in Isaiah 18:1-2 as ancient Cush, which is modern Sudan.

The Land of Tarshish (Ezekiel 38:13). According to Ezekiel 38:13, when the great northern military coalition invades Israel in the end times, a small group of nations will lamely protest the invasion: "Sheba and Dedan and the merchants of Tarshish with all its villages will say to you, 'Have you come to plunder? Have you gathered your hordes to loot, to carry off silver and gold, to take away livestock and goods and to seize much plunder?'"

Without going into too much detail, a good number of Bible expositors believe the Tarshish of ancient times may be a reference to Spain. Others say Tarshish may refer to Great Britain. Still others say Tarshish might represent all the western nations of the end times, which would at least include the U.S. It is difficult to come to a definitive conclusion on the matter.

America Is Not Mentioned in Bible Prophecy at All. My assessment is that America is not mentioned in Bible prophecy at all. Using proper hermeneutics and sound exegesis, I cannot see America in any of the verses so often suggested by prophecy buffs. If I am correct in this belief, then the key question becomes, *Why isn't* America mentioned in Bible prophecy? There are a number of possible explanations.

1. Foundationally, most nations in the world are not mentioned in Bible prophecy, so it really may be no big deal if the United States is not mentioned. Still, the United States is the world's single remaining superpower that also happens to be Israel's principal ally. One therefore might naturally expect at least a passing mention to be made of this country.
2. It may be that America is not mentioned simply because America plays no significant role in the unfolding of God's end-time plans. Again, however, because the United States is the world's single remaining superpower that also happens to be Israel's principal ally (financially supporting Israel with vast sums of money), one might naturally expect at least some reference. So, again, why no reference?
3. Perhaps the reason America is not mentioned in Bible prophecy is that our country may eventually implode due to ever-escalating moral and spiritual degeneration. There are lots of statistics that show the trouble this country is in morally and spiritually. At present, four out of five adults—some 83 percent—say they are concerned about the moral condition of the United States. If the moral

fiber of this country continues to erode, then the demise of this country is only a matter of time.

4. Perhaps the United States is not mentioned in Bible prophecy because it will be destroyed or at least greatly weakened by nuclear weapons, and so will play no significant role in the end times. There is certainly a good chance that the United States will be attacked with nuclear weapons at some point in the future. Government advisors are presently saying that a nuclear attack on U.S. soil within the next ten years is "more likely than not." Of course, it may be a stretch to say that the entire United States could be destroyed, but if one major city—such as New York City—were destroyed, this would have an absolutely devastating effect on the U.S. economy.

5. Perhaps the United States is not mentioned in Bible prophecy because the country will become incapacitated due to an electromagnetic pulse (EMP) attack. This is not a sensationalistic speculation of prophecy fanatics. It is a potential, realistic scenario documented in a report issued in 2004 by a blue-ribbon commission created by Congress. It is called the "Commission to Assess the Threat to the United States from Electromagnetic Pulse Attack." Based on this report, some government officials lamented that the technology is now here to bring America's way of life to an end.

   The commission found that a single nuclear weapon, delivered by a missile to an altitude of a few hundred miles over the United States, would yield catastrophic damage to the nation. Such a missile could easily be launched off of a freighter off the coast of the United States. The commission explained that the higher the altitude of the weapon's detonation, the larger the affected geographic area would be. At a height of 300 miles, the entire continental United States would be exposed, along with parts of Canada and Mexico.

The commission warned that the electromagnetic pulse produced by such a weapon would have a high likelihood of severely damaging electrical power systems, electronics, and information systems—all of which Americans depend on. At high risk would be electronic control, the infrastructures for handling electric power, sensors and protective systems of all kinds, computers, cell phones, telecommunications, cars, boats, airplanes, trains, transportation, fuel and energy, banking and finance, emergency services, and even food and water. Anything electrical is at risk.

The consequences of an EMP attack would be especially harmful to American society today. The infrastructure of our society—civilian *and* military—virtually runs on electricity and electronic components. The commission estimated that it could take "months to years" to fully recover from such an attack.

It is not infeasible that starvation and disease could ultimately result following an EMP attack. Expert testimony presented before the U.S. Congress indicated that an EMP attack could reduce the United States to a pre-Industrial-Age capacity in terms of transportation options and the ability to provide vital food and water to the general population. Instead of cars, buses, and trains, people would be reduced to using bikes, horses, and buggies.

Of great concern is the fact that U.S. intelligence has discovered that Iran has performed tests on its Shahab-3 medium-range ballistic missile in a manner consistent with an EMP attack scenario. Worse, many of our military systems are arguably as vulnerable as our civilian technologies. The hard reality is that the U.S. Defense Department has not spent the funds necessary to shield equipment from electromagnetic pulses. (There have been too many budget cuts!)

6. Perhaps the United States is not mentioned in Bible

prophecy because the country will suffer substantial economical weakening due to its gross overdependence on oil. Experts are now telling us that a progressive lessening in the oil supply will progressively weaken the economy of our oil-driven society. Once supply begins to dwindle, it is possible that the years to follow will see shortages that at best will cause global recession, or worse.

7. One final possible reason the United States is not mentioned in Bible prophecy is that the United States will be affected catastrophically by the rapture. It seems fair to say that the United States will be negatively affected by the rapture more so than most other nations. That is because there are more Christians per square mile in the United States than anywhere else on earth. Following the moment of the rapture, many factory workers (and workers of all kinds) will no longer show up for work, many bills and mortgages will go unpaid, many college tuition bills and loans will go unpaid, many business leaders will no longer show up to lead their companies, many law enforcement personnel will no longer be here to keep the peace, and the stock market will likely crash because of the panic over millions of people suddenly vanishing. This and much more will result following the rapture.

Amillennialism

Amillennialism, which takes a spiritualized approach in interpreting biblical prophecy, teaches that when Christ comes, eternity will begin with no prior literal thousand-year reign on earth. *Amillennial* literally means "no millennium." Instead of believing in a literal rule of Christ on earth, amillennialists generally interpret prophetic verses related to the reign of Christ metaphorically and say they refer to Christ's present (spiritual) rule from heaven. Old Testament predictions made to Israel are viewed as being fulfilled in the New Testament church.

Among arguments suggested in favor of amillennialism are: 1) The Abrahamic and Davidic covenants were conditional, and hence do not require a future fulfillment because the conditions were not met. (Premillennial dispensationalists rebut that these covenants were *un*conditional—see *Abrahamic Covenant* and *Davidic Covenant* in this dictionary.) 2) Prophecy should be interpreted symbolically, for apocalyptic literature is highly symbolic in nature. (Premillennialists rebut that prophecy ought to be interpreted literally—see *Literal Interpretation of Scripture* in this dictionary.) 3) Israel and the church are not two distinct entities but rather one people of God united by the covenant of grace. (However, see *Church and Israel, Distinction* in this dictionary.) 4) This view is most compatible with the idea that the Old Testament is fulfilled in the New Testament; and 5) The New Testament contains many examples which demonstrate that Old Testament prophecies are fulfilled in the church (for example, Jeremiah 31:31; Hebrews 8:8-13). (However, see *Replacement Theology* in this dictionary.)

This view was held by the later Augustine, as well as by Reformers Martin Luther (A.D. 1483–1546) and John Calvin (1509–1564). Most Puritans were amillennial, as are most Roman Catholics. Famous proponents of the view in more recent history include Oswald Allis (1880–1973), Louis Berkhof (1873–1957), and Anthony Hoekema (1913–1988).

Amos

The book of Amos was written by a prophet of the same name about 755 B.C. Amos, whose name means "burden-bearer," was a prophet to the northern kingdom of Israel (Amos 7:14-15). By trade, he was a lowly shepherd and a dresser of fig trees. He lived in Tekoa, south of Jerusalem (1:1). He was a contemporary of Jonah, Hosea, and Isaiah, and prophesied during the reigns of Uzziah and Jeroboam II.

Amos focused heavy attention on the social injustice of his day (see Amos 5:24). During his time the land was prosperous and there were many rich people. Yet the rich did not aid those who were disadvantaged. This was not as it should be. Amos, the farmer-turned-prophet, therefore prophesied that a day of judgment was forthcoming in which destruction would be inevitable (7:1–9:10).

Ironically, the rich people of Amos's day thought they were bestowed with such great wealth because they were so religious. The falsity of this viewpoint is evident in that they did not use their wealth to do God's work of caring for the poor and disadvantaged. Rather, they exploited the poor to become even richer. From the vantage point of Amos, these rich people were nothing more than hypocrites. It was not long after Amos wrote his book that the Assyrians invaded the land and took the people into captivity. Judgment came just as Amos had prophesied.

Ancient of Days

In a vision of the prophet Daniel, the term "Ancient of Days" was ascribed to Yahweh, the God and divine Judge of the universe (Daniel 7:9,13,22). The portrayal of the Ancient of Days is awesome and majestic, for "his clothing was white as snow, and the hair of his head was white like wool; his throne was flaming with fire" (verse 9). Indeed, "a river of fire was flowing, coming out from before him. Thousands upon thousands attended him; ten thousand times ten thousand stood before him" (verse 10). The great age of this majestic individual is not intended to communicate that God actually ages, but rather this is a symbolical representation of the eternity of God (see Isaiah 9:7; Exodus 3:6,14). This is in obvious contrast to the temporal rulers of finite earth. Some also see the great age as portraying the qualities of wisdom and venerability of God.

It is interesting to observe how similar the description of Yahweh as the "Ancient of Days" in Daniel 7 is to the resurrected, glorified Christ in Revelation 1. For example, we read of Christ that "his head and hair were white like white wool, as white as snow, and his eyes were like blazing fire" (Revelation 1:14).

A

Angels

Angels are ministering spirits (Hebrews 1:14). They have not existed forever, but are created beings. Psalm 148:2-5 affirms that God spoke the word and the angels were created at a specific point in time. Theologians believe the angels were created some time prior to the creation of the earth. After all, Job 38:7 (NASB) makes reference to the "sons of God" (who are angels—see Job 1:6; 2:1 NASB) singing at the time the earth was created.

We learn a great deal about the nature of angels by studying what the Bible says about their characteristics:

Angels are incorporeal and invisible (Hebrews 1:14). The word *incorporeal* means "lacking material form or substance." Angels, then, are not material, physical beings; they are spiritual beings, and are therefore invisible.

Angels are localized beings. Scripture portrays them as having to move from one place to another. An example of this is when the angel Gabriel had to engage in "swift flight" to travel from heaven to Daniel's side (Daniel 9:21-23).

Not all angels have wings. Many angels in the Bible are described as having wings (Isaiah 6:1-5; Ezekiel 1:6; Revelation 4:8). But some Bible verses about angels make no mention of wings (for example, Hebrews 13:2). We conclude that though it is possible all angels have wings, this is not a necessary inference. There is no explicit reference indicating that angels as a whole are winged.

Angels can appear as men. Though angels are by nature incorporeal and invisible, they can nevertheless appear as men (Genesis 18). Their resemblance to men can be so realistic that the angel is actually taken to be a human being (Hebrews 13:2).

Angels are powerful beings. Scripture portrays angels as being extremely powerful and mighty beings. Psalm 103:20 calls them "mighty ones who do his [God's] bidding." Second Thessalonians 1:7 makes reference to God's "powerful angels." Yet, none of them are omnipotent (all-powerful) like God is. They are creatures with creaturely limitations.

Angels are holy. The word "holy" comes from a root that means "set apart." God's angels are set apart from sin and set apart unto God, to serve Him and carry out His assigned tasks. Angels are often called God's "holy ones" (Job 5:1; 15:15; Psalm 89:7).

Angels are obedient. The angels do not do their own bidding. They do only God's bidding (Psalm 103:20).

Angels have great knowledge. Though angels are not all-knowing like God is, they nevertheless possess great intelligence. Angels were created as a higher order of creatures than humans are (see Psalm 8:5), and innately possess a greater knowledge. Beyond this, angels gain ever-increasing knowledge through long observation of human activities.

Angels are immortal. Angels are not subject to death (Luke 20:36). Since angels are immortal and do not die—and since they do not propagate baby angels (Matthew 22:30)—it seems obvious that the number of angels is and always will be the same.

Innumerable. Scripture makes reference to "a great company of the heavenly host" (Luke 2:13), and the angels are spoken of as "tens of thousands and thousands of thousands" (Psalm 68:17). Their number is elsewhere described as "myriads of myriads" (Revelation 5:11 NASB). (The word *myriad* means "vast number," "innumerable.") Daniel 7:10, speaking of God, says that "ten thousand times ten thousand stood before him." The number "ten thousand times ten thousand" is 100,000,000 (one-hundred million). This is a number almost too vast to fathom. Job 25:3 understandably asks, "Can his forces be numbered?"

Roles. Angels are engaged in fulfilling various roles:

Messengers. The word *angel* literally means "messenger." Angels serve as God's messengers—bringing revelation, announcements, warnings, and other information to the people of God. For example, angels appeared to the prophet Daniel to reveal the future (Daniel 9). An angel appeared to Joseph and to Mary to announce the coming birth of the Savior, Jesus Christ (Matthew 1).

Guardians. God has assigned angels to watch over believers. Psalm 91:9-11 affirms that the angels guard believers in all their ways (see 2 Kings 6:17).

Ministry at death. At the moment of death, when the soul separates from the body, angels are there to escort the believer's soul into his or her eternal inheritance (Luke 16:22).

Restraining evil. Angels sometimes restrain evil among humans. For example, in Genesis we read about angels that struck some wicked men with blindness so they could not carry out their evil intentions when they came to Lot's house (Genesis 18:22; 19:1,10,11).

Executing judgments. Angels are sometimes found in Scripture executing God's judgments. A prime example is found in Acts 12 where an angel executed Herod in judgment (Acts 12:22-23).

End times. The book of Revelation portrays a number of different angels involved in the outworking of God's sovereign plan in the end times (for example, Revelation 8–10). Angels are portrayed as God's "reapers" at the end of the age. In His parable of the weeds, Jesus speaks about sowing good seed in a field, pulling up weeds and burning them, and bringing in the harvest. In Matthew 13:37-42, Jesus explains the symbolism of this parable:

> The one who sowed the good seed is the Son of Man. The field is the world, and the good seed stands for the sons of the kingdom. The weeds are the sons of the evil one, and the enemy who sows them is the devil. The harvest is the end of the age, and the harvesters are angels. As the weeds are pulled up and burned in the fire, so it will be at the end of the age. The Son of Man will send out his angels, and they will weed out of his kingdom everything that causes sin and all who do evil. They will throw them into the fiery furnace, where there will be weeping and gnashing of teeth.

What this sobering passage tells us is that at the end of the age,

God's angels will actually take hold of Christ-rejecting evildoers and toss them into the "fiery furnace."

Animal Sacrifices, Future Temple

See *Millennial Temple and Sacrifices.*

Annihilationism

The doctrine of annihilationism teaches that man was created immortal. But those who continue in sin and reject Christ are by a positive act of God deprived of the gift of immortality and are ultimately destroyed.

Another view, called "conditional immortality," argues that immortality is not a natural endowment of man, but is rather a gift of God in Christ only to those who believe. The person who does not accept Christ is ultimately annihilated and loses all consciousness. Some of the advocates of these doctrines teach a limited duration of conscious suffering for the wicked after death, after which time they are annihilated.

A key verse that refutes annihilationism is Matthew 25:46: "Then they will go away to eternal punishment, but the righteous to eternal life." By no stretch of the imagination can the punishment spoken of in this verse be defined as a nonsuffering extinction of consciousness. Indeed, if actual suffering is lacking, then so is punishment. Let us be clear on this: Punishment entails suffering. And suffering necessarily entails consciousness. One can exist and not be punished, but no one can be punished and not exist.

How do we know that the punishment referred to in Matthew 25:46 does not entail an extinction of consciousness and annihilation? There is a lot of evidence.

For example, consider the fact that there are no degrees of annihilation. One is either annihilated or one is not. The Scriptures, by contrast, teach that there will be degrees of punishment on the day of judgment (Matthew 10:15; 11:21-24; 16:27; Luke 12:47-48; John 15:22; Hebrews 10:29; Revelation 20:11-15; 22:12).

The very fact that people will suffer varying degrees of punishment in hell shows that annihilation or the extinction of consciousness is not taught in Matthew 25:46 or anywhere else in Scripture. These are incompatible concepts.

Moreover, one cannot deny that for one who is suffering excruciating pain, the extinction of his or her consciousness would actually be a blessing—not a punishment (see Luke 23:30-31; Revelation 9:6). Any honest seeker after truth must admit that one cannot define "eternal punishment" as an extinction of consciousness.

We must emphasize that torment cannot, by definition, be anything but conscious torment. One cannot torment a tree, a rock, or a house. By its very nature, being tormented requires consciousness.

A critical point to make in regard to Matthew 25:46 is that this punishment is said to be eternal. There is no way that annihilationism or an extinction of consciousness can be forced into this passage. Indeed, the adjective *aionion* in this verse literally means "everlasting, without end." This same adjective is predicated of God (the "eternal" God) in 1 Timothy 1:7, Romans 16:26, Hebrews 9:14, 13:8, and Revelation 4:9. The punishment of the wicked is just as eternal as our eternal God.

Antichrist

The apostle Paul warned of a "man of lawlessness," which is the Antichrist (2 Thessalonians 2:3,8,9). This individual will perform counterfeit signs and wonders and deceive many people during the future Tribulation period (2 Thessalonians 2:9-10). The apostle John describes this anti-God individual in the book of Revelation as "the Beast" (Revelation 13:1-10).

This Satan-inspired individual will rise to prominence in the Tribulation period, initially making a peace treaty with Israel (Daniel 9:27). But he will then seek to dominate the world, double-cross and then seek to destroy the Jews, persecute believers, and set up his own kingdom (Revelation 13). He will speak arrogant and boastful words in glorifying himself (2 Thessalonians 2:4). His assistant, the false prophet, will seek to make the world worship him (Revelation 13:11-12). People around the world will be forced to receive his mark, without which they cannot buy or sell, thereby controlling the global economy (Revelation 13:16-17). However, to receive this mark insures one of being the recipient of God's wrath. The Antichrist will eventually rule the whole world (Revelation 13:7), with his headquarters in Rome (Revelation 17:8-9). This beast will be defeated and destroyed by Jesus at His second coming (Revelation 19:11-16).

A Jew? Some interpreters have tried to argue that the Antichrist will be a Jew. For example, an early tradition claimed that the Antichrist would come from the tribe of Dan (in the twelve tribes of Israel). Some relate this to the fact that the tribe of Dan fell into deep apostasy and idolatry, setting up for themselves a graven image (Judges 18:30). In the Testament of Dan (5:6), Satan is said to be the prince of the tribe. Irenaeus, writing in the latter part of the second century, noted that the omission of Dan was due to a tradition that the Antichrist was to come from that tribe (*Adv. Haer.* v.30.2.). However, Revelation 13:1 and 17:15 picture the Antichrist as rising up *out of the sea,* and the term "sea" in Scripture is often used as a way of referring to the Gentile nations. Antiochus Epiphanes, a Gentile, seems to typify the future Antichrist in Daniel 11. Hence, it is unlikely the Antichrist will be a Jew.

A Muslim? More recently, for understandable reasons, many have claimed that the Antichrist will be a Muslim. However, such a view has significant problems in terms of theological consistency. For one thing, Daniel 11:36 tells us the Antichrist "will exalt and magnify himself above every god." We also read in 2 Thessalonians 2:4 that the Antichrist ultimately "will oppose and exalt himself over everything that is called God or is worshiped, so that he sets himself up in God's temple, proclaiming himself to be God." To say the very least, the idea of a Muslim Antichrist claiming to be God would represent an absolute and heinous trashing of the Muslim creed, which affirms that "there is one God named Allah, and Muhammad is his prophet." No *true* Muslim would make any claim that he was God. Just as it is anathema to Muslims to call

Jesus "God incarnate" or the "Son of God," so it would be anathema to Muslims for any human to claim he was God. (Keep in mind that Muslims are radical monotheists.) A Muslim Antichrist would thus be viewed as an infidel among Quran-believing Muslims.

In keeping with this is the Muslim teaching that "God can have no partners." Muslims generally say this as a means of arguing against the Trinity. But it is certainly applicable to human leaders on earth who claim to be God.

Still further, it is the Muslim teaching that Allah is so radically unlike any earthly reality—so utterly transcendent and beyond anything in the finite realm—that he can scarcely be described using earthly terms. How, then, could a human Muslim (the Antichrist) claim (as the Antichrist) to be God—a God described in earthly terms?

One must also wonder why a Muslim Antichrist would make a covenant with Israel (Daniel 9:24-27), guaranteeing protection for Israel. Many evangelical expositors have believed that this covenant is what allows Israel to live in "peace and safety" so that she can rebuild the Jewish temple. It seems hard to believe that a Muslim leader would protect Israel in this regard.

Gog? Contrary to the assumptions of some today, Gog (the leader of the northern military coalition that will one day invade Israel—Ezekiel 38) is not another name for the Antichrist. The Bible interpreter will end up in prophetic chaos if he or she tries to make this identification. The Antichrist heads up a revived Roman empire (Daniel 2,7), while Gog heads up an invasion force made up of Russia and a number of Muslim nations (Ezekiel 38:1-6). Moreover, Gog's invasion into Israel constitutes a direct challenge to the Antichrist's covenant with Israel (Daniel 9:27). Further, Gog's moment in the limelight is short-lived (it's all over when God destroys the invading force—Ezekiel 39), whereas the Antichrist is in power over the span of a significant part of the Tribulation (see Revelation 4–18).

Christ Himself will defeat the Antichrist. Scripture reveals that the Antichrist is destined for the lake of fire. Revelation 19:20 tells us:

"The beast was captured, and with him the false prophet who performed the miraculous signs on his behalf. With these signs he had deluded those who had received the mark of the beast and worshiped his image. The two of them were thrown alive into the fiery lake of burning sulfur." Satan, too, will eventually experience this destiny: "The devil, who deceived them, was thrown into the lake of burning sulfur, where the beast and the false prophet had been thrown. They will be tormented day and night forever and ever" (20:10).

This will mark the end of influence of this satanic trinity.

Antichrist, Spirit of

Scripture reveals that not only will there be a future person known as the Antichrist who comes to power in the future Tribulation, the spirit of Antichrist is already at work, promoting heretical doctrine. For example, the apostle John wrote, "Beloved, do not believe every spirit, but test the spirits to see whether they are from God, for many false prophets have gone out into the world. By this you know the Spirit of God: every spirit that confesses that Jesus Christ has come in the flesh is from God, and every spirit that does not confess Jesus is not from God. This is the spirit of the antichrist, of which you have heard that it is coming, and now it is already in the world" (1 John 4:1-3 NASB). He then repeats this warning in 2 John 7: "Many deceivers have gone out into the world, those who do not acknowledge Jesus Christ as coming in the flesh. This is the deceiver and the antichrist."

A major theological system promoting this false doctrine in the first century was Docetism. The Docetists in the first century believed in a form of dualism, the view that matter is evil and spirit is good. Because of this, they believed Jesus couldn't have had a real material human body because that would have involved a union of spirit and matter (good and evil). Jesus therefore must have had a phantom-like body—that is, He only had the appearance of flesh, without substance or reality. ("Docetism" comes from a Greek word, *dokeo,* meaning "to seem" or "to appear.") Jesus' suffering and death on the cross was therefore not real, for it is inconceivable that a Supreme God (spirit) would give Himself up to the evil and destructive power of matter (evil). Bible passages that specifically refute Docetism include Colossians 1:15-18, 2:9, Hebrews 2:14, 1 John 2:22f., 4:2-6, 5:1-6, and 2 John 7.

Antiochus Epiphanes

Daniel 11:31 and Matthew 24:15 speak of a future "abomination that causes desolation" that will take place during the future Tribulation (see also Daniel 9:27). This refers specifically to the Antichrist, who will set up an image of himself inside the Jewish temple, and then demand that the world worship and pay idolatrous homage to him. This will utterly desecrate the temple, making it abominable, and therefore desolate.

Such an abomination took place once before—though to a lesser degree—in 168 B.C. At that time, Antiochus Epiphanes erected an altar to Zeus upon the altar of burnt offering in the Temple at Jerusalem and sacrificed a pig—considered an unclean animal by the Jews—on it. He thereby dedicated a holy temple to a pagan deity. We may therefore consider Antiochus Epiphanes an idolatrous prototype of the final Antichrist.

Some try to argue that all references to the abomination of desolation in Scripture were fulfilled in this act of Antiochus Epiphanes. However, Paul's prophetic discussion of this event in 2 Thessalonians 2 would seem to demand that this "abomination" will occur in reference to the Antichrist during the future Tribulation. Indeed, the Antichrist will seek to take God's place in the Temple and make people bow down and worship him (see verses 3-4).

Apocalypse

This term is an alternate way of referring to the book of Revelation, the last book of the New Testament (see Revelation 1:1). It derives from a Greek word meaning "revelation, or "uncovering," or "unveiling," or "disclosure of truth." The book of Revelation literally reveals, uncovers, and unveils what lies in the future.

Apocalyptic Literature

Scholars tell us that apocalyptic literature is a special kind of writing that arose among the Jews and Christians to reveal certain mysteries about heaven and earth, especially regarding the world to come. This type of literature is often characterized by visions, the necessity of making ethical and moral decisions or changes as a result of such visions, and a pervasive use of symbols. Many of the symbols in the book of Revelation are found (or alluded to) in the Old Testament.

Certain themes are common to apocalyptic literature, such as 1) a growing sense of hopelessness as wicked powers grow in strength; 2) the promise that the sovereign God will intervene; 3) heavenly visions which provide readers with a heavenly perspective that helps them endure present suffering; 4) the intervention of God in overcoming and destroying evil; 5) the call to believers to live righteously; 6) the call to persevere under trial; and 7) God's final deliverance and restoration, with the promise to dwell with His people.

The book of Revelation is a good example of apocalyptic literature. This book was written to persecuted believers for the purpose of giving them hope, inspiration, and comfort, so that they would be able to patiently endure the persecution and struggle they were facing. The book clearly demonstrates that in the end God wins, and we will one day live face-to-face with Him forever in a new heaven and a new earth.

Another well-known apocalyptic book is Daniel. Like the book of Revelation, the book of Daniel contains Bible prophecy of the end times. One critically important reference involves the seventieth week of Daniel (Daniel 9:24-27), which speaks of the future Tribulation period that precedes the second coming of Christ.

Nonbiblical apocalyptic books include the Apocalypse of Abraham, Apocalypse of Baruch, Ascension of Isaiah, Assumption of Moses, 2 Baruch, Book of Jubilees, 1 and 2 Enoch, Life of Adam and Eve, the

Sibylline Oracles, Testament of Abraham, and the Testaments of the 12 Patriarchs. Most of these books are found in the Pseudepigrapha (literally, "false writings") of the Old Testament.

Apostasy

The word "apostasy" comes from the Greek word *apostasia* and means "falling away." The word refers to a determined, willful "defection from the faith," or "abandonment of the faith."

In the New Testament, Judas Iscariot and his betrayal of Jesus for 30 pieces of silver is a classic example of apostasy and its effects (see Matthew 26:14-25,47-57; 27:3-10). Other examples include Hymenaeus and Alexander, who experienced a "shipwreck" of their faith (1 Timothy 1:19-20), and Demas, who turned away from the apostle Paul because of his love for the present world (2 Timothy 4:10).

Apostasy is often encouraged by false teachers (Matthew 24:11; Galatians 2:4), and escalates during times of trial (Matthew 24:9-10; Luke 8:13). The apostles often warned of the danger of apostasy (Hebrews 6:5-8; 10:26). Apostasy also occurred in Old Testament times among the Israelites (Joshua 22:22; 2 Chronicles 33:19; Jeremiah 2:19; 5:6). Scripture prophesies a great end times apostasy involving a massive defection from the truth (2 Thessalonians 2:3; see also Matthew 24:10-12).

In keeping with this, 1 Timothy 4:1-2 warns: "The Spirit expressly says that in latter times some will depart from the faith, giving heed to deceiving spirits and doctrines of demons, speaking lies in hypocrisy, having their own conscience seared" (NKJV). Likewise, 2 Timothy 4:3-4 warns: "The time is coming when people will no longer listen to sound and wholesome teaching. They will follow their own desires and will look for teachers who will tell them whatever their itching ears want to hear. They will reject the truth and chase after myths" (NLT).

Ark of the Covenant

The Ark of the Covenant was constructed from the wood of an

Acacia tree (which grows in the Sinai desert), and was coated with gold. It had rings at the four corners, through which poles were inserted to make it easier to carry. About 45 by 27 by 27 inches in volume, it was built by a talented craftsman named Bezalel (Exodus 37:1).

In the Ark were placed the two stone tablets of the law written by the finger of God on Mount Sinai, which were a continual reminder of the covenant between God and Israel (Exodus 25:16,21). It also contained a pot of manna, which symbolized the bread of God from heaven (Exodus 16:33). Aaron's rod was later placed in it as a witness to Israel of God's choice of the priesthood (Numbers 17:10).

Scripture indicates that the Ark symbolized God's presence (1 Samuel 4:3-22). It was kept in the Holy of Holies, the innermost shrine, of the tabernacle and the temple (Exodus 26:33).

The lid of the Ark held great significance. It was known as the Mercy Seat or Atonement Cover. On each annual Day of Atonement, the high priest sprinkled the blood of a sacrificial animal on it to symbolize the nation's repentance for the sins committed the previous year. Israel's guilt was transferred to the animal (Leviticus 23:27; Numbers 29:7).

Eventually, the Ark disappeared following the days of Jeremiah (Jeremiah 3:16). It may be that the Ark was destroyed when the Babylonians wrecked the temple in 586 B.C. Others believe the Ark has not been destroyed, but that it is hidden somewhere. Some suggest it may be hidden on Mount Nebo. Others suggest it may be hidden in a cave beneath Jerusalem. Many archaeologists—both Christian and non-Christian—have continued to search for its whereabouts.

The significance of the Ark of the Covenant for prophecy relates to the biblical teaching that the Jewish temple will be rebuilt by the middle of the future seven-year Tribulation (see Daniel 9:24-27; Matthew 24:15; 2 Thessalonians 2:4; Revelation 11:1-2; 13:14-15). A number of prophecy students have suggested that although the evidence is not conclusive, there is some biblical support—particularly in the writings of Ezekiel—that the Ark of the Covenant may be rediscovered and placed in the rebuilt Temple in association with the restoration of the glory of God to Israel. After all, in Old Testament times, God's glory attended the Ark (see 1 Samuel 4:21).

Armageddon

Human suffering will steadily escalate during the Tribulation period. First are the seal judgments, involving bloodshed, famine, death, economic upheaval, a great earthquake, and cosmic disturbances (Revelation 6). Then come the trumpet judgments, involving hail and fire mixed with blood, the sea turning to blood, water turning bitter, further cosmic disturbances, affliction by demonic scorpions, and the death of a third of humankind (Revelation 8:6–9:21). Then come the bowl judgments, involving horribly painful sores on human beings, more bodies of water turning to blood, the death of all sea creatures, people being scorched by the sun, total darkness engulfing the land, a devastating earthquake, and much more (Revelation 16). Worse comes to worse, however, when these already traumatized human beings find themselves engaged in a catastrophic series of battles called Armageddon (see Daniel 11:40-45; Joel 3:9-17; Zechariah 14:1-3; Revelation 16:14-16).

The word *Armageddon* literally means "Mount of Megiddo," and refers to a location about 60 miles north of Jerusalem. This is the location of Barak's battle with the Canaanites (Judges 4; 5:19) and Gideon's battle with the Midianites (Judges 7). This will be the site for the final horrific battles of humankind just prior to the second coming (Revelation 16:16).

Napoleon reportedly commented once that this site is perhaps the greatest battlefield he had ever witnessed. Of course, the battles Napoleon fought will dim in comparison to Armageddon. So horrible will Armageddon be that no one would survive if it were not for Christ coming again (Matthew 24:22).

There are a number of stages that comprise the campaign of Armageddon, including the assembling of the Antichrist's allies (Psalm 2:1-6; Joel 3:9-11; Revelation 16:12-16), Babylon's destruction (Isaiah 13–14;

Jeremiah 50–51; Zechariah 5:5-11; Revelation 17–18), Jerusalem's fall (Micah 4:11–5:1; Zechariah 12–14), the Antichrist's armies at Bozrah (Jeremiah 49:13-14), Israel's national regeneration (Psalm 79:1-13; Isaiah 64:1-12; Hosea 6:1-13; Joel 2:28-32; Zechariah 12:10; Romans 11:25-27), the second coming (Isaiah 34:1-7; Micah 2:12-13; Habakkuk 3:3), the horrific battle from Bozrah to the Valley of Jehoshaphat (Jeremiah 49:20-22; Joel 3:12-13; Zechariah 14:12-15), and the ascent on the Mount of Olives (Joel 3:14-17; Zechariah 14:3-5; Matthew 24:29-31; Revelation 16:17-21; 19:11-21). In view of all that occurs in Armageddon, it would be wrong to refer to it as the "battle" of Armageddon, as if it were a single event.

Astrology

Astrology is a form of divination that seeks to forecast events on earth and among humans by observing and interpreting the planets, stars, sun, and moon. More specifically, astrology makes forecasts of a person's life by drawing up a horoscope chart that shows the positions of the planets and zodiacal signs at the moment of the person's birth, taking into account where on earth the person was born. It is believed that the positions of the planets at the moment of one's birth reflect one's character and destiny. The credo is, "As above, so below." The planets and stars above are viewed as being mystically connected to earth and human beings below.

Historically, astrology can trace its roots back to Babylon around 3000 B.C. The ancient Babylonians observed how orderly and rhythmically the planets moved across the sky, and concluded that the planets were "gods of the night." Hence, the planets were assigned godlike powers and character, and were worshipped. These gods were believed to control the fate of human beings on earth in a broad sense—that is, they controlled the destiny of nations. In view of this, the priests of Babylon sought to understand and predict the movements of these planets so that perhaps they could use this knowledge beneficially on their nation's behalf. With a view to studying and worshiping these deities, the Babylonians built towers called ziggurats. Apparently, the Tower of Babel was such a ziggurat.

Today astrology is a bit different. Instead of focusing broadly on nations, astrology is used to gain information about individual human beings. Moreover, whereas the old school of thought in astrology was fatalistic in the sense that it was considered deterministic (with little or no room for free will decisions to change the course of one's destiny), astrology today speaks more in terms of forecasting trends, likelihoods, and influences. Contemporary astrology generally does not say that everyone has an absolute predetermined future. Based on the trends and influences one discovers from horoscope charts, one can then seek to make wise decisions for the future.

The horoscope chart has three primary components: the planets, the signs of the zodiac, and the twelve houses. A person's horoscope constitutes a map of precisely where the planets and zodiac constellations were at the moment of that person's birth, and this chart is used to forecast trends and influences for that person's life. More specifically:

- *Planets.* The planets are placed on the chart based on a calculation made via mathematical formulas. These formulas consider two primary facts: one's time of birth, and the latitude and longitude of one's birthplace. The fact that each planet is viewed as having its own personality or character is an important aspect of astrology. For example, Venus is associated with love and beauty. Mars is associated with aggression and spontaneity. These characteristics can be modified by the "house" in which the planet is found (see below) as well as by the signs of the zodiac.
- *Signs of the Zodiac.* The zodiac is an imaginary belt in the heavens that comprises the twelve signs of the zodiac. The horoscope chart—a chart of the zodiac—is a circular diagram that contains 360 degrees. The twelve zodiac signs are equally divided among these 360 degrees, each being allotted

30 degrees. These zodiac signs are: Aries the Ram, Taurus the Bull, Gemini the Twins, Cancer the Crab, Leo the Lion, Virgo the Virgin, Libra the Scales, Scorpio the Scorpion, Sagittarius the Archer, Capricorn the Goat, Aquarius the Water Bearer, and Pisces the Fish. These zodiac signs allegedly describe the ways that planets are limited or expanded.

- *Twelve houses.* The twelve houses on the horoscope chart represent various areas of one's life, including one's home, one's marriage, one's career, and so forth. As earth rotates, and the houses with it, the planets move into these various houses. The planets then influence that particular area of life with their distinct characteristics.

This may seem complicated to the uninitiated. The important point to remember is that as the astrologer looks at a person's horoscope chart, his goal is to interpret how the planets, houses, and signs of the zodiac relate to each other, and influence each other. He thereby seeks to forecast trends, likelihoods, and influences in that person's future. The astrologer's interpretation is based on his personal knowledge of the meanings of the planets and their positions on the chart at the time of the client's birth.

One thing the astrologer watches for are "angular relationships." For example, if there is a 90-degree aspect between two planets (called a "square aspect"), this reveals tension and disagreement. If there is a 120-degree aspect between two planets (called a "trine aspect"), this reveals sympathy and cooperation. By analyzing such angular relationships, the astrologer draws conclusions regarding what to forecast for the client's future.

In recent years it has been popular for astrologers to deny any connection with occultism and to argue that astrology is an objective science that uses scientific methodology. It is claimed that mathematical calculations are made, and then the data is interpreted.

Critics, however, maintain that the mere use of mathematical formulas to plot the position of planets at the time and place of one's birth does not remove astrology from the realm of occultism. It is widely known that astrologers often delve into other forms of occultism, such as palmistry and numerology, and they often develop psychic powers. Some astrologers admit that their practice is a form of occultism. Others admit that spirit guides help them properly interpret horoscope charts. Still others suggest that they have become adept at reading horoscope charts because they were astrologers in their past lives. All of this reeks with occultism.

Astrology, of course, is strictly off-limits for the Christian. In Isaiah 47, we find a strong denunciation of astrologers and their craft (verses 13-15). Verse 15 explicitly states that "each of them goes on in his error," and "there is not one that can save you." The book of Daniel confirms that astrologers lack true discernment, and that the only source of accurate revelation is God Almighty (Daniel 2:2,10). Further, anything bordering on worship of heavenly bodies is strictly forbidden (Deuteronomy 4:19). As well, astrology is a form of occultism, and occultism in all forms is condemned in Scripture (Deuteronomy 18:9-12; 2 Kings 17:16; Jeremiah 10:2; Acts 7:42).

Aside from these biblical warnings against astrology, there are other problems to make note of:

- Different astrologers often give different interpretations, even though they are looking at the same horoscope chart.
- Astrologers do not agree on how many signs of the zodiac there are. Many say twelve, others say eight, or ten, or fourteen, or twenty-four. The number of signs influences how one interprets the data.
- What is the basis of authority in matters relating to astrology? Who definitively determines how many signs of the zodiac there are? How do we definitively know the meanings of the various planets? All this seems arbitrary.
- How do we explain the different experiences of twins?

Consider Jacob and Esau as an example. If astrology is really true, why so much difference in their lives?

- How do we explain disasters where many people of different zodiac signs experience the same fate (like a plane crash)?
- Scientific studies show a prediction failure rate of 90 percent or worse for astrologers.

Astronomical Signs

See *Cosmic Disturbances*.

B

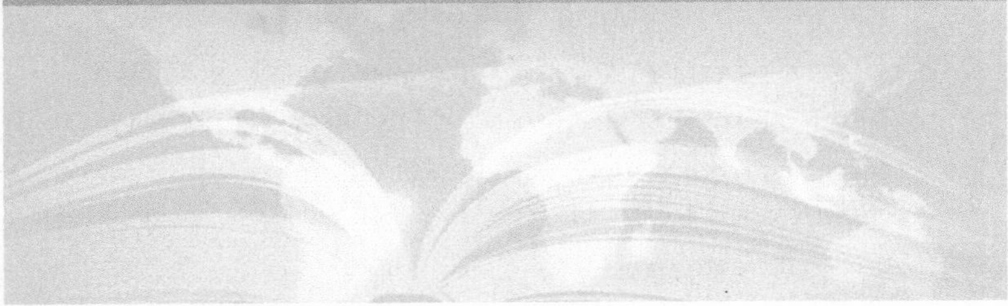

Babylon

Babylon lay in the land of Shinar (Genesis 10:10). This influential civilization, ruled by kings and priests, was situated on the banks of the Euphrates River, a little over 50 miles south of modern Baghdad. Because of its ideal location, Babylon was an important commercial and trade center in the ancient world. It became a powerful kingdom under the leadership of Hammurabi (1792–1750 B.C.).

Archaeologists have discovered a variety of Babylonian documents. For example, Babylonian collections of wisdom literature include Counsels of Wisdom (ca. 1500–1000 B.C.), Akkadian Proverbs (ca. 1800–1600 B.C.), and The Words of Ahiqar (ca. 700–400 B.C.). Many of the proverbs contained in these works are secular in nature, and some are even quite crass in their moral tone.

Like other pagan nations of the Ancient Near East, the Babylonians believed in many false gods and goddesses. These gods were thought to control the entire world of nature, and hence if one sought to be successful in life, one would do well to placate the gods. In Babylonian religion, the behavior of the gods was considered unpredictable at best.

Each city in Babylon had a patron god with an accompanying temple. There were also a number of small shrines scattered about each city where people often met to worship various other deities. The chief of the Babylonian gods was Anu, considered the king of heaven, while the patron god of Babylon was Marduk.

Belief in an afterlife permeated the thinking of the Babylonians. The dead were thought to live in the underworld, and found their sustenance in offerings made by their living descendants. If no offerings of food or drink were made by descendants, the ghosts of the dead would allegedly return to haunt them. Hence, there was strong motivation to make such offerings.

The Babylonians were well known for their practice of divination. Astrology can trace its roots back to Babylon around 3000 B.C. The ancient Babylonians observed how orderly and rhythmically the planets moved across the sky, and concluded that the planets were "gods of the night." Hence, the planets were assigned godlike powers and character, and were worshiped. These gods were believed to control the fate of human beings on earth in a broad sense—that is, they controlled the destiny of nations (see Daniel 1:20; 2:2,10,27; 4:7; 5:7,11,15). In view of this, the priests of Babylon sought to understand and predict the movements of these planets so that perhaps they could use this knowledge beneficially on their nation's behalf. With a view to studying and worshiping these deities, the Babylonians built towers called ziggurats. Apparently, the Tower of Babel was such a ziggurat.

Babylon is often represented in Scripture as being arrayed against God and His people (2 Kings 24:10). In 597 B.C., for example, some 3,000 Jews went into exile in Babylon by Nebuchadnezzar. Jerusalem and the temple were obliterated (Lamentations 1:1-7). Though God sovereignly used Babylon as His powerful whipping rod in chastening Israel, Babylon was to be utterly destroyed by God's hand of judgment for its continual standing against His people (Isaiah 13:1-16).

Based upon a literal approach to Scripture, there would appear to be a revived Babylon in the end times, rebuilt by the Antichrist (see

Revelation 18). It is noteworthy that when the late Saddam Hussein was in power, he spent over one billion dollars in oil money to enhance the city—essentially as a monument to himself. Scripture reveals that when Christ comes again to set up His millennial kingdom, He will destroy the city of Babylon, along with its false religious system, commerce, and government (see Revelation 17–18).

See *Iraq*.

Balaam, Teaching of

We learn of the teaching of Balaam by consulting the account of Balaam in the Old Testament (Numbers 22–25:31). Balaam had been hired by Balak, the king of Moab, to lure the hearts of the Israelites away from the Lord God by having Moabite women seduce Israelite men into intermarriage. Israel thus succumbed to fornication and idolatrous feasts.

Later, something similar took place in the church at Pergamos, one of the seven churches in Asia Minor mentioned in Revelation 2 and 3. Believers were apparently being lured away from the Lord and into idolatry and sexual immorality (Revelation 2:14).

Beast(s)

Revelation 13:1-3 makes reference to the Antichrist as a "beast." He is personally empowered by "the dragon," or Satan (verse 2). Apparently the symbol of the beast was chosen by God to designate the beastly or animal nature of the Antichrist. This does not mean that the beast is just the metaphorical personification of evil in the world, as some have tried to argue. Even though a symbol is used to describe this still-future human being, the symbol indicates that the Antichrist will display an ungodly and anti-God character as a real historical person (2 Thessalonians 2:3-12).

We read of another beast in Revelation 13:11 who will serve as the Antichrist's lieutenant. This second beast will seek to bring about the worship of the Antichrist through performing great and miraculous signs, such as bringing fire down from heaven (verse 13). Those who refuse bring the death sentence upon themselves (verse 15). In those days no one will be able to buy or sell without having received the mark of the beast (verses 16-17). These three—Satan, the Antichrist, and this second beast—form a counterfeit Trinity.

In Revelation 19:20 we read that the beast and the False Prophet—two malevolent foes who will come into power during the future Tribulation period—will be "thrown alive into the fiery lake of burning sulfur." This takes place before the beginning of Christ's millennial kingdom—that 1,000-year period following the second coming of Christ in which Christ will physically rule on earth on the throne of David.

What is sobering to realize is that at the end of the millennial kingdom—1,000 years after the beast and the False Prophet have been thrown into the lake of burning sulfur—the devil will be "thrown into the lake of burning sulfur, where the beast and the false prophet have been thrown. They will be tormented *day and night for ever and ever*" (Revelation 20:10, emphasis added).

Notice that the beast and False Prophet will not be burned up or annihilated at the time the devil is thrown into the lake of burning sulfur. "They" will still be burning after 1,000 years. These sinister beings, along with unbelievers of all ages, will be tormented day and night forever (Revelation 20:14-15).

Beginning of Sorrows

Matthew 24–25 records Jesus' Olivet discourse, in which He teaches on the prophetic future. Matthew 24:8 in the King James Version reads, "All these are the beginning of sorrows." The English Standard Version translates it, "All these are but the beginning of the birth pains." What are "all these" things? In the preceding verses, Jesus speaks of specific signs of the end times, including the rise of false Christs, wars and rumors of wars, nation rising against nation,

B

famines, and earthquakes in various places. These are the "beginning of sorrows" or "beginning of the birth pains," events that will apparently take place in the Tribulation period.

Of course, such things as false Christs, wars, famines, and earthquakes have been around for a very long time. By calling specific attention to these items as the "beginning of the birth pains," Jesus indicates that there would be a marked increase in these things—in *rate* and *intensity*—at the end of the age, during the Tribulation. This increase marks the beginning of what will eventually lead to the second coming of Christ and the setting up of His millennial kingdom on earth (see 1 Thessalonians 5:3; Revelation 6:1-17; 8:1-9:21; 16:1-21).

Some have noted a parallel between these words of Jesus and the seal judgments in the book of Revelation. Jesus speaks of the rise of false Christs (Matthew 24:4-5), just as the first seal speaks of the rise of Antichrist (Revelation 6:1-2). Jesus speaks of wars and rumors of wars (Matthew 24:6), just as the second seal speaks of warfare in which nations rise up against each other (Revelation 6:3-4). Jesus speaks of famines (Matthew 24:7), just as the third seal speaks of famine (Revelation 6:5-6). Jesus speaks of earthquakes (Matthew 24:7), just as the sixth seal speaks of an earthquake (Revelation 6:12-14).

Bema

See *Judgment Seat of Christ.*

Beth-togarmah

In Hebrew, "Beth" means "house." "Beth-togarmah" is a Hebrew term that literally means "the House of Togarmah." Ezekiel 38:6 makes reference to Beth-togarmah as being from the remote parts of the north. Hence, Beth-togarmah must be located to the north of Israel.

Some expositors believe Beth-togarmah is a reference to modern-day Turkey, which is to the far north of Israel. This is in keeping with the geography of Ezekiel's time, for in that day there was a city in Cappodocia (modern Turkey) known as Tegarma, Tagarma, Tilgarimmu, and Takarama. If this identification is correct, this means that Turkey will be one of the nations in the northern military coalition that will invade Israel in the end times (Ezekiel 38:1-6).

Some scholars suggest that Beth-togarmah may refer to Turkey *and* some neighboring geographical territories. In support of this view, the ancient historian Josephus identified the people of Togarmah as Phrygians. Phrygia was located in Asia Minor, in the geographical territory we now know as Turkey. Around 700 B.C., some of the inhabitants of Phrygia crossed over to a different territory in order to found Armenia. This is confirmed by no less a scholar than Wilhelm Gesenius. Beth-togarmah thus apparently could refer to Turkey, Armenia, and perhaps other Turkic-speaking peoples who spread into other areas in central Asia.

Binding of Satan

Revelation 20:1-3 speaks specifically of the future binding of Satan:

> Then I saw an angel coming down from heaven, holding the key of the abyss and a great chain in his hand. And he laid hold of the dragon, the serpent of old, who is the devil and Satan, and bound him for a thousand years; and threw him into the abyss, and shut it and sealed it over him, so that he would not deceive the nations any longer, until the thousand years were completed; after these things he must be released for a short time (NASB).

Satan is referred to as a "dragon," an apt metaphor that points to the ferocity and cruelty of this evil spirit being. He is also called an "ancient serpent," apparently an allusion to Satan's first appearance in the Garden of Eden where he deceived Eve (Genesis 3; see also 2 Corinthians 11:3; 1 Timothy 2:14).

The "pit" referenced here is the bottomless pit that serves as the place of imprisonment of some demonic spirits (Luke 8:31; see also 2 Peter 2:4). The devil—along with all demonic spirits—will be bound here for 1,000 years, during Christ's millennial kingdom. This quarantine will effectively remove a powerful destructive and deceptive force in all areas of human life and thought during Christ's kingdom.

At the end of the 1,000 years, Satan will be loosed from the abyss and have one last opportunity to deceive the nations (Revelation 20:7-9). He will then be judged and eternally cast into the lake of fire (Revelation 20:10; see also Matthew 25:46).

In view of the fact that only believers enter into Christ's millennial kingdom (these are believers who survive the Tribulation period—see Matthew 25:31-46), one might wonder how Satan would succeed in leading many astray following the 1,000 years. Scripture reveals that some of the descendants of these believers will not be believers themselves. It is these that Satan will gather against God in one final rebellion. Christ will quickly and decisively crush this rebellion. Following the millennial kingdom, the Great White Throne judgment—which is the judgment of the wicked—will take place and the lake of fire will be populated (Revelation 20:11-15). The eternal state will then be established (Revelation 21).

Birth Pangs

Matthew 24–25 records Jesus' Olivet discourse, in which He teaches on the prophetic future. In Matthew 24:8 He affirms that "all these are the beginning of the birth pains." What is He speaking of? In the preceding verses, He refers to the rise of false Christs, wars and rumors of wars, famines, and earthquakes (verses 4-7). *These* are the beginning of birth pains. By using such phraseology, Jesus indicates that these things will get noticeably worse and increase in frequency during the future Tribulation period, leading up to the second coming of Christ (see Mark 13:8).

Blasphemy

The root meaning of the Greek word for blasphemy involves injuring the reputation of another. Biblically, it can range from showing a lack of reverence for God to a more extreme attitude of contempt for either God or something considered sacred (see Leviticus 24:16; Matthew 26:65; Mark 2:7). It can involve speaking evil against God (Psalm 74:18; Isaiah 52:5; Romans 2:24; Revelation 13:1,6; 16:9,11,21). It can also involve showing contempt for the true God by making claims of divinity for oneself (see Mark 14:64; John 10:33). Those who deny the true identity of Jesus as Messiah also commit blasphemy (Luke 22:65; John 10:36).

There are biblical evidences for the manifestation of blasphemy in the end times, especially in regard to the Antichrist. For example, we read John's account of the Antichrist: "I saw a beast coming up out of the sea. He had ten horns and seven heads, with ten crowns on his horns, and on each head a blasphemous name" (Revelation 13:1). We are told that the Antichrist "was given a mouth to utter proud words and blasphemies and to exercise his authority for forty-two months. He opened his mouth to blaspheme God, and to slander his name and his dwelling place and those who live in heaven" (Revelation 13:5-6; see also 17:3). The Antichrist's blasphemous words are in keeping with his blasphemous nature (see 2 Thessalonians 2:3-11).

Blessed Hope

The term "blessed hope" is a general reference to the rapture of the church. This event is *blessed* in the sense that it brings *blessedness* to believers. The term carries the idea of joyous anticipation. Believers can hardly wait for it to happen!

We read of this in Titus 2:13, where Christians are urged to look "for the blessed hope and glorious appearing of our great God and Savior Jesus Christ" (NKJV). At this momentous event, the dead in Christ will be resurrected while believers still alive on earth will be

B

instantly translated into their resurrection bodies (see Romans 8:22-23; 1 Corinthians 15:51-58; Philippians 3:20-21; 1 Thessalonians 4:13-18; 1 John 3:2-3). These bodies will never again be subject to sickness, pain, and death. While we live in this fallen world as "pilgrims," were are empowered by this magnificent hope.

Blindness, Israel's

The apostle Paul, himself once a blinded Jew, helps us to understand Israel's judicial blindness. In Romans 11:25 he writes, "I do not want you to be ignorant of this mystery, brothers, so that you may not be conceited: Israel has experienced a hardening in part until the full number of the Gentiles has come in [that is, until the full number of Gentiles who *will* be saved *have become* saved]" (insert added). The backdrop is that Israel had "pursued a law [literally 'kept on pursuing a law'—the Mosaic Law] of righteousness, but they have 'not attained it.' Why not? Because they pursued it not by faith, but as if it were by works. They have stumbled over the 'stumbling stone,' which is Jesus Christ" (Romans 9:31-33, insert added).

Put another way, Israel had sought a relationship with God via a righteousness earned by keeping the law. Instead of seeking a faith-relationship with God, they instead sought to do everything that the law prescribed so they could earn a relationship with God in that way (see Galatians 2:16; 3:2,5,10). Failure was unavoidable, for attaining a righteousness by observing the Law requires it to be kept perfectly (James 2:10), which no man is capable of doing.

To make matters worse, they refused to admit their inability to perfectly keep the law and turn by faith to God for His forgiveness. They rejected Jesus Christ as the Messiah, refusing to turn to Him in faith, because He did not fit their preconceived ideas about the Messiah (see, for example, Matthew 12:14,24). So, they "stumbled" over Him.

Hence, a partial judicial blindness or hardness of heart came upon Israel. Israel thus lost her favored position before God, and the gospel was then preached to the Gentiles, with the aim of causing the Jews to become jealous and *then* become saved (Romans 11:11).

Israel's hardening and casting off is only *temporary*. In dire threat at Armageddon, Israel will finally recognize their Messiah and then plead for Him to return. They will "mourn for Him, as one mourns for an only son" (Zechariah 12:10 NASB; see also Matthew 23:37-39; see also Isaiah 53:1-9), at which point their deliverance will surely come (see Romans 10:13-14). Moreover, Israel's hardening and casting off is only *partial*, for there is a remnant of Israel who will be saved in this present age and become members of the church, the Body of Christ (see Romans 11:25).

Book of Life

The Book of Life (Greek: *biblion zōēs*) is a heavenly book in which are recorded the names of the redeemed who will inherit heaven (Revelation 3:5; 13:8; 17:8; 20:12,15; 21:27; see also Luke 10:20; Philippians 4:3). The names of God's elect have been inscribed in this book "from the foundation of the world" (Revelation 17:8 NASB).

The concept of a Book of Life apparently harkens back to Old Testament times. For example, Moses requested that God blot his name from God's book rather than dooming his fellow Israelites (Exodus 32:32–33). In Psalm 69:28, the author requested that God blot out his enemies from "the book of life." In the end times, those whose names are not found in God's Book of Life will be cast into the lake of fire (Revelation 20:15).

Some scholars suggest that when each human being is born, his or her name is automatically written in the Book of Life. The name remains there as long as he or she is alive. Upon death, if the person has sinned (as all do) and has not received salvation in Jesus Christ, and/or if the person takes away from God's prophecy in the book of Revelation (Revelation 22:19), that person's name is blotted out of the Book of Life.

Some people have been concerned that perhaps Revelation 3:5 indicates the possibility of a Christian losing salvation: "He who overcomes will, like them, be dressed in white. I will never blot out his name from the book of life, but will acknowledge his name before my Father and his angels." One might interpret this as saying that the Christian can have his name blotted out of the Book of Life. But this is probably not the intent of Jesus' words.

First, there are many clear passages of Scripture that point to the security of one's salvation. In fact, the same John who wrote the book of Revelation wrote elsewhere about the security of salvation of each individual believer (see John 5:24; 6:35-37,39; 10:28-29; compare with John 10:28-30; Romans 8:29-39; Ephesians 4:30). Hence, however Revelation 3:5 is interpreted, it should probably not be taken to mean a believer can lose his or her salvation.

While this passage may imply that a believer's name could be erased from the Book of Life, actually it only gives a positive affirmation that their names *will not* be erased. Jesus' statement may thus be considered not a threat but indeed an assurance that saved peoples' names will always be in the Book of Life.

This seems to be the gist of what other verses communicate about the Book of Life. For example, in Luke 10:20 Jesus said to the disciples, "Do not rejoice that the spirits submit to you, but rejoice that your names are written in heaven." In Hebrews 12:23 we read of "the church of the firstborn, whose names are written in heaven."

Bottomless Pit

See *Abyss*.

Bowl Judgments

Human suffering will steadily escalate throughout the Tribulation period. First are the seal judgments, involving bloodshed, famine, death, economic upheaval, a great earthquake, and cosmic disturbances (Revelation 6). Then come the trumpet judgments, involving hail and fire mixed with blood, the sea turned to blood, water made bitter, further cosmic disturbances, affliction by demonic scorpions, and the death of a third of humankind (Revelation 8:6–9:21). Then come the increasingly worse bowl judgments, involving horribly painful sores on human beings, more bodies of water turning to blood, the death of all sea creatures, people being scorched by the sun, rivers drying up, total darkness engulfing the land, a devastating earthquake, widespread destruction, and much more (Revelation 16). Such is the judgment of God on a Christ-rejecting world.

Bridegroom, Bride of Christ

The bridegroom motif comes into play several times in the New Testament in regard to end times prophecy—and in several different senses. For example, the church is regarded as a virgin bride awaiting the coming of her heavenly bridegroom (2 Corinthians 11:2; see also Revelation 19:7-9).

In a different context, Jesus' parable of the ten virgins in Matthew 25:1-13 compares the kingdom of heaven to ten virgins who went out to meet the bridegroom (verse 1). Five of the virgins were foolish and five of them were wise. The foolish virgins did not take oil for their lamps (verse 3) while the wise virgins did (verse 4). All the virgins subsequently went to sleep while awaiting the bridegroom (verse 5). When the bridegroom arrived they all began to trim their lamps, but the foolish virgins did not have any oil (verses 6-8). While the foolish virgins were away buying oil, the door to the wedding feast was shut after the wise virgins had entered (verses 9-10). When the foolish virgins returned, they begged to get into the feast but they were told that they were not known (verses 11-12). The main point of the parable seems to be that only those who are watchful for the kingdom of God and alert for the coming of the Son of Man (that is, believers) will be able to enter it (verse 13).

Contextually, this refers to true believers who are living during the future Tribulation period, prior to the second coming of Christ. His coming will be sudden, when it is not expected. Believers are those who anticipate Jesus' coming and seek to be prepared for it, living their lives accordingly. Jesus' return will terminate the opportunity for people to "prepare themselves" (trust in Jesus) to enter His kingdom. Only those who are previously prepared (saved, by trusting in Christ) will be permitted to enter. No unprepared (unsaved) person will be permitted to enter.

We also see the bridegroom motif in relation to the marriage of the lamb. Jesus is the bridegroom, while the church—redeemed Christians—are the bride of Christ. We read in Revelation 19:7-9:

> Let us rejoice and exult and give him the glory, for the marriage of the Lamb has come, and his Bride has made herself ready; it was granted her to clothe herself with fine linen, bright and pure—for the fine linen is the righteous deeds of the saints. And the angel said to me, "Write this: Blessed are those who are invited to the marriage supper of the Lamb." And he said to me, "These are the true words of God."

The backdrop to this imagery is rooted in Hebrew weddings. There were three phases: 1) the marriage was legally consummated by the parents of the bride and groom; 2) the bridegroom came to claim his bride; and 3) the marriage supper, which was a feast lasting several days.

All three of these phases are seen in Christ's relationship to the church, or bride of Christ: 1) As individuals living during the Church Age come to salvation, they become a part of the Bride of Christ (or the church); 2) the Bridegroom (Jesus Christ) comes to claim His bride at the rapture, at which time He takes His bride to heaven, the Father's house (John 14:1-3), with the actual marriage taking place in heaven right prior to the second coming (Revelation 19:11-16); and 3) the marriage supper of the Lamb, which apparently takes place on earth at the beginning of the millennial kingdom. That this will be an earthly feast celebrated in the millennial kingdom seems to correspond to the illustrations of weddings in Scripture (see Matthew 22:1-14; 25:1-13).

C

Chiliasm

Chiliasm is another name for millennialism, the theological idea that Jesus Christ will reign on earth for a thousand years before the eternal state begins.

See *Millennial Kingdom.*

Church Age

From the perspective of the time of Christ, the establishment of the church was yet future (Matthew 16:12). Scripture reveals that the church age was inaugurated following the resurrection of Christ (Ephesians 1:20-22) and His ascension into heaven (Ephesians 4:7-12). Since every single believer in this age is baptized into the body of Christ (1 Corinthians 12:13), it seems clear that the church age must have begun on the day of Pentecost, since this is when this phenomenon first occurred (Acts 2; see also 11:15-16).

The church did not exist in Old Testament times. In fact, the church is called a "mystery" that was not revealed to past generations, but was revealed for the first time in the New Testament era. This mystery involved the idea of uniting Jewish and Gentile believers in one spiritual body (Ephesians 3:3-5,9; Colossians 1:26-27). This lends support to the idea that the church age began on the day of Pentecost.

This age will last up till the time the church is raptured off the earth, with the dead in Christ resurrecting and all living believers on the earth being instantly translated into their resurrection bodies (1 Thessalonians 4:13-17; 1 Corinthians 15:50-58). Pretribulationists believe this event takes place prior to the Tribulation period.

Church and Israel, Distinction

There are some similarities between Israel and the church. For example: 1) Both are part of the people of God; 2) Both are part of God's spiritual kingdom; and 3) Both participate in the spiritual blessings of both the Abrahamic and new covenants.

Beyond this, however, there are notable distinctions, including: 1) While the roots of Israel predate Moses, the church began on the day of Pentecost (Acts 1:5; 1 Corinthians 12:13); 2) While Israel is an earthly political entity (Exodus 19:5-6), the universal church is the invisible spiritual body of Christ (Ephesians 1:3); 3) While Israel was composed of Jews, the church is composed of both Jews and Gentiles (see Ephesians 2:15); and 4) One becomes a Jew by physical birth, whereas one becomes a member of the church via a spiritual birth (John 3:3).

Covenantalists like to argue that the New Testament church is spiritual Israel, a continuation of Old Testament ethnic Israel. Dispensationalists respond that such a view is wrong for the following reasons: 1) A consistent use of the historical-grammatical method demands that the unconditional land and throne promises be literally fulfilled in Israel (Genesis 13:1-7; 2 Samuel 7:12); 2) from the perspective of Jesus Christ Himself, Israel was in no sense a continuation of Old Testament Israel, but rather the church was viewed as an entity that was *yet future* from the time He spoke (Matthew 16:18; see also Ephesians 3:1-10). It was the advent of the Holy Spirit on the day of Pentecost that inaugurated the church (Acts 2:1-12; 1 Corinthians 12:13); 3) John the

Baptist offered a literal kingdom to national Israel (Matthew 3:2), as did Jesus (Matthew 19:28; 24:30) and Peter later (Acts 3:19-21); 4) the apostle Paul was clear that national Israel will be restored before Christ returns (Romans 11:1-2,29).

Church in Prophecy, The

The church is related to prophetic elements in Scripture in many different ways. This includes (but is not limited to):

- predictions of apostasy in the end times (2 Thessalonians 2:3; 1 Timothy 4:1-5; 2 Timothy 3:1-5),
- the emergency of heresy in the last days (2 Timothy 4:3),
- the imminent rapture of the church prior to the Tribulation (1 Thessalonians 4:13-17),
- the Tribulation taking place on earth while the church is in heaven (Revelation 4–18),
- the church as the bride of Christ who is not only married to Christ but participates in the marriage supper of the lamb (Revelation 19:7),
- the church reigning with Christ (2 Timothy 2:12; Revelation 20:6),
- and the church living in the New Jerusalem (Revelation 21; see also John 14:1-3).

Such prophetic factors ought to motivate Christians, as members of the church, to live in righteousness and purity as they await their Savior from heaven!

City of God

The term "City of God" is found in both the Bible and in popular Christian literature. In the Bible, the term is a name that is given to Jerusalem. For example, in Psalm 46:4 we read, "There is a river

C

whose streams make glad the city of God, the holy place where the Most High dwells." In this verse, the presence of God is compared to a peaceful flowing river that brings blessing to Jerusalem, the city of peace (see also Psalm 48:1,8).

The term is also used in Scripture to refer to the New Jerusalem, the heavenly city in which the saints of all ages will eternally dwell. It is referred to as the "city that has foundations, whose designer and builder is God" (Hebrews 11:10; see also John 14:1-3). In the book of Revelation, Jesus refers to it as "the city of my God, the new Jerusalem" (Revelation 3:12).

Augustine once wrote a philosophy of history entitled *The City of God.* In this volume, he suggested that there are two cities (or kingdoms)—the city of God and the city of man. These cities are different in a number of ways. One's origin lies in God, while the other is rooted in Satan. One is characterized by love for God, while the other is characterized by love of self. One is the habitat of Christians, while the other is the habitat of non-Christians.

Augustine taught that at the end of history, God—who is sovereign over all things—will be victorious over Satan and evil. The paradise that was lost by humankind in the beginning will be restored by God in the end.

Conversion of Israel

At present, Israel is in a state of judicial blindness (see *Blindness, Israel's*). Largely as a result of rejecting the divine Messiah (Romans 9:32), a partial judicial blindness or hardness of heart (causing a turning away from the gospel) has come upon Israel. Israel thus lost her favored position before God, and the gospel was then preached to the Gentiles, with a view to causing the Jews to become jealous and then become saved (Romans 11:11).

Israel's hardening and casting off is only *temporary.* In dire threat at Armageddon, Israel will finally recognize their Messiah and then plead for Him to return (they will "mourn for Him, as one mourns for an only son" (Zechariah 12:10 NASB; see also Matthew 23:37-39; see also Isaiah 53:1-9), at which point their deliverance will surely come (see Romans 10:13-14). Moreover, Israel's hardening and casting off is only *partial,* for there is a remnant of Israel who will be saved in this present age and become members of the church, the Body of Christ (see Romans 11:25).

See *Israel, Rebirth of.*

Cosmic Disturbances

Scripture reveals that there will be notable cosmic disturbances during the future Tribulation period. For example, there are cosmic disturbances associated with the seal judgments. We read, "I watched as he opened the sixth seal. There was a great earthquake. The sun turned black like sackcloth made of goat hair, the whole moon turned blood red" (Revelation 6:12). The same will be true of the trumpet judgments: "The fourth angel sounded his trumpet, and a third of the sun was struck, and a third of the moon, and a third of the stars, so that a third of them turned dark. A third of the day was without light, and also a third of the night" (8:12).

There will also be cosmic disturbances associated with the second coming of Christ. For example, Matthew 24:29-30 (NASB) tells us, "Immediately after the tribulation of those days the sun will be darkened, and the moon will not give its light, and the stars will fall from the sky, and the powers of the heavens will be shaken. And then the sign of the Son of Man will appear in the sky, and then all the tribes of the earth will mourn, and they will see the Son of Man coming on the clouds of heaven with power and great glory" (see also Isaiah 13:10; 24:23; Ezekiel 32:7; Joel 2:10,31; 3:15; Amos 5:20; 8:9; Zephaniah 1:15; Acts 2:20).

Covenants

A covenant is an agreement between two parties. Covenants were used among the ancients in the form of treaties or alliances between nations (1 Samuel 11:1); treaties between individual people (Genesis 21:27); friendship pacts (1 Samuel 18:3-4); and agreements between God and His people.

In the Bible, God made specific covenant promises to a number of people, including Noah (Genesis 9:8-17), Abraham (Genesis 15:12-21; 17:1-14), the Israelites at Mount Sinai (Exodus 19:5,6), David (2 Samuel 7:13; 23:5), and God's people in the new covenant (Jeremiah 31:31; Hebrews 8:6-13). *God is a God of promises.*

Covenants and Hermeneutics, The Debate over

A primary debate among Christians today relates to whether one should use a literal or an allegorical approach in interpreting Bible prophecy (including the prophetic covenants). While both sides claim to subscribe to the historical-grammatical method of Bible interpretation, classical dispensationalists believe that schools of thought that use an allegorical approach to biblical prophecy distort the true historical-grammatical method, as will become clear below.

The classical covenant view. In this view, a strict literal interpretation of prophetic Scripture is rejected. Jesus is viewed as the fulfillment of Old Testament promises made to Israel—including the land promises (in the Abrahamic covenant, Genesis 13:14-17) and the throne promises (in the Davidic covenant, 2 Samuel 7:12). The New Testament church is viewed as spiritual Israel, a continuation of Old Testament ethnic Israel. Hence, there will be no literal fulfillment of land promises (or other Old Testament prophecies) to Israel.

Dispensationalists view this position as practicing more eisegesis (reading a meaning into the text) than exegesis (deriving the meaning out of the text). They charge that this position is not consistent in using the historical-grammatical method, but rather incorporates allegory in prophetic portions of Scripture.

The modified covenantal view. While this view also rejects a strict literal interpretation of biblical prophecy, it also "modifies" things by allowing for a future literal fulfillment of land and throne promises made to Israel. There will allegedly be an initial spiritual fulfillment of these promises in the church, but the future will provide a more fully realized and literal fulfillment in which both Israel and the church share.

Again, dispensationalists respond that this view is built upon a faulty and inconsistent hermeneutic that ultimately allegorizes Old Testament promises made strictly to Israel. This view also fails to recognize the church's status as a "new creation" of God (2 Corinthians 5:17; Ephesians 3:3-5,9; Colossians 1:26-27).

Progressive dispensationalism. Progressive dispensationalism's openness to allegorism in interpreting Bible prophecy is evident in that it rejects that there is a fixed objective meaning of the biblical text. Rather, it holds that there are many meanings in a biblical text, and that we ought to seek a deeper understanding than the author's expressed meaning. This view also suggests there will be a literal fulfillment of the Abrahamic, Davidic, and new covenants in ethnic Israel, but also claims there is a present inaugural fulfillment of these covenants in the church.

Classical dispensationalists respond by asserting: 1) Those who approach prophecy in such an allegorical way are inconsistent, for they approach the rest of Scripture in a literal fashion; 2) there are no objective criteria by which one can determine the alleged correct allegorical truth; and 3) it goes against the precedent set by prophecies of Christ's first coming, all of which were fulfilled quite literally—including Christ being born of a virgin (Isaiah 7:14), in Bethlehem (Micah 5:2), from the line of Abraham (Genesis 15:1-6) and David (2 Samuel 7:12-16.).

Traditional dispensationalism versus revised dispensationalism. Both traditional dispensationalism and revised dispensationalism use a literal hermeneutic in interpreting Bible prophecy, and thus both believe in a national fulfillment of the Abrahamic covenant for Israel. Traditional dispensationalists, however, hold that there are two new covenants:

one for Israel (yet to be fulfilled) and one for the church (presently being fulfilled). As well, Israel and the church are viewed as two separate peoples with different destinies: one in heaven (the church) and the other on earth (Israel).

Revised dispensationalists, by contrast, hold that there is only one new covenant, which, while having a later literal fulfillment in national Israel, has a present application to the church. And even though revised dispensationalists see distinctives between Israel and the church, both are viewed as collectively composing one overall people of God who share in the spiritual redemption wrought by Christ.

Covenant, Antichrist Signs with Israel

Daniel 9:24-27 contains an important prophecy in reference to the future seven-year Tribulation. The event that will mark the beginning of this period is a covenant that the Antichrist will sign with Israel: "He will make a firm covenant with the many for one week" (verse 7 NASB).

Some prophecy experts believe this covenant may relate to the future Ezekiel invasion in which Russia and a group of Muslim nations—including Iran, Sudan, Turkey, Libya, Kazakhstan, Kyrgyzstan, Uzbekistan, Turkmenistan, Tajikistan, Armenia, and possibly northern Afghanistan—invade Israel in the end times (Ezekiel 38:1-6). After all, Ezekiel's prophecy indicates that the invasion will take place when Israel is *living in security and at rest* (Ezekiel 38:11). It is suggested that Israel will not have this strong sense of security and rest *until* the leader of the revived Roman empire—the Antichrist—signs a peace pact, guaranteeing Israel's protection (Daniel 9:27). Up till the signing of this covenant, Israel will remain as she presently is—always on "high alert" because of the possibility of attack. On any given day, it is possible that a Muslim suicide bomber could walk into a pizza parlor in Israel and blow everyone up. On any given day, Palestinian militants might try to sneak in and take sniper shots at Israel's citizens.

On any given day, missiles might come flying in overhead and blow up buildings in Israel. Many believe this will not stop until the peace pact is signed.

Whether or not this is so, it is clear that this covenant is a key event in the prophetic timetable, for the seven years that follow the signing of this agreement will be the seven worst years of human history, and will lead directly up to the second coming of Christ.

Crowns

All believers will one day stand before the Judgment Seat of Christ (Romans 14:10). At that time each believer's life will be examined in regard to deeds done while in the body. Personal motives and intents of the heart will also be weighed.

The idea of a judgment seat relates to the athletic games of Paul's day. When the races and games were over, a dignitary or perhaps the emperor himself would take a seat on an elevated throne in the arena. Then, one by one, the winning athletes would come up to the throne to receive a reward—usually a wreath of leaves, a victor's crown. In the case of Christians, each of us will stand before Christ the Judge and receive (or lose) rewards.

Scripture indicates that some believers at this judgment may have a sense of deprivation and suffer some degree of forfeiture and shame. Indeed, certain rewards may be forfeited that otherwise might have been received, and this will involve a sense of loss. The fact is, Christians differ radically in holiness of conduct and faithfulness in service. God in His justice and holiness takes all this into account. For this reason, 2 John 8 warns us, "Watch out that you do not lose what you have worked for, but that you may be rewarded fully." In 1 John 2:28 John wrote about the possibility of a believer actually being ashamed at Christ's coming.

What kinds of rewards will believers receive (or forfeit) at the Judgment Seat of Christ? Scripture often speaks of them in terms of crowns that we wear. In fact, there are a number of different crowns that symbolize the various spheres of achievement and award in the Christian life.

The *crown of life* is given to those who persevere under trial, and especially to those who suffer to the point of death (James 1:12; Revelation 2:10). The *crown of glory* is given to those who faithfully and sacrificially minister God's Word to the flock (1 Peter 5:4). The *crown incorruptible* is given to those who win the race of temperance and self-control (1 Corinthians 9:25). The *crown of righteousness* is given to those who long for the second coming of Christ (2 Timothy 4:8).

It is highly revealing that in Revelation 4:10 we find believers casting their crowns before the throne of God in an act of worship and adoration. This teaches us something very important. Clearly the crowns (as rewards) are bestowed on us not for our own glory but ultimately for the glory of God. We are told elsewhere in Scripture that believers are redeemed in order to bring glory to God (1 Corinthians 6:20). It would seem that the act of placing our crowns before the throne of God is an illustration of this.

Here is something else to think about. The greater reward or crown one has received, the greater capacity one has to bring glory to the Creator. The lesser reward or crown one has received, the lesser is his capacity to bring glory to the Creator. Because of the different rewards handed out at the judgment seat of Christ, believers will have differing capacities to bring glory to God.

Still, we should not take this to mean that certain believers will have a sense of lack throughout eternity. After all, each believer will be glorifying God to the fullness of his capacity in the next life. Each one of us, then, will be able to "declare the praises of him who called [us] out of darkness into his wonderful light" (1 Peter 2:9).

Cush

One of the nations that is part of the end-times northern military coalition that will launch an invasion against Israel is "Ethiopia" (NASB) or "Cush" (NIV) (Ezekiel 38:5). These terms refer to the geographical territory just south of Egypt on the Nile River—what is today known as Sudan.

Sudan is a hard-line Islamic nation, a kindred spirit with Iran in its venomous hatred of Israel. In fact, these nations are already such close allies that a mutual stand against Israel would not in the least be unexpected. This nation is infamous for its ties to terrorism and its harboring of Osama bin Laden from 1991 to 1996.

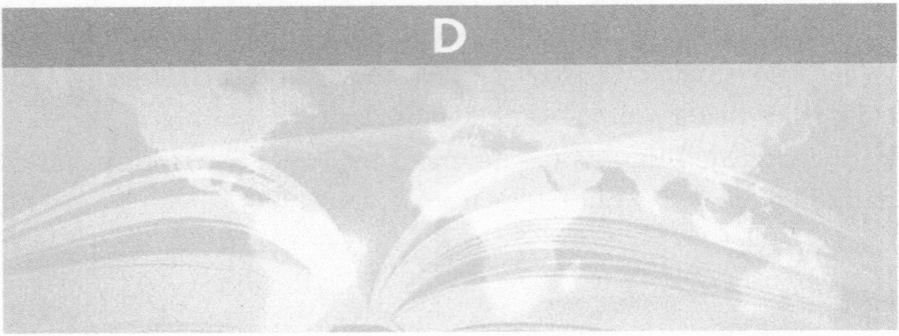

Daniel and the Seventy Weeks

Like the book of Revelation, the book of Daniel is categorized as apocalyptic literature. It contains Bible prophecy of the end times. The book was written by Daniel in about 537 B.C.

Daniel was a Jewish youth who had been deported to Babylon along with many other Jews in exile as a result of Nebuchadnezzar's siege of Jerusalem in 605 B.C. In Babylon Daniel rose to a position of prominence through his commitment to God and through the skills God had given him.

There is a great deal of hope in Daniel's writing. Even though God's people were presently suffering great persecution in their exile in Babylon, God was nevertheless in control and He had not abandoned them. There would come a day when He would deal with Israel's oppressors and set Israel free (Daniel 12). There would be justice in the end. God is sovereign over human history.

In Daniel 9 God provided a prophetic timetable for the nation of Israel. The prophetic clock began ticking when the command went out to restore and rebuild Jerusalem following its destruction by Babylon (Daniel 9:25). According to this verse, Israel's timetable was divided into 70 groups of seven years, totaling 490 years.

The first 69 groups of seven years—or 483 years—counted the years "from the issuing of the decree to restore and rebuild Jerusalem until the Anointed One, the ruler, comes" (Daniel 9:25). The "Anointed One" is Jesus Christ. "Anointed One" means Messiah. The day that Jesus rode into Jerusalem to proclaim Himself Israel's Messiah was exactly 483 years to the day after the command to restore and rebuild Jerusalem had been given.

At that point God's prophetic clock stopped. Daniel describes a gap between these 483 years and the final seven years of Israel's prophetic timetable. Several events were to take place during this "gap," according to Daniel 9:26: 1) The Messiah will be killed; 2) the city of Jerusalem and its temple would be destroyed (which occurred in A.D. 70); and 3) the Jews would encounter difficulty and hardship from that time on.

The final "week" of seven years will begin for Israel when the Antichrist confirms a "covenant" for seven years (Daniel 9:27). When this peace pact is signed, this will signal the beginning of the Tribulation period. That signature marks the beginning of the seven-year countdown to the second coming of Christ, which follows the Tribulation period.

Date-Setting

Christians can be excited about the coming of the Lord, but they should never set dates (for example, setting a date when the rapture is expected to occur). There are at least eight reasons for this:

1. Over the past 2,000 years, the track record of those who have predicted and/or expected "the end" has been 100 percent wrong. The history of doomsday predictions is little more than a history of dashed expectations. Though it is possible we are living in the last days, it is also possible that Christ's second coming may be a long way off.
2. Those who succumb to setting dates may end up making

harmful decisions for their lives. Selling one's possessions and heading for the mountains, purchasing bomb shelters, stopping education, leaving family and friends—these are destructive actions that can ruin one's life.

3. Christians who succumb to setting dates may end up damaging their faith in the Bible (especially prophetic sections) when their expectations fail.
4. If one loses confidence in the prophetic portions of Scripture, biblical prophecy ceases to be a motivation to purity and holiness in daily life (see Titus 2:12-14).
5. Christians who succumb to setting dates may damage the faith of new and/or immature believers when predicted events fail to materialize.
6. Date-setters tend to be sensationalistic, and sensationalism is unbefitting to a Christian. Christ calls His followers to live soberly and alertly as they await His coming (Mark 13:32-37).
7. Christians who get caught up in date setting can do damage to the cause of Christ. Humanists enjoy scorning Christians who have put stock in end-time predictions—especially when specific dates have been attached to specific events. Why give "ammo" to the enemies of Christianity?
8. The timing of end-time events is in God's hands, and we haven't been given the details (Acts 1:7). As far as the second coming is concerned, it is better to live as if Jesus were coming today and yet prepare for the future as if He were not coming for a long time. Then you are ready for time and eternity.

Davidic Covenant

God made a covenant with David in which He promised that one of his descendants would rule forever (2 Samuel 7:12-13; 22:51). This is an example of an unconditional covenant. It did not depend on David in any way for its fulfillment. David realized this when he received the promise from God, and responded with an attitude of humility and a recognition of God's sovereignty over the affairs of men.

The three key words of the covenant are *kingdom, house,* and *throne.* Such words point to the political future of Israel. The word *house* here carries the idea of "royal dynasty." This covenant finds its ultimate fulfillment in Jesus Christ, who was born from the line of David (Matthew 1:1), and will one day rule on the throne of David in Jerusalem during the future millennial kingdom (Ezekiel 36:1-12; Micah 4:1-5; Zephaniah 3:14-20; Zechariah 14:1-21).

Davidic Throne

Jesus Christ, the son of David (Matthew 1:1), will one day fill David's throne! This is promised in the David covenant of 2 Samuel 7:11-16 and 1 Chronicles 17:10-14. This covenant with David promised an *eternal kingdom,* an *eternal throne,* and an *eternal rule.* This will be fulfilled in the millennial kingdom with Jesus Christ Himself ruling over God's redeemed people in their land (see Isaiah 9:6-7; Jeremiah 23:5-6; 33:17-26; Amos 9:11-12; Luke 1:32-33). This reign of Christ during the millennial kingdom will extend beyond the Jews to include the Gentile nations as well.

Day of the Lord

The term *day of the Lord* is used in several senses in Scripture. The Old Testament prophets sometimes used the term of an event to be fulfilled in the near future. At other times, they used the term of an event in the distant eschatological future (the future Tribulation period). The immediate context of the term generally indicates which sense is intended. In both cases, the day of the Lord is characterized by God actively intervening supernaturally in order to bring judgment against sin in the world. The day of the Lord is a time in which

God actively controls and dominates history in a direct way, instead of working through secondary causes.

The New Testament writers generally use the term of the judgment that will climax in the future seven-year Tribulation period (2 Thessalonians 2:2; Revelation 16–18), as well as the judgment that will usher in the new earth in the end times (2 Peter 3:10-13; Revelation 20:7–21:1; see also Isaiah 65:17-19; 66:22; Revelation 21:1). It is this theme of judgment against sin that runs like a thread through the many references to the day of the Lord.

Days of Noah

See *Noah, Days of.*

Death

The New Testament word for "death" carries the idea of separation. At the moment of physical death, man's spirit separates or departs from his body (2 Corinthians 5:8). This is why, when Stephen was being put to death by stoning, he prayed, "Lord Jesus, receive my spirit" (Acts 7:59). At the moment of death "the spirit returns to God who gave it" (Ecclesiastes 12:7). Verses such as these indicate that death for the believer involves his or her spirit departing from the physical body and immediately going into the presence of the Lord in heaven. Death for the believer is thus an event that leads to a supremely blissful existence (Philippians 1:21).

For the unbeliever, however, death holds grim prospects. At death the unbeliever's spirit departs from the body and goes not to heaven but to a place of great suffering (Luke 16:19-31; 2 Peter 2:9).

Both believers and unbelievers remain as spirits, in a disembodied state, until the future day of resurrection. The resurrection bodies of believers will be specially suited to dwelling in heaven in the direct presence of God—the perishable will be made imperishable and the mortal will be made immortal (1 Corinthians 15:53). Unbelievers, too, will be resurrected, but they will spend eternity apart from God (John 5:29; Revelation 20:15).

Death is described in a rich variety of ways in the Bible, enabling us to understand a great deal about this mysterious event:

The way of all the earth. Sometimes death is described as "the way of all the earth," emphasizing the universality of the death experience. When David was about to die, he said to Solomon his son, "I am about to go the way of all the earth...So be strong, show yourself a man" (1 Kings 2:1-2).

The journey of no return. Job spoke of his eventual death by saying, "Only a few years will pass before I go on the journey of no return" (Job 16:22). Such words remind us of the permanence of passing from mortal life.

Breathing one's last. Job reflected that "man dies and is laid low; he breathes his last and is no more" (Job 14:10). This description of death focuses solely on the cessation of life in the physical body.

A withering away. Scripture says that man "springs up like a flower and withers away; like a fleeting shadow, he does not endure" (Job 14:2). The flower fades. Its beauty quickly vanishes. So it is with human life.

Departing. The apostle Paul said, "If I am to go on living in the body, this will mean fruitful labor for me. Yet what shall I choose? I do not know! I am torn between the two: I desire to depart and be with Christ, which is better by far" (Philippians 1:22-23). Paul considered departure from earthly life and into the Lord's presence something to be desired.

Dismissal from earthly life. Recognizing that God alone is sovereign over the timing and circumstances of death, Simeon, after beholding the Christ-child as God had promised, said, "Sovereign Lord, as you have promised, you now dismiss your servant in peace" (Luke 2:29).

Earthly tent being destroyed. The apostle Paul graphically described death as an earthly tent being destroyed (2 Corinthians 5:1). Our present bodies are temporary and flimsy abodes. They are weak, frail, and vulnerable. But a time is coming when these "habitations" will be resurrected, and our resurrection bodies will be permanent and indestructible.

Paradise. To one of the thieves being crucified with Him, Jesus said, "I tell you the truth, today you will be with me in paradise" (Luke 23:43). Paradise is a place of incredible bliss and serene rest in the very presence of God (2 Corinthians 12:2).

The physical body "sleeps." Death is often described in the Bible as "sleep," for the body takes on the appearance of sleep. The soul, however, does not sleep. It is fully conscious. The believer's soul in the afterlife is fully awake and active in the presence of God (Revelation 6:9-11). The unbeliever's soul is fully conscious in a place of great suffering (Luke 16:19-31).

Death, First and Second

The "first death" is physical death—that is, the separation of the spirit or soul from the body (Genesis 35:18). Virtually all people—except those Christians alive on earth at the future rapture of the church, at which point they will instantly receive glorified bodies—will experience the first death (1 Corinthians 15:50-55; 1 Thessalonians 4:13-17).

The "second death"—which is for unbelievers only—refers to eternal separation from God in the lake of fire, which is eternal hell. For the evil, "their portion will be in the lake that burns with fire and sulfur, which is the second death" (Revelation 20:14). The lake of fire will be populated immediately following the Great White Throne judgment, which is the judgment of the wicked (Revelation 20:11-15). No believer will experience the second death.

Deception, End Times

There will be broad and penetrating deception in the end times. For example, 1 Timothy 4:1 warns that "the Spirit clearly says that in later times some will abandon the faith and follow deceiving spirits and things taught by demons." Second Timothy 4:3-4 likewise warns that "the time is coming when people will no longer listen to sound and wholesome teaching. They will follow their own desires and will look for teachers who will tell them whatever their itching ears want to hear. The will reject the truth and chase after myths" (NLT).

A key verse pertaining to end times deception is 2 Thessalonians 2:3, which speaks of the coming day of the Lord. The English Standard Version renders the verse this way: "Let no one deceive you in any way. For that day will not come, *unless the rebellion comes first,* and the man of lawlessness is revealed, the son of destruction" (emphasis added). The New American Standard Version renders the critical part of this verse, "Let no one in any way deceive you, for it will not come *unless the apostasy comes first...*" (emphasis added). The King James Version puts it this way: "Let no man deceive you by any means: for that day shall not come, *except there come a falling away first...*" (emphasis added). These various translations give us insight into the apostle Paul's intended meaning. In the end times, there will be a great "apostasy," a "falling away" from the truth, a "rebellion" against God and His Word (see also 1 Timothy 4:1-3; 2 Timothy 3:1-5; 4:3-4; James 5:1-8; 2 Peter 2; 3:3-6). Apparently, this rebellious apostasy will prepare the way for the emergence of the Antichrist, who will be empowered by Satan, the Father of lies (John 8:44). This "falling away" must take place before the man of sin will be revealed.

Delay of the Second Coming

The reason the Lord continues to delay the second coming is clear from 2 Peter 3:9: "The Lord is not slow in keeping his promise, as some understand slowness, but is patient with you, not wanting any to perish, but everyone to come to repentance." God is patient and is awaiting people to repent. God has a long track-record of showing immense patience before bringing people to judgment (see Joel 2:13; Luke 15:20; Romans 9:22).

One should be careful to note that although God desires that "everyone to come to repentance" (2 Peter 3:9), this verse does not teach universalism, for not all *will* reach repentance. In the end, there will be many who refuse to turn to God and will therefore spend eternity apart from Him (Matthew 25:46). God longs that all be saved (see 1 Timothy 2:4), but not all will receive God's gift of salvation (see Matthew 7:13-14).

Demons

Many scholars believe Revelation 12:4 contains a mini-history of the fall of the angels who followed Lucifer's rebellion: "His [Satan's] tail swept a third of the stars out of the sky and flung them to the earth." It has long been recognized that the word "stars" is sometimes used of angels in the Bible (see Job 38:7). If "stars" refers to angels in Revelation 12:4, it would appear that after Lucifer rebelled against God (Isaiah 14:12-15; Ezekiel 28:12-19), he was able to draw a third of the angelic realm after him in this rebellion. Lucifer apparently led a massive angelic revolt against God. These fallen angels are the demons of the New Testament (see Revelation 12:7; Ephesians 3:10; 6:12).

Nature. Demons are portrayed in Scripture as being evil and wicked. They are designated "unclean spirits" (Matthew 10:1), "evil spirits" (Luke 7:21), and "spiritual forces of wickedness" (Ephesians 6:12). All these terms point to the immoral nature of demons.

Activities. Demons, under Satan's lead, seek to disseminate false doctrine (1 Timothy 4:1). As well, they wield influence over false prophets (1 John 4:1-4) and seek to turn men to the worship of idols (see Leviticus 17:7; Deuteronomy 32:17; Psalm 106:36-38). Demons hinder answers to the prayers of believers (Daniel 10:12-20), and instigate jealousy and faction among believers (James 3:13-16). Scripture also portrays them as inflicting physical diseases on people (such as dumbness, Matthew 9:33; blindness, 12:22; and epilepsy, 17:15-18). They also afflict people with mental disorders (Mark 5:4-5; 9:22; Luke 8:27-29; 9:37-42). They cause people to be self-destructive (Mark 5:5; Luke 9:42). They are even responsible for the deaths of some people (Revelation 9:14-19).

Classes. Presently there are two classes or groups of demons. One group of demons is free and active in opposing God and His people (Ephesians 2:1-3). The other group is confined (2 Peter 2:4). These confined demons are apparently being punished for some sin other than the original rebellion against God. Some theologians believe these angels are guilty of the unnatural and heinous sin mentioned in Genesis 6:2-4, and because of the gross depravity of this sin they are confined to Tartarus, which is translated as "hell" in 2 Peter 2:4.

Ranks. Just as God's holy angels are organized according to rank, so fallen angels are organized according to rank—including principalities, powers, rulers of the darkness of this world, and spiritual wickedness in high places (see Ephesians 6:12). All fallen angels, regardless of their individual ranks, follow the leadership of their malevolent commander-in-chief—Satan, the prince of demons.

Last days. In the last days, demons will be increasingly active in promulgating doctrines of demons (false doctrines) to deceive the masses of humanity (1 Timothy 4:1). Their goal is to keep as many human beings from going to heaven as possible. As well, during the future Tribulation they will be active in tormenting those who dwell on the earth (see Revelation 9:3). After the Tribulation, prior to the beginning of Christ's millennial kingdom, Satan and demonic spirits will be bound (Revelation 20:2). Their eventual destiny is the lake of fire (Revelation 20:10).

Destruction of the Jerusalem Temple (A.D. 70)

Jesus prophesied the destruction of Jerusalem and the Jewish temple. In Luke 23:28-29, Jesus—shortly to be crucified—turned to a group of women who were following Him and said, "Daughters of Jerusalem, do not weep for me; weep for yourselves and for your children. For the time will come when you will say, 'Blessed are the barren women, the wombs that never bore and the breasts that never nursed!'" Barren women living during that time would be considered blessed, for it would be better for women not to have any children than for them to have children experience such suffering as would come in A.D. 70. Jesus thus sadly told these women to "weep for yourselves."

The Jewish historian Flavius Josephus documented that some Jewish mothers were reduced to eating their own children during the famine that followed Rome's siege against Jerusalem. This adds all the more to the graveness of Jesus' words about the blessing of being barren during that time.

Archaeological finds now reveal that Roman soldiers looted the destroyed temple. Indeed, in the Arch of Titus in the ancient Roman forum is a scene in which Roman soldiers are portrayed carrying sacred items looted from the destroyed temple. Looted items include the Table of Showbread and the Golden Lampstand.

While Jesus prophesied the destruction of Jerusalem and the Jewish temple in Luke 23, some Bible interpreters—*preterists* and *partial preterists*—allege that Jesus' Olivet discourse in Matthew 24–25 and the book of Revelation also refer to this event. For more on this faulty view, see *Preterism*.

Devil

See *Satan*.

Discerning Signs of the Times

See *Fig Tree, Parable*.

Dispensationalism

Dispensationalism is a system of theology that is characterized by 1) a consistent literal method of interpreting the Bible, 2) a clear distinction between Israel and the church, and 3) the glory of God as God's ultimate purpose in the world. The word *dispensation*—from the

Greek *oikonomia* (meaning "stewardship")—refers to a distinguishable economy in the outworking of God's purpose. This system of theology views the world as a household run by God. In this "household," God delegates duties and assigns humankind certain responsibilities. If human beings obey God during that dispensation, God promises blessing; if human beings disobey, He promises judgment. In each dispensation, we generally see 1) the testing of humankind, 2) the failure of humankind, and 3) judgment as a consequence. As things unfold, God provides progressive revelation of His plan for history.

The present dispensation is the church age. Prior to that was the dispensation of the law. A future dispensation is the millennial kingdom (see Ephesians 1 and 3; John 1:17; Romans 6:14; Galatians 3:19-25). These three dispensations might be categorized as Old Testament, New Testament, and Kingdom. Dispensationalism recognizes that God deals differently with people in different ages or economies, as illustrated in how God related to people in Moses' time, in our day, and in the future millennium.

There is some disagreement among dispensationalists on some issues—one example being the proper way to interpret the covenants. For example, both traditional dispensationalism and revised dispensationalism use a literal hermeneutic in interpreting Bible prophecy, and thus both believe in a national fulfillment of the Abrahamic covenant for Israel (Genesis 12:3; 13:14-17; 15:18-21). Traditional dispensationalism, however, holds that there are two new covenants: one for Israel (yet to be fulfilled) and one for the church (presently being fulfilled). As well, Israel and the church are viewed as two separate peoples with different destinies: one in heaven (the church) and the other on earth (Israel).

Revised dispensationalism, by contrast, holds there is only one new covenant, which, while having a later literal fulfillment in national Israel, has a present application to the church. And even though revised dispensationalists see distinctives between Israel and the church, both are viewed as collectively composing one overall people of God who share in the spiritual redemption wrought by Christ.

D

Dispensations

There are seven dispensations that are part and parcel of traditional dispensationalism:

Innocence (Genesis 1:28–3:6). This dispensation relates to Adam and Eve, up till the time they fell into sin at the Fall.

Conscience (Genesis 3:7–8:14). This dispensation describes the time between the Fall and the Flood (see Romans 2:15).

Human Government (Genesis 8:15–11:9). Following the Flood, God began a new dispensation when He instituted human government to mediate and restrain evil on the earth.

Promise (Genesis 11:10–Exodus 18:27). This dispensation relates to God's call of Abraham, and the specific promises God made to Him and His descendants, both physical and spiritual.

Law/Israel (Exodus 19–John 14:30). This dispensation is characterized by God's giving of the law to Israel as a guide to live by, governing every aspect of their lives. Note that the law was not presented as a means of salvation. Note also that the law's status as a tutor was temporary—lasting only until the coming of and fulfillment by Christ (Galatians 3:23-25).

Grace/Church (Acts 2:1–Revelation 19:21). In this dispensation, the rule of life in the church is grace.

Kingdom (Revelation 20:1-15). This dispensation relates to Christ's future millennial kingdom, over which He will rule for 1,000 years on the throne of David. The church will rule with Christ as His bride.

Dragon

In the book of Revelation, Satan is metaphorically referred to as "the dragon, the serpent of old" (20:2 NASB). The names and titles used of Satan in Scripture reveal something about his character. In the present case, the term "dragon" reveals that he is ferocious and cruel, particularly in his attacks against believers.

The reference to Satan as the "serpent of old" hearkens back to the

Garden of Eden. It was here that Satan through the serpent deceived Eve (Genesis 3; see also 2 Corinthians 11:3; 1 Timothy 2:14).

Though this "dragon" is a powerful foe, Scripture reveals that his destiny is the lake of fire (Revelation 20:10). He will be confined there for all eternity, forever quarantined from believers who are in eternal bliss in heaven.

E

Earthquakes

Scripture reveals there will be an increase in earthquakes in the end times. Speaking of signs of the end, Jesus in Matthew 24:7 affirms that "nation will rise against nation, and kingdom against kingdom, and there will be famines and earthquakes in various places" (see also Mark 13:8; Luke 21:11).

Earthquakes certainly play a pivotal role during the seven-year Tribulation period, as documented in the book of Revelation. A "great earthquake" is associated with the sixth seal judgment (Revelation 6:12 NASB). Revelation 11:13 speaks of a "great earthquake" so strong that "a tenth of the city fell," and "seven thousand people were killed in the earthquake" (NASB). Revelation 16:18 speaks of another "great earthquake, such as there had never been since man came to be upon the earth, so great...was it, and so mighty" (NASB). Earthquakes in the book of Revelation are connected with judgment, for each of the three series of judgments—the seal judgments, the trumpet judgments, and the bowl judgments—end with an earthquake.

Related to this, Scripture also reveals that in the end times, a northern military coalition involving Russia, Iran, Turkey, Libya, and other nations will invade Israel (see Ezekiel 38), and God Himself will destroy these invaders. One of the means of doing this is via a great earthquake (verses 19-20). Ezekiel described this devastating earthquake as one in which "the mountains...will be thrown down, the steep pathways will collapse and every wall will fall to the ground" (verse 20 NASB), and it will cause many troops to die. Transportation will be utterly disrupted, and apparently the armies of the multinational forces will be thrown into utter chaos. So intense will this earthquake be that all the creatures on the earth will feel its effect.

Such verses indicate that earthquakes are one means by which God unleashes judgment on sinners on earth. God is in absolute control over the world of nature!

Eclectic View of Revelation

There are four primary interpretive approaches to studying the book of Revelation:

1. The *historicist* view holds that the book of Revelation supplies a prophetic overview of the entire panoramic sweep of church history, from the first century to the second coming of Christ.
2. The *futurist* view holds that most of the events described in the book of Revelation will take place in the end times, just prior to the second coming of Jesus Christ.
3. The *idealist* view holds that the book of Revelation is primarily a symbolic description of the ongoing battle between God and the devil, between good and evil. Seen in this light, the book of Revelation gives strength to believers as they suffer through persecution and various injustices.
4. The *preterist* approach holds that the prophecies of Revelation were fulfilled in the first century A.D.—more specifically, in A.D. 70, when Titus and his Roman warriors overran Jerusalem and destroyed the Jewish temple.

There is also what is called the *eclectic* view, which is a mixed view that combines the features of these four views. The eclectic view says that there is both a present and a future fulfillment of the prophecies contained in the book of Revelation, or perhaps some of the events described in Revelation were fulfilled in the past but there will still be some fulfilled in the future.

Elders, 24

In Revelation 4:4 we are told that around the throne of God were "twenty-four…thrones, and seated on them were twenty-four elders. They were dressed in white and had crowns of gold on their heads" (see also 4:10; 5:5,6,8,11,14; 7:11,13; 11:16; 14:3; 19:4). It is difficult to say with certainty who these 24 elders are. Some hold that they must be counselors who are enthroned. It is difficult to see, however, what role or purpose such counselors might have. Moreover, throughout the rest of the book of Revelation, we see no evidence of them engaging in actual counseling.

Other interpreters suggest that the 24 elders are angelic beings—perhaps as some kind of heavenly ruling council (see Jeremiah 23:18,22). If this view is correct, it might explain Michael's role as a "chief prince" (Daniel 10:13). Against this view, however, is the fact that they seem to be glorified, crowned, and enthroned, something that seems more in keeping with redeemed human beings. Scripture elsewhere reveals that believers will be judged (1 Corinthians 3:10-15; 2 Corinthians 5:10) and then rewarded with crowns (for example, 2 Timothy 4:8; James 1:12; 1 Peter 5:4; Revelation 2:10), something that is never said to be true of angels.

If the elders are representative of believers, as many other interpreters hold, the question becomes whether they represent the redeemed of both the Old and New Testaments, or just the redeemed of the New Testament. Some expositors hold to one view, and other expositors embrace the other view.

If the 24 elders—who are portrayed as being in heaven—represent the redeemed of the New Testament, then it would seem that the church is in view. This would seem to coincide best with the pretribulational view of the rapture, which holds that the church will be "raptured" and brought to heaven prior to the beginning of the Tribulation. The fact that they are dressed in white may be significant, for these same words were previously used of believers within the churches (see Revelation 3:5,18). Moreover, as noted previously, the fact that the elders have crowns may be significant, because believers in the churches were promised crowns (see 2:10; 3:11).

Because so many respected biblical scholars have such different views on the identity of the 24 elders, it is probably best not to be dogmatic on the issue. This is an issue over which Christians can agree to disagree in an agreeable way.

Elect, The

The elect are those who have been chosen by God for salvation before the foundation of the world. There are two primary views as to how these individuals actually become elect: 1) the foreknowledge view and 2) the sovereignty view. Let's us briefly consider both:

Foreknowledge view. This view says that God used His foreknowledge to look down the corridors of time to see who would respond favorably to His Gospel message, and on that basis He elected certain persons to salvation. Several arguments are offered in favor of this view:

- Scripture teaches that God's salvation has appeared to all men, not merely the elect (Titus 2:11).
- The Bible teaches that Christ died for all (1 Timothy 2:6; 4:10; Hebrews 2:9; 2 Peter 2:1; 1 John 2:2).
- There are numerous exhortations in Scripture to turn to God (Isaiah 31:6; Joel 2:13; Matthew 18:3; Acts 3:19), to repent (Matthew 3:2; Luke 13:3,5; Acts 2:38; 17:30), and to believe (John 6:29; Acts 16:31; 1 John 3:23).

- Scripture seems to indicate that election is based on God's foreknowledge of who would respond positively to such exhortations (Romans 8:28-30; 1 Peter 1:1).

Among the arguments offered against this view are statements in Scripture indicating that the Father gave certain ones to Christ (John 6:37; 17:2,6,9). Christ said, "No one can come to Me, unless the Father who sent Me draws him" (John 6:44 NASB). Moreover, in Romans 9:10-16 God is said to have chosen Jacob rather than Esau, even before they were born and before they had done either good or bad.

We read in Acts 13:48 that "as many as had been appointed to eternal life believed" (NASB). Ephesians 1:5-8 and 2:8-10 represent salvation as originating in the choice of God and as being all of grace (see also Acts 5:31; 11:18; Romans 12:3; Ephesians 2:8-10; 2 Timothy 2:25). Finally, many claim that if election is not unconditional and absolute, then God's whole plan is uncertain and liable to miscarriage.

Sovereignty view. The second view is that God's election is based on His sovereign choice. A number of arguments are offered in favor of this view:

- Biblical statements support election by choice (Acts 13:48).
- The whole process of salvation is a gift of God (Romans 12:3; Ephesians 2:8-10).
- Certain verses speak of human beings having been given to Christ (John 6:37; 17:2), and of the Father drawing men to Christ (John 6:44).
- There are examples in Scripture of the sovereign calling of God upon individuals, like Paul (Galatians 1:15) and Jeremiah (Jeremiah 1:5), even before they were born.
- Election is necessary in light of man's total depravity (Job 14:1; Jeremiah 13:11; Romans 3:10-20).
- Election is necessary in light of man's inability (Ephesians 2:1).

- Election is compatible with God's sovereignty (Jeremiah 10:23; Proverbs 19:21).
- Election is portrayed as being from all eternity (2 Timothy 1:9).
- It is on the basis of election by choice that the appeal to a godly life is made (Colossians 3:12; 2 Thessalonians 2:13; 1 Peter 2:9).

Two primary arguments have been suggested against this view:

1. First, it is argued that if election is limited by God, then surely the atonement must be limited as well (providing salvation only for the elect). However, this conclusion is clearly refuted by John 1:29, 3:16, 1 Timothy 2:6, Hebrews 2:9, and 1 John 2:2.
2. It is argued that election by choice makes God responsible for "reprobation." However, those not included in election suffer only their due reward. God does not "elect" a person to hell. Those not elected to salvation are left to their own self-destructive ways.

Commonalities. Whichever view one concludes is the correct one, the following facts should be kept in mind: God's election is loving (Ephesians 1:4-11); election glorifies God (Ephesians 1:12-14); and the product of election is a people who do good works (Ephesians 2:10; Colossians 3:12; Romans 11:33-36).

End Times

The term *end times* is a general phrase that embraces a number of events that take place in the eschatological last days—including the rapture, the Judgment Seat of Christ (for Christians), the Tribulation (and all the events that take place during that seven-year period, such as the emergence and reign of the Antichrist and Armageddon), the second coming of Jesus Christ, Christ's millennial kingdom, the

Great White Throne judgment (for the wicked), a destiny in hell for the wicked, and the destiny of heaven for believers. (This dictionary fully explains each of these events.)

E

Ephesus

Ephesus was a city characterized by luxurious homes, elegant buildings, and wide avenues. A hundred or so wealthy aristocrats owned most of the land around the city; these individuals also controlled the local government. Ephesus was a leading commercial and trade center of the ancient world, and was understandably one of the more prominent cities in the province of Asia.

Ephesus is well known for its temple of the Roman goddess Diana (Greek: Artemis), a structure that was considered one of the seven wonders of the world. Hence, this was a city where many pagans lived. It is a city that needed the gospel.

During his third missionary tour, the apostle Paul spent about three years in Ephesus building up the church there (Acts 19). When he left, Paul's young associate Timothy pastored there for another year or so, seeking to establish them in sound doctrine (1 Timothy 1:3,20).

Sometime later, Paul wrote his epistle to the Ephesians while a prisoner in Rome in A.D. 61. However, he intended it to be a circular letter to be read not just at the church at Ephesus but other churches as well. This conclusion is based on several factors. First, the phrase "To the Ephesians" is missing from some ancient biblical manuscripts. Further, the letter does not aim to solve any specific problems of any specific church, but rather contains general truths relevant to all churches.

In this epistle, Paul speaks of God's eternal sovereign purpose for the church (Ephesians 1:6-14), as well as the spiritual blessing and spiritual endowment that are ours in Jesus Christ (see 2:4-10). Believers should therefore live a life worthy of the high calling with which they have been called (4:1; see also 2:10).

Paul also speaks of how all things in the universe find their ultimate unity in the person of Jesus Christ (Ephesians 4:1-16). This especially includes the church, where both Jews and Gentiles—believers from every nation in the world—are united in Christ. In Christ there are no racial, religious, cultural, or social barriers. In view of this unity, believers should act with love toward one another, whether husbands and wives, masters and slaves, or parents and children (chapter 5).

Ephesus is one of the seven churches addressed in the book of Revelation (see 2:1-7). The church was commended for not going along with those who were evil, and for testing and standing against false apostles (verse 2). However, the church was also chastised for abandoning their first love (verse 4). Christ called on them to repent and do the works they did at first (verse 5). Christ also adds a special commendation for hating the works of the Nicolaitans (verse 6).

See *Nicolaitans.*

Eschatology

The study of prophecy or the end times is known in theological circles as eschatology. This term is derived from two Greek words: *eschatos,* meaning "last" or "last things," and *logos,* meaning "study of." Eschatology is the study of last things, or study of the end times, particularly as related to the second coming of Christ and the events preceding and following this great event. The importance of eschatology is found in the fact that 25 percent of divine revelation was prophetic when written. Subjects dealt with include Jesus Christ, Israel, the church, the Gentiles, Satan, the Antichrist, apostasy, judgments, Armageddon, and much more.

Eschatology can logically be broken down into two primary areas of study. *Personal eschatology* concerns such things as death, the future judgment, heaven, and hell. (These are matters related to each person.) *General eschatology* concerns more general matters, such as the rapture, the Tribulation, the second coming, and the millennial kingdom.

A major benefit of eschatology is that it provides encouragement to suffering believers, particularly in their witness for Jesus Christ (Matthew 24:14; 1 Corinthians 15:58). Moreover, a strong view on the prophetic events in Scripture has a purifying effect in the lives of believers (Titus 2:13-14).

E

Eschaton

Eschaton is a term that literally means "last," and is often used in reference to the end of the present world, or to a final event that brings about the end of the present world. The Eschaton includes the second coming of Christ, the millennial kingdom, and the eternal state.

See *Eschatology.*

Eternal Life

God is the only being in the universe that is intrinsically eternal, never having been created. He has always existed. He never came into being at a point in time. He is beyond time altogether. He is the King eternal (1 Timothy 1:17) who alone is immortal (6:16). But those who trust in Christ are the recipients of "eternal life," and they will live with Him forever in heaven (John 3:16-17). It is a life forever uninterrupted by death. This gift of eternal life is available to those who believe in Christ as Savior (John 3:15-16; 5:24; 6:40,47; 12:25).

The eternal life of believers is not just *quantitative* in the afterlife (that is, never-ending life in the afterlife). It is also a *qualitative* kind of life that the believer receives *in the now,* and continues into eternity (see John 3:15-16,36; 5:24; 6:27; 17:3; Acts 17:25). Seen in this light, eternal life refers to the quality of our new existence in Christ as well as the unending character (or quantity) of that life in the afterlife.

The actual term "eternal life" appears most often in the writings of John. He emphasizes that eternal life is the present possession of the Christian (see John 3:36; 5:24; 1 John 5:13). The "now" sense of that salvation is evident in John 17:3: "Now this is eternal life: that they know you, the only true God, and Jesus Christ, whom you have sent" (see also John 5:24; Romans 6:4; 1 John 1:2).

Conversely (and sadly), those who do not know the only true God, and Jesus Christ, will experience "eternal punishment" (Matthew 25:46). Those who reject Jesus Christ put themselves at utmost peril.

Eternal Perspective

As Christians ponder the awesome greatness of God, as well as the many prophecies He has revealed in Scripture, it creates an excitement in the heart—an excitement that is rooted in the reality of a future eternity in heaven with our wondrous God. No matter what takes place on this earth, Christians have a splendorous destiny ahead. A daily pondering of the incredible glory of the afterlife is one of the surest ways to stay motivated to live faithfully during this relatively short stay on earth. Christians are but pilgrims en route to another land—to the final frontier of heaven where God Himself dwells (Revelation 21).

Eternal State

Christ will set up His thousand-year millennial kingdom on earth following His second coming. It is after the millennial kingdom that the eternal state will begin.

There is both an eternal state for the redeemed and an eternal state for the lost. John's vision of the eternal state of the redeemed is found in Revelation 21:1-8:

> Then I saw a new heaven and a new earth, for the first heaven and the first earth had passed away, and there was no longer any sea. And I saw the holy city, new Jerusalem, coming down out of heaven from God...And I heard a loud voice from the throne saying, "Now, the dwelling place of God is with men, and he will live with them. They will be his people, and God himself will be with them and be their God. He will wipe away every tear from their eyes. There will be no more death or mourning or crying or pain, for the old order of things has passed away." He who was seated

> on the throne said, "I am making everything new!" Then he said, "Write this down, for these words are trustworthy and true." He said to me: "It is done. I am the Alpha and the Omega, the Beginning and the End."

By contrast, the eternal state of the lost is the lake of fire, which is hell. John describes the judgment of the wicked and their eternal destiny in Revelation 20:11-15:

> Then I saw a great white throne and him who was seated on it...And I saw the dead, great and small, standing before the throne, and books were opened. Another book was opened, which is the book of life. The dead were judged according to what they had done as recorded in the books... Then death and Hades were thrown into the lake of fire. The lake of fire is the second death. If anyone's name was not found written in the book of life, he was thrown into the lake of fire.

Theologians and Bible expositors have been careful to distinguish between the *present* heaven where God now dwells and where believers go at the moment of death (2 Corinthians 5:8; Philippians 1:21-23), and the *future* heaven where believers will spend all eternity (that is, in the eternal state—see 2 Peter 3:13; Revelation 21:1). God will one day create new heavens and a new earth. It is upon this new earth that the New Jerusalem, the heavenly city, will rest (Revelation 21:10). It will be this glorious city where believers will reside for all eternity (Revelation 21–22).

The description of the New Jerusalem—the heavenly city—in the book of Revelation is astounding. Presented to our amazed gaze in Revelation 21 is a scene of such transcendent splendor that the human mind can scarcely take it in. This is a scene of ecstatic joy and fellowship of sinless angels and redeemed glorified human beings. The voice of the One identified as the Alpha and the Omega, the beginning and the end, utters a climactic declaration: "Behold, I am making all things new" (Revelation 21:5). The heavenly city will be far more wondrous than we can possibly imagine.

Euphrates River

The Euphrates River—also referenced in Scripture as "the river" (Exodus 23:31), or "the great river" (Deuteronomy 1:7)—is mentioned several times in the book of Revelation. For example, in Revelation 9:14 an angel is instructed, "Release the four angels who are bound at the great river Euphrates." In Revelation 16:12 we read that this same angel "poured out his bowl on the great river Euphrates, and its water was dried up to prepare the way for the kings from the East."

The Euphrates River—the longest river of Western Asia (almost 1,800 miles)—begins in modern-day Turkey, heads toward the Mediterranean Sea, then turns south, flows over 1,000 miles to eventually converge with the Tigris River, and then flows into the Persian Gulf. Many ancient cities, including Ur and Babylon, are located at various points along the river.

Interestingly, the Euphrates was one of the rivers that flowed from the Garden of Eden (see Genesis 2:14). Moreover, according to the Abrahamic covenant (Genesis 15:18), the Euphrates River constituted the northern boundary of the land promised to Abraham's descendants (see Deuteronomy 11:24; Joshua 1:4), something that became a reality under the rule of David (2 Samuel 8:3).

It is noteworthy that this river finds significance in both the first and the last books of the Bible!

Ezekiel

The book of Ezekiel was written by the prophet Ezekiel, the son of Buzi, between 593 and 570 B.C., and his messages were for the Jews in exile. God had called him into service as a prophet when he was about 30 years of age. At the time, he was training to be a priest. Like all the other Jews, however, he soon found himself living in exile in Babylon, and this captivity would last 70 years.

Ezekiel's name literally means "God is strong" or "strengthened by God." To carry on his work of confronting the people regarding their sins, and bringing comfort to them while in exile, Ezekiel would surely need God's strength.

As a prophet, Ezekiel was quite unique. He would often dramatize God's message by using signs, symbols, and parables. (For example, he said the dispersed Jews are like dry bones in the sun, Ezekiel 37.) By using such techniques, Ezekiel graphically communicated that God's judgment falls as a result of human sin. This is the message he proclaimed during the first part of his ministry.

In 597 B.C., when he and some 3,000 other Jews went into exile in Babylon by Nebuchadnezzar (the uncontested ruler of the world at that time), Ezekiel started to speak a new message—words of hope and comfort, teaching that God would regather His people from the ends of the earth, and a new temple would one day be built (Ezekiel 40). He tried to give the people something to look forward to.

Ezekiel Invasion

Some 2,600 years ago, the ancient prophet Ezekiel prophesied that the Jews would be regathered from "many nations" to the land of Israel in the end times (Ezekiel 36–37). He then prophesied that, sometime later, there would be an all-out invasion of Israel by a massive northern assault force, with Russia heading up a coalition of Muslim nations, including modern Iran, Sudan, Turkey, and Libya. Their goal will be to utterly obliterate the Jews. And with the sheer size of this assault force, Israel will have virtually no chance of defending itself. God, however, will intervene and supernaturally destroy the invaders (38–39).

More than a few students of the Bible have recognized that the very nations prophesied to join this alliance in the end times are, in fact, already coming together in our own day. The fact that this alliance is beginning to emerge after Israel became a nation again in 1948—with Jews continuing to stream into their homeland ever since, so that today there are more Jews in Israel than anywhere else on earth—is considered by many to be highly significant. It appears that the stage may be being set for this prophesied future invasion into Israel.

Of course, it is always possible for things to reverse course, in which case the invasion could still be a long way off. Nevertheless, seeking to obey Jesus' injunction to accurately discern the times (Matthew 16:1-3; Luke 21:29-33), it very well may be that what we witness happening today is preparing the way for the eventual invasion of this northern alliance into Israel.

Some interpreters have tried to deny that these chapters have reference to a future invasion into Israel, holding instead that perhaps they refer to an invasion in past history. The evidence, however, is in favor of a future invasion:

1. There has never been an invasion into Israel on the scale of what is described in Ezekiel 38–39. Nor has there ever been an invasion into Israel involving the specific nations mentioned in the passage. Since it hasn't been fulfilled yet, its fulfillment must yet be future.

2. Ezekiel was clear that the things of which he spoke would be fulfilled "in the latter years" (Ezekiel 38:8 NASB) and "in the last days" (38:16 NASB) from the standpoint of his day. Such phrases point to the end times.

3. The unique alignment of nations as described in Ezekiel 38–39 has never occurred in the past, but is apparently occurring in modern days.

4. Related to this, it can be observed that an alliance between many of the nations mentioned in Ezekiel 38–39 may not necessarily have made good sense in Ezekiel's day (since some are not located near each other), but it makes great sense today because the nations that make up the coalition

are predominantly Muslim. That in itself is more than enough reason for them to unify in attacking Israel—especially given current Islamic hatred for Israel.

5. Ezekiel affirmed that the invasion would occur after Israel would have been regathered from all around the earth—"gathered from many nations" (Ezekiel 38:8; see also verse 12)—to a land that had been a wasteland. Certainly there were occasions in Israel's history where the Jews were held in bondage. For example, they were held in bondage in Egypt. They went into captivity in Assyria, as well as in Babylon. But in each of these cases, their deliverance involved being set free from a single nation, not many nations around the world. The only regathering of Jews from "many nations" around the world in Israel's history is that which is occurring in modern days.
6. Since chapters 36–37 are apparently being literally fulfilled (a regathering from "many nations"), it is reasonable and consistent to assume that chapters 38–39 will likewise be literally fulfilled. This is in keeping with the well-established precedent of biblical prophecies throughout the Old Testament being literally fulfilled.
7. Without a literal approach, we are left in a sea of relativism regarding what prophetic passages teach. Unless prophetic statements are taken in their normal sense, it is almost impossible to determine their meaning with any consistency. As the well known dictum puts it, when the plain sense makes good sense, seek no other sense.

F

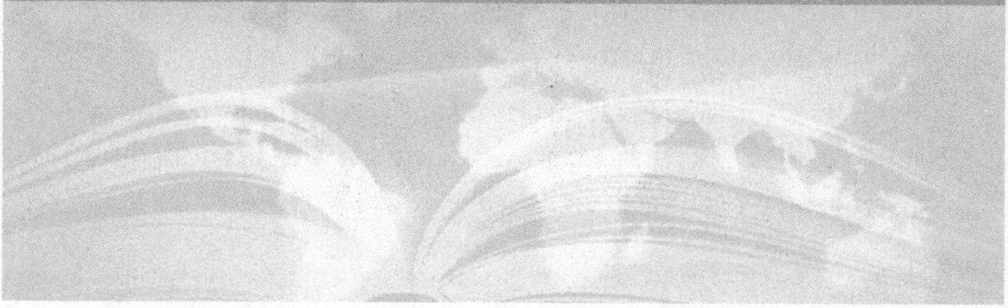

Fallen Angels

See *Demons.*

Fallen Angels, Judgment of

Within the pages of Scripture we find that there are six distinct judgments against Satan, himself a fallen angel, and leader and representative of all other fallen angels:

- Following Satan's initial rebellion against God, he was cast from his original position of privilege in heaven (Ezekiel 28:16).
- He was judged in the Garden of Eden following his role in leading Adam and Eve into sin (Genesis 3:14-15).
- He was judged at the cross (John 12:31; see also Colossians 2:15; Hebrews 2:14). Christ partook of humanity, and through His substitutionary death on the cross He defeated Satan, rendering him impotent in the believer's life.
- He will be cast out of heaven in the middle of the seven-year Tribulation period (Revelation 12:13). During this time he will be barred from all further access to heaven.

- He will be confined in the abyss (bottomless pit) during the future 1,000-year millennial kingdom over which Christ will rule (Revelation 20:2).
- He will ultimately be cast into the lake of fire at the end of the millennial kingdom, where he will be quarantined for all eternity (Revelation 20:10; see also Matthew 25:41).

What we learn from the above passages is that even though Satan (like other fallen angels) is presently active in our world, he is a judged being and is destined for eternal suffering. While the *execution* of this final judgment is not yet *enforced*, the judgments have been *pronounced* and it's just a matter of time before Satan's final doom is brought about, along with all other fallen angels.

False Apostles

The apostle Paul warned of false apostles who are "deceitful workmen, masquerading as apostles of Christ" (2 Corinthians 11:13). The two key characteristics we see here are that these individuals 1) deceive people doctrinally and 2) pretend to be true apostles of Jesus Christ.

Christ commends those who take a stand against false apostles. In Revelation 2:2, we read Christ's commendation to the church of Ephesus: "I know your deeds, your hard work and your perseverance. I know that you cannot tolerate wicked men, that *you have tested those who claim to be apostles but are not, and have found them false*" (emphasis added).

How can the claims of apostles be "tested"? Like the ancient Bereans, all Christians should make a regular habit of testing all things against Scripture (Acts 17:11), for Scripture is our only infallible barometer of truth. No true apostle will ever say anything that will contradict the Word of God (see Galatians 1:8).

False Christs

In Matthew 24:24 Jesus Himself warned about the end times: "For false Christs and false prophets will appear and perform great signs and miracles to deceive even the elect—if that were possible" (see also Mark 13:22). The apostle Paul also warned of a different Jesus (2 Corinthians 11:4). The danger, of course, is that a *counterfeit Jesus* who preaches a *counterfeit gospel* yields a *counterfeit salvation* (compare with Galatians 1:8). There are no exceptions to this maxim.

Even in our own day, we witness an unprecedented rise in false Christs and self-constituted messiahs affiliated with the kingdom of the cults and the occult. This will no doubt continue as we move further into the end times.

False Prophet, The

During the Tribulation period, a diabolic trinity will emerge—the Antichrist (the beast), the False Prophet (a second beast, who is a lieutenant of the Antichrist), and Satan (also called the dragon). The book of Revelation reveals that the False Prophet will control religious affairs on earth (Revelation 13:11), will be motivated by Satan (verse 11), will promote the worship of the Antichrist (verse 12), will execute those who refuse to worship the Antichrist (verse 15), will control economic commerce on the earth with a view to enforcing worship of the Antichrist (verse 17), will perform apparent signs and miracles (verse 13), and bring deception and false doctrine upon the whole world (verse 14).

The diabolical trinity is destined for doom. In Revelation 19:20 we read that the Antichrist and the false prophet will be "thrown alive into the fiery lake of burning sulfur." This will take place before the beginning of Christ's millennial kingdom. Then, at the end of the millennial kingdom—1,000 years *after* the Antichrist and the False Prophet had been thrown into the lake of burning sulfur—the devil will be "thrown into the lake of burning sulfur, where the beast and the False Prophet had been thrown. They will be tormented day and night for ever and ever" (Revelation 20:10).

Notice that the Antichrist and False Prophet will not be burned up or annihilated at the time the devil is thrown into the lake of burning sulfur. "They" will *still be burning* after one thousand years. These sinister beings, along with unbelievers of all ages, will be tormented *day and night forever* (Revelation 20:14-15).

False Prophets and Teachers

Scripture contains many warnings against false prophets and false teachers for the simple reason that it is possible for God's own people to be deceived. Ezekiel 34:1-7, for example, indicates that God's sheep can be abused and led astray by wicked shepherds. Jesus warned His followers: "Watch out for false prophets. They come to you in sheep's clothing, but inwardly they are ferocious wolves" (Matthew 7:15-16). Why would Jesus warn His followers to "watch out" if there was no possibility that they could be deceived? The apostle Paul likewise warned his Christian readers about the possibility of deception (2 Corinthians 11:2-3; see also Acts 20:28-30). It is in view of this that the Bible exhorts believers to "test" those who claim to be prophets (see 1 John 4:1).

How can believers recognize a false prophet? Deuteronomy 18:21-22 indicates that false prophets are those who give false prophecies that do not come true. Other verses in the Bible indicate that false prophets sometimes cause people to follow false gods or idols (Exodus 20:3-4; Deuteronomy 13:1-3); they often deny the deity of Jesus Christ (Colossians 2:8-9); they sometimes deny the humanity of Jesus Christ (1 John 4:1-2); they sometimes advocate abstaining from certain foods and/or meats for spiritual reasons (1 Timothy 4:3-4); they sometimes deprecate or deny the need for marriage (1 Timothy 4:3); they often promote immorality (Jude 4-7); and they often encourage legalistic self-denial (Colossians 2:16-23). A basic rule of thumb is that if a so-called prophet says anything that clearly contradicts any part of God's Word, his teachings should be rejected (Acts 17:11; 1 Thessalonians 5:21).

Famine

In biblical times, there were always threats to the food supply—even in Palestine, the land of "milk and honey" (Exodus 13:5). An enemy might invade and destroy all the crops. Locusts might swoop in out of nowhere and consume the crops in less than an hour. If there was not enough rain, the crops would not grow. Because of such factors, famines often occurred in biblical times. So long as everything went well, however, people could generally produce enough food for daily needs.

In the book of Joel, we read of a devastating swarm of locusts that ripped through the land of Judah, resulting in famine. This black cloud of devouring insects struck like a firestorm. As these consuming locusts ate up the agricultural produce and caused the light of the sun to be hidden and darkened, Joel saw in this catastrophe a little foretaste of the day of judgment that was surely coming upon God's people (Joel 1:15–2:11). In fact, Joel indicated that as bad as the locust plague was, it would pale by comparison to God's day of judgment. He therefore called the people to repentance (2:12-17). The reality is, Joel said, that God cannot ignore sin. Blessing can only follow obedience.

The book of Revelation speaks of famine as part and parcel of the judgments unleashed during the seven-year Tribulation period. For example, in Revelation 6:8, we read, "I looked, and there before me was a pale horse! Its rider was named Death, and Hades was following close behind him. They were given power over a fourth of the earth to kill by sword, famine and plague, and by the wild beasts of the earth" (see also Revelation 18:8). A famine makes sense during this period, for crops will be destroyed, workers (including food workers) will be killed, and transportation—including the transportation of food—will be greatly disrupted.

Feasts, Related to Biblical Prophecy

There are some Bible expositors who believe that Jewish fall feasts typologically point forward to end time events. The seven fall feasts are Passover, Unleavened Bread, First Fruits, Feast of Weeks, Feast of

Trumpets, Day of Atonement, and the Feast of Tabernacles. It is suggested that the Feast of Trumpets is a reference to the rapture (see Leviticus 23:24), for when the great trumpet sounds, the rapture will occur (see 1 Corinthians 15:51-52; 1 Thessalonians 4:16-17). The problem with this viewpoint is that Israel's feasts relate to Israel alone. The rapture is an event that is related to the church, and hence it seems unlikely that it would be predicted through Old Testament revelation regarding Jewish feasts. Still, it is wise not to be dogmatic on the issue.

Fig Tree, Parable

Scripture says we should seek to be accurate observers of the times. Consider the words of Jesus in Matthew 16:1-3:

> The Pharisees and Sadducees came up, and testing Jesus, they asked Him to show them a sign from heaven. But He replied to them, "When it is evening, you say, 'It will be fair weather, for the sky is red.' And in the morning, 'There will be a storm today, for the sky is red and threatening.' Do you know how to discern the appearance of the sky, but cannot discern the signs of the times?" (NASB).

What a rebuke! The religious elite of the time were supposed to know the teachings of Scripture, and yet they were completely blind to properly discerning the times. The Pharisees and Sadducees had been bombarded by spiritual signs relating to the person of Jesus Christ and they had missed them all. They were blinded to the reality that the Messiah was in their midst. The miracles Jesus wrought were just as clear a sign to His divine identity as dark clouds in the sky are a sign of impending rain. These miracles had been prophesied of the Messiah in the Old Testament (Isaiah 35:5-6), and the Pharisees and Sadducees—experts in the Old Testament—should have seen Jesus as being the fulfillment of these messianic verses. But in their blindness, they could not discern the "signs of the times." All Christians ought to resolve not to follow the example of the Pharisees and Sadducees!

Jesus urged, "Now learn the parable from the fig tree: when its branch has already become tender and puts forth its leaves, you know that summer is near; so, you too, when you see all these things, recognize that He is near, right at the door" (Matthew 24:32-33). Jesus indicates in this verse that there are certain things God has revealed via prophecy which ought to cause people who know the Bible to understand that a fulfillment of prophecy is taking place—or perhaps the stage is being set for a prophecy to eventually be fulfilled. Jesus is thus informing His followers to seek to be accurate observers of the times so that when biblical prophecies are fulfilled, they will recognize it (see also Luke 21:25-28).

Figurative Language

See *Allegory*.

Final Revolt

The bottomless pit serves as the place of imprisonment of some demonic spirits (Luke 8:31; 2 Peter 2:4). The devil—along with all demonic spirits—will be bound here for 1,000 years, during Christ's millennial kingdom (Revelation 20:1-3). This quarantine will effectively remove a powerful destructive and deceptive force in all areas of human life and thought during Christ's kingdom.

At the end of the 1,000 years, Satan will be loosed from the bottomless pit and have one last opportunity to deceive the nations (Revelation 20:7-9). He will then be judged and eternally cast into the lake of fire (Revelation 20:10; see also Matthew 25:46).

In view of the fact that only believers who survive the Tribulation will enter into Christ's millennial kingdom (Matthew 25:31-46), one might wonder how Satan would succeed in leading many astray following the 1,000 years. Apparently, some of the *descendants* of these believers will *not* be believers themselves. It is these that Satan gathers against God in one final rebellion. Christ will quickly and decisively crush this rebellion. The Great White Throne judgment, which is the judgment of the wicked, will then take place and the lake of fire will be populated (Revelation 20:11-15). The eternal state will then be established (Revelation 21).

F

First and the Last

The phrase "I am the first and I am the last" is used of Almighty God in the Old Testament. Isaiah 44:6, for example, records God as saying, "I am the first and I am the last; apart from me there is no God." Again, in Isaiah 48:12, God affirmed, "I am he; I am the first and I am the last," and God said this right after His pronouncement that "I will not yield my glory to another" (verse 11b).

All this is significant, for in the book of Revelation, Jesus Himself claims to be the First and the Last. In Revelation 1:17, He urges, "Do not be afraid. I am the First and the Last." In addressing the church in Smyrna, Jesus said: "These are the words of him who is the First and the Last, who died and came to life again" (Revelation 2:8). Then, in Revelation 22:13, Jesus again affirmed, "I am the Alpha and the Omega, the First and the Last, the Beginning and the End."

Christ's use of this title was undoubtedly intended to be taken as a claim to equality with God. And it is precisely this that was to bring comfort and encouragement to Christ's followers who were undergoing great persecution. Christ wanted them to be absolutely assured that He is the all-powerful Sovereign who will be victorious in the end. As the First and the Last, Christ is the all-powerful One of eternity past and eternity future.

First Death

See *Death, First and Second.*

First Resurrection

See *Resurrection, First and Second.*

Forehead, Mark of the Beast on

In Revelation 14:9-11, an angel issues this warning:

> If anyone worships the beast and his image and receives his mark on the forehead or on the hand, he, too, will drink of the wine of God's fury, which has been poured full strength into the cup of his wrath. He will be tormented with burning sulfur in the presence of the holy angels and of the Lamb. And the smoke of their torment rises for ever and ever. There is no rest day or night for those who worship the beast and his image, or for anyone who receives the mark of his name.

Such words are sobering. Any who express loyalty to the Antichrist and his cause will suffer the wrath of our holy and just God. How awful it will be for these to experience the full force of God's divine anger and unmitigated vengeance (see Psalm 75:8; Isaiah 51:17; Jeremiah 25:15-16)!

Four Beasts of Daniel

Daniel 7:3-8 makes reference to four beasts—representing kingdoms—that play an important role in biblical prophecy. Daniel begins in verse 3 by affirming, "Four great beasts, each different from the others, came up out of the sea."

The first, Daniel says, was "like a lion, and it had the wings of an eagle," but "its wings were torn off" (verse 4). This imagery apparently represents Babylon, its lionlike quality indicating power and strength. It is interesting to observe that winged lions guarded the gates of Babylon's royal palaces (see Jeremiah 4:7,13). The wings indicate rapid mobility, while the plucking of the wings indicate a removal of mobility (perhaps a reference to Nebuchadnezzar's insanity, or to Babylon's deterioration following his death).

Daniel continued in verse 5 by referring to a "second beast which looked like a bear. It was raised up on one of its sides, and it had three ribs in its mouth between its teeth. It was told, 'Get up and eat your fill of flesh.'" This kingdom is Medo-Persia, and the "ribs" are vanquished nations—perhaps Lydia, Babylon, and Egypt. Medo-Persia was well-known for its strength and fierceness in battle (see Isaiah 13:17-18).

Daniel then referred to a third beast, "like a leopard, with four wings of a bird on its back. And the beast had four heads, and dominion was given to it" (Daniel 7:6). The leopard was an animal that was known for its swiftness, cunning, and agility. This imagery represents Greece under Alexander the Great. The reference to the "four heads" are the four generals who divided the kingdom following Alexander's death, ruling Macedonia, Asia Minor, Syria, and Egypt.

Finally, in verse 7, Daniel makes reference to the fourth beast—a mongrel beast composed of parts of a lion, bear, and leopard that was more terrifying and powerful than the three preceding beasts:

> Behold, a fourth beast, terrifying and dreadful and exceedingly strong. It had great iron teeth; it devoured and broke in pieces and stamped what was left with its feet. It was different from all the beasts that were before it, and it had ten horns. I considered the horns, and behold, there came up among them another horn, a little one, before which three of the first horns were plucked up by the roots. And behold, in this horn were eyes like the eyes of a man, and a mouth speaking great things.

This wild imagery refers to the Roman Empire. Rome already existed in ancient days, but it fell apart in the fifth century A.D. It will be revived, however, in the end times, apparently comprised of ten nations ruled by ten kings (ten horns). An eleventh horn—a little horn (the Antichrist)—starts out apparently in an insignificant way, but grows powerful enough to uproot three of the existing horns (kings). He eventually comes into absolute power and dominance over this revived Roman Empire.

Four Horsemen of the Apocalypse

The four horsemen of the apocalypse relate to the seal judgments that are poured out on humankind during the Tribulation (see Revelation 6). We first find reference to a person riding a white horse (6:2). Some have speculated that perhaps the rider is Jesus Christ, since Jesus is said to ride a white horse in Revelation 19:11. However, the contexts are entirely different. In Revelation 19 Christ returns to the earth as a conqueror on a horse at the end of the Tribulation. By contrast, Revelation 6 deals with a rider on a horse at the beginning of the Tribulation, in association with three other horses and their riders, all associated with the seal judgments. Most scholars believe the rider of the white horse in Revelation 6:2 is none other than the Antichrist (Daniel 9:26). The crown suggests that this individual is a ruler. It may be that the mention of the bow without an arrow is symbolic of the idea that the Antichrist's world government will be accomplished without warfare. It would seem that his government begins with a time of peace, but it is short-lived, for destruction will surely follow (see 1 Thessalonians 5:3).

A second horse mentioned in Revelation 6:3-4 is red—a color that represents bloodshed, killing with the sword, and war (see also Matthew 24:6-7). The rider carries a large sword. These verses symbolize that man's efforts at bringing about peace will be utterly frustrated, for peace will be taken from the entire earth. As bad as this will be, however, it will only represent the initial "birth pangs" of what is yet to come upon the earth (see Matthew 24:8; Mark 13:7-8; Luke 21:9).

A third horse mentioned in Revelation 6:5-6 is black. The rider is carrying a pair of scales in his hand. This apparently symbolizes famine (with subsequent death), as the prices for wheat and barley are extravagantly high, requiring a day's wages just to buy a few meals (see Lamentations 5:8-10). Such a famine would not be unexpected following global war.

A fourth horse mentioned in Revelation 6:7-8 is pale—literally, "yellowish-green," the color of a corpse. The rider of this horse is appropriately named Death. It would seem that the death symbolized here is the natural consequence of the previous three judgments. The death toll will be catastrophic (a fourth of earth's population).

Woe to those who dwell on the earth during this time!

Fullness of the Gentiles

The phrase "fullness of the Gentiles" is used by the apostle Paul in Romans 11:25-26 in reference to Israel and the Gentiles in the end times. More specifically, near the end of the Tribulation period, Israel will experience national conversion. However, up till that time, Gentiles will largely comprise the people of God. Once the predetermined number of Gentiles have become believers—once the "fullness of the Gentiles" has been reached—large numbers of Jews will also find salvation. As Paul points out in Romans 9–11, God is not finished with Israel yet.

See *Israel, Rebirth of.*

Future Events

Future events ought to be a concern for all Christians. The fact that over one fourth of the Bible is prophetic in nature shows that God considers it an important issue. The Bible often uses terms such as "the last days" or "the latter times" to speak of the end times. In the eschatological last days, many events will take place, including the rapture, the Judgment Seat of Christ (for Christians), the Tribulation (and all the events that take place during that seven-year period, such as the emergence and reign of the Antichrist and Armageddon), the second coming of Jesus Christ, Christ's millennial kingdom, the Great White Throne judgment (for the wicked), a destiny in hell for the wicked, and the destiny of heaven for believers.

Futurist View of Revelation

The futurist approach to interpreting the book of Revelation holds that most of the events described in the book will take place in the end times, just prior to the second coming of Jesus Christ. This view is in contrast to 1) the preterist approach, which sees most of the prophecies as having already been fulfilled in A.D. 70; 2) the historicist view, which holds that the book of Revelation supplies a prophetic overview of the entire panoramic sweep of church history, from the first century to the second coming of Christ; and 3) the idealist view, which holds that Revelation is primarily a symbolic description of the ongoing battle between God and the devil, between good and evil. It seems evident that the early church took a futurist view inasmuch as it saw the Tribulation, second coming, and millennium as yet-future events. Later writers who took a futurist approach include Jesuit Francisco Ribera (1537–1591) and John Nelson Darby (1800–1882).

G

Gehenna

Gehenna is one of the more important New Testament words for hell (Matthew 10:28; see also 2 Kings 23:10). This word has an interesting history. For several generations in ancient Israel, atrocities were committed in the Valley of Ben Hinnom—atrocities that included human sacrifices, even the sacrifice of children (2 Chronicles 28:3; 33:6; Jeremiah 32:35). These unfortunate victims were sacrificed to the false Moabite god Molech. Jeremiah appropriately called this valley a "Valley of Slaughter" (Jeremiah 7:31-34).

Eventually the valley came to be used as a public rubbish dump into which all the filth in Jerusalem was poured. Not only garbage but also the bodies of dead animals and the corpses of criminals were thrown on the heap where they—like everything else in the dump—would perpetually burn. The valley was a place where the fires never stopped burning. And there was always a good meal for a hungry worm.

This place was originally called (in the Hebrew) *Ge ben hinnom* (the valley of the son of Hinnom—see Joshua 15:8 NASB). It was eventually shortened to *Ge-Hinnom* (see Nehemiah 11:30). The Greek translation of this Hebrew phrase is *Gehenna.* It became an appropriate and graphic term for the reality of hell. Jesus Himself used the word eleven times as a metaphorical way of describing the eternal place of suffering of unredeemed humanity.

See *Hell.*

See *Lake of Fire.*

Generation, This

In Matthew 24:34 Jesus said, "Truly I say to you, *this generation* will not pass away until all these things take place" (emphasis added). Evangelical Christians have generally held to one of two interpretations of Matthew 24:34. One is that Christ was simply saying that those people who witness the signs stated earlier in Matthew 24 (dealing with the future Tribulation period) will see the coming of Jesus Christ within *that* very generation. In other words, the generation alive when "these things" (the abomination of desolation [verse 15], the great Tribulation such as has never been seen before [verse 21], the sign of the Son of Man in heaven [verse 30], and the like) begin to come to pass will still be alive when these judgments are completed. Since it is commonly believed that the Tribulation is a period of seven years (Daniel 9:27; Revelation 11:2) at the end of the age, then Jesus would be saying that "this generation" alive at the beginning of the Tribulation will still be alive at the end of it.

Other evangelicals say the word *generation* is to be taken in its basic usage of "race, kindred, family, stock, or breed." Jesus' statement could mean that the Jewish race would not pass away until all things are fulfilled. Since there were many promises to Israel, including the eternal inheritance of the land of Palestine (Genesis 12; 15; 17) and the Davidic kingdom (2 Samuel 7), then Jesus could be referring to God's preservation of the nation Israel in order to fulfill His promises to them. Indeed, Paul speaks of a future of the nation of Israel when they will be reinstated in God's covenantal promises (Romans 11:11-26).

G

Gentiles, Times of the

The phrase, "times of the Gentiles" (referred to by Christ in Luke 21:24), refers to the time of Gentile domination of Jerusalem. This period began with the Babylonian captivity that started in 606 B.C. The "times of the Gentiles" was well entrenched by A.D. 70 when Titus and his Roman warriors overran Jerusalem and destroyed the Jewish temple. This does not rule out the possibility of temporary Jewish control over Jerusalem, but such Jewish control will be temporary until the second coming. This "time" will last into the seven-year future Tribulation period (Revelation 11:2), and will not end until the end of the great Tribulation and the second coming of Jesus Christ.

To clarify, in our own day the Israelis control much of Jerusalem, but they do not control the Arab quarter or the area of the temple site. Hence, the times of the Gentiles have not yet ended.

Jerusalem will one day be restored under the rule of the divine Messiah, Jesus Christ. In dire threat at Armageddon, Israel will finally recognize their Messiah and then plead for Him to return. They will "mourn for Him, as one mourns for an only son" (Zechariah 12:10 NASB; Matthew 23:37-39; see also Isaiah 53:1-9), at which point their deliverance will surely come (see Romans 10:13-14). These regenerated Jews will enter into Christ's millennial kingdom (see Daniel 7:22,27; Zechariah 14:5; Matthew 19:28).

Glorious Appearing

Titus 2:11-14 speaks of "our blessed hope—the glorious appearing of our great God and Savior, Jesus Christ." This will be a magnificent event accompanied by cosmic phenomena involving the sun, moon, and stars (Matthew 24:29), the sign of the Son of Man will appear in the heavens (Matthew 24:30), He will be on a white horse (Revelation 19:11), followed by the armies of heaven (Revelation 19:14), in great power and glory (Matthew 24:30). The Antichrist and his forces will confront Christ (Revelation 19:19), but both he and the False Prophet will be promptly cast into the lake of fire (Revelation 19:20). All those who reject Christ are executed (Revelation 19:21), Satan is imprisoned in the pit for 1,000 years (Revelation 20:1-3), the Tribulation saints will be resurrected from the dead (Revelation 20:4), and Christ will judge the nations and set up His millennial kingdom (Matthew 25:31-46). Truly it will be a "glorious appearing."

It is important to note that the "glorious appearing" will be different than the rapture. Every eye will see Jesus at the second coming (Revelation 1:7), but the rapture is never described as being visible to the whole world. At the rapture, Jesus will come *for* His church (John 14:1-3; 1 Thessalonians 4:13-17), while at the second coming (the "glorious appearing") Jesus will come *with* His church (Colossians 3:4; Jude 14; Revelation 19:14). At the rapture, Christians will meet Jesus in the air (1 Thessalonians 4:13-17) whereas at the second coming Jesus' feet will touch the Mount of Olives (Zechariah 14:4). At the rapture, Christians will be taken and unbelievers will be left behind (1 Thessalonians 4:13-17), whereas at the second coming unbelievers will be taken away in judgment (Luke 17:34-36), while mortal believers will remain to enter into Christ's millennial kingdom (Matthew 25:31-46). At the rapture, Jesus will receive His bride, whereas at the second coming or "glorious appearing," He executes judgment (Matthew 25:31-46). The rapture will take place in the blink of an eye (1 Corinthians 15:52), whereas the second coming will be more drawn out, and every eye will see Him (Matthew 24:30; Revelation 1:7).

God, Protector of Israel

Scripture reveals that God is always watchful—"He who keeps Israel will neither slumber nor sleep" (Psalm 121:4 NASB)—and He will be Israel's defender. So, for example, the invaders who are a part of the end-times northern military coalition against Israel (Ezekiel 38) may think their success is all but guaranteed, but Israel's attackers stand no chance of success. God had earlier promised His people that "no weapon that is formed against you will prosper" (Isaiah 54:17 NASB). In fulfilling this promise, we often witness God in the Old Testament playing the definitive role in battling against Israel's enemies (see, for example, Exodus 15:3 and Psalm 24:8). God is even sometimes described in military terms—the "Lord of Hosts" (2 Samuel 6:2,18).

G

God is certainly powerful enough to defeat Israel's enemies. Scripture portrays God as being all-powerful (Jeremiah 32:17). He has the power to do all that He desires and wills. Some 56 times Scripture declares that God is almighty (for example, Revelation 19:6). God is abundant in strength (Psalm 147:5) and has incomparably great power (2 Chronicles 20:6; Ephesians 1:19-21). No one can hold back His hand (Daniel 4:35). No one can reverse Him (Isaiah 43:13) and no one can thwart Him (Isaiah 14:27). Nothing is impossible with Him (Matthew 19:26; Mark 10:27; Luke 1:37) and nothing is too difficult for Him (Genesis 18:14; Jeremiah 32:17,27). The Almighty reigns (Revelation 19:6).

God, Sovereign over Human Affairs

God is absolutely sovereign over human affairs, and this is a primary reason that Christians can trust Bible prophecy. God rules the universe, controls all things, and is Lord over all (see Ephesians 1). There is nothing that can happen in this universe that is beyond the reach of His control. All forms of existence are within the scope of His absolute dominion. Psalm 50:1 makes reference to God as the Mighty One who "speaks and summons the earth from the rising of the sun to the place where it sets." Psalm 66:7 affirms that "He rules forever by his power." We are assured in Psalm 93:1 that "the LORD reigns" and "is armed with strength." God asserts, "My purpose will stand, and I will do all that I please" (Isaiah 46:10). God assures us, "Surely, as I have planned, so it will be, and as I have purposed, so it will stand" (Isaiah 14:24).

God is also absolutely sovereign over the affairs of individual nations in the world. In the book of Job we read, "He makes the nations great, then destroys them; He enlarges the nations, then leads them away" (Job 12:23 NASB). We are told that "from one man he created all the nations throughout the whole earth. He decided beforehand which should rise and fall, and he determined their boundaries" (Acts 17:25-26). Daniel 2:21 tells us that "it is He who changes the times and the epochs; He removes kings and establishes kings" (NASB).

Gog

The word *Gog* is a reference to the powerful leader of the end-times northern military coalition that will launch an invasion against Israel (Ezekiel 38). Gog is referred to as the "prince of Rosh, Meshech and Tubal" (verse 2 NASB). This term appears eleven times in Ezekiel 38–39, thereby indicating that he plays a significant role in this end-times invasion.

The term *Gog* may or may not be a proper name. There is a reference to an altogether different Gog in 1 Chronicles 5:4, where we read that among the sons of Joel were "Shemaiah his son, Gog his son, Shimei his son," and others. This verse at least indicates that the term *can* be used as a proper name. It would seem, however, that the term is not intended as a proper name in the context of Ezekiel 38–39. The term may refer to a king-like role—such as Pharaoh, Caesar, czar, or president. The term literally means "high," "supreme," "a height," or "a high mountain." Apparently, then, this leader—this czar-like military leader—will be a man of great stature who commands tremendous respect.

It is critical to understand that Gog is not just another name for the Antichrist. One will end up in prophetic chaos if one tries to make this identification. The Antichrist heads up a revived Roman Empire (Daniel 2,7), while Gog heads up an invasion force made up of Russia and a number of Muslim nations (Ezekiel 38:1-6). Moreover, Gog's invasion into Israel constitutes a direct challenge to the Antichrist's covenant with Israel (Daniel 9:27). Further, Gog's moment in the limelight is short-lived (it's all over when God destroys the invading force—Ezekiel 39), whereas the Antichrist is in power over the span of a significant part of the Tribulation period.

Gomer

Gomer is one of the nations that is part of the northern military coalition that will launch an invasion against Israel in the end times (Ezekiel 38:1-6). Identifying Gomer is difficult. There is no clear consensus among Bible scholars. The "best guess" is that it refers either to modern-day Turkey or perhaps to modern-day Germany.

In support of the Turkey hypothesis, the ancient historian Josephus said Gomer founded those whom the Greeks called the Galatians. The Galatians of New Testament times lived in the region of central Turkey. Hence, there is a direct connection of ancient Gomer to modern Turkey.

Moreover, many claim Gomer may be a reference to the ancient Cimmerians or Kimmerioi. History reveals that from around 700 B.C., the Cimmerians occupied the geographical territory that is modern Turkey.

In support of the Germany hypothesis, the Jewish Talmud claims Gomer refers to Germani, or the Germans. This was the rabbinic view. The Midrash calls Gomer Germania.

Gospel of the Kingdom

In Matthew 24:14 we read of the gospel of the kingdom: "This gospel of the kingdom shall be preached in the whole world as a testimony to all nations, and then the end will come" (NASB). This "gospel" will be preached in the future seven-year Tribulation and concerns the coming of the divine Messiah and the setting up of His millennial kingdom, in fulfillment of the Davidic covenant (2 Samuel 7:16). Those who respond positively to this "gospel" and turn to the Savior for salvation will be allowed entrance into the kingdom (see Matthew 25:46).

Since this gospel will be preached, we can naturally assume that God will have witnesses on the earth during the Tribulation who do the preaching! Some expositors believe this will be the two witnesses of Revelation 11 and the 144,000 Jews mentioned in Revelation 7. The book of Revelation indicates that many will respond to this gospel (Revelation 7:9-10).

Great Prostitute

Prostitution is often a graphic metaphor in Scripture that symbolizes unfaithfulness to God, idolatry, and religious apostasy (see Jeremiah 3:6-9; Ezekiel 20:30; Hosea 4:15; 5:3; 6:10; 9:1). In the book of Revelation, the great prostitute symbolizes the apostate religious system of Babylon—probably apostate Christendom, embracing all those who were "left behind" following the rapture, and perhaps referring to the ecumenical church. Revelation 17:1 tells us that this prostitute "sits on many waters," which symbolizes various peoples, multitudes, nations, and languages. Scripture reveals that the kings of the earth commit adultery with this harlot, and become a part of the religious system she symbolizes (see Revelation 14:8). This false religious system, then, is pervasive in its influence, working hand-in-hand with the political system of the end times.

Revelation 19:2 tells us that God's judgments are true and just, "for He has judged the great harlot who was corrupting the earth with her immorality, and He has avenged the blood of his servants on her" (NASB). This false religious system will fall hard!

Great Tribulation

See *Tribulation, The.*

Great White Throne Judgment

Unlike believers, whose judgment deals only with rewards and loss of rewards, unbelievers face a horrific judgment that leads to their being cast into the lake of fire. The judgment that unbelievers face is called the Great White Throne judgment (Revelation 20:11-15). Christ is the divine Judge, and those who are judged are the unsaved dead of all time. The judgment takes place at the end of the millennial kingdom, Christ's 1,000-year reign on planet earth.

Those who face Christ at this judgment will be judged on the basis of their works (Revelation 20:12-13). It is critical to understand that they actually *get* to this judgment because they are *already* unsaved. This judgment will not separate believers from unbelievers, for all who will experience it will have already made the choice during their lifetimes to reject God. Once they are before the divine Judge, they are judged according to their works not only to justify their condemnation but to determine the degree to which each person should be punished throughout eternity.

When Christ opens the Book of Life, no name of anyone present at the Great White Throne judgment is in it. Their names do not appear in the Book of Life because they have rejected the source of life—Jesus Christ. Because they rejected the source of life, they are cast into the lake of fire—which constitutes the "second death" and involves eternal separation from God.

Resurrected unto judgment. Those who participate in the Great White Throne judgment are resurrected unto judgment. Jesus Himself affirmed that "a time is coming when all who are in their graves will hear his voice and come out—those who have done good will rise to live, and those who have done evil will rise to be condemned" (John 5:28-29).

To clarify, Jesus is not teaching that there is just one general resurrection that will take place at the end of time. Contrary to this idea, the Scriptures indicate that there are two types of resurrection—the first resurrection and the second resurrection (Revelation 20:5-6,11-15). The first resurrection is the resurrection of Christians, while the second resurrection is the resurrection of the wicked.

More specifically, the term *first resurrection* refers to all the resurrections of the righteous, even though they are widely separated in time. There is one resurrection of the righteous at the rapture (before the Tribulation period); another at the end of the Tribulation period; and still another at the end of the 1,000-year millennial kingdom (1 Thessalonians 4:16; Revelation 20:4). They all are "first" in the sense of being before the second (final) resurrection of the wicked. Accordingly, the term *first resurrection* applies to all the resurrections of the saints regardless of when they occur, including the resurrection of Christ Himself.

The "second" resurrection is an awful spectacle. All the unsaved of all time will be resurrected at the end of Christ's millennial kingdom, judged at the Great White Throne judgment, and then cast alive into the lake of fire (Revelation 20:11-15).

Degrees of punishment. The Scriptures indicate that all those who are judged at the Great White Throne judgment have a horrible destiny ahead. Indeed, their destiny generally will involve weeping and gnashing of teeth (Matthew 13:41-42), condemnation (Matthew 12:36-37), destruction (Philippians 1:28), eternal punishment (Matthew 25:46), separation from God's presence (2 Thessalonians 1:8-9), and trouble and distress (Romans 2:9).

Nevertheless, the Scriptures also indicate that there will be degrees of punishment in hell (Matthew 10:15; Luke 12:47-48; Revelation 20:12-13; 22:12). And these degrees of punishment will be determined at the Great White Throne judgment when Christ examines each person with His penetrating eyes.

Common observation shows that unsaved people vary as much in their quality of life as saved people do. Some saved people are spiritual and charitable (for example), and other saved people are carnal and unloving. Some unbelievers are terribly evil (like Hitler), while others—such as unbelieving moralists—are much less evil.

Just as believers differ in how they respond to God's law, and hence in their reward in heaven, so unbelievers differ in their response to God's law, and hence in their punishment in hell. Just as there are degrees of reward in heaven, so there are degrees of punishment in hell.

H

Habakkuk

The book of Habakkuk was written by a prophet of the same name about 606 B.C. Aside from the fact that he was a prophet, little is known about the man.

A contemporary of Jeremiah, Habakkuk, in the seventh century B.C., wrestled with the issue as to why good and innocent people suffer, while evil people so often seem to prosper. Habakkuk, like many people today, asked, "Why do you let this happen, O God?" More specifically, he asked why God allowed the Babylonians (hardcore pagans) to successfully invade and injure the people of God (Habakkuk 1:1-11). It seemed that wicked nations were being allowed to prosper, while God's people were getting squashed. The answer Habakkuk received from God was that, in the end, the wicked Babylonians and all like them would be destroyed, but those who trust in God will remain and be blessed (1:12–2:20). The bottom line is that we must live by total faith in God (2:4).

There is at least one key reference to end times prophecy in the book of Habakkuk. Habakkuk 2:14 tells us that "the earth will be filled with the knowledge of the glory of the LORD, as the waters cover the sea."

This prophecy will ultimately be fulfilled in the 1,000-year millennial kingdom (see also Numbers 14:21; Psalm 72:19; Isaiah 6:3; 11:9). Truly the Lord's glory—a full manifestation of His person, presence, and wonder—will be manifest in the millennium and acknowledged throughout the entire earth. So extensive will knowledge of the Lord and His glory be that it is compared to water that inescapably covers the sea.

Hades

In the Old Testament, the English word *hell* sometimes translates the Hebrew word *Sheol.* The term *Sheol* can have different meanings in different contexts. Sometimes the word means "grave" (Psalm 49:15). Other times it refers simply to the place of departed people. The Old Testament often characterizes this place as being full of horror (Psalm 30:9) and punishment (Job 24:19).

Hades is the New Testament counterpart to Sheol, and came to refer to the state or place of the dead. In the Septuagint—the Greek translation of the Hebrew Old Testament that predates the time of Christ—the term *Sheol* is actually translated as "Hades."

The New Testament tells us that the rich man, during the intermediate state, endured great suffering in Hades (Luke 16:19-31). Jesus, who sovereignly holds "the keys of death and Hades," determines who dies and when, and who goes to Hades and who does not (Revelation 1:18).

Hades, however, is a temporary abode and will one day be cast into the lake of fire (hell). In the future, wicked evildoers will be raised from the dead and judged at the Great White Throne judgment (Revelation 20:11). They will then be cast into the lake of fire, which will be their permanent place of suffering throughout all eternity (verses 14-15).

Haggai

The book of Haggai was written by a prophet of the same name around 520 B.C. Aside from the fact that he was a prophet, we know little of the man. His name literally means "festival," perhaps because he was born on the day of a major festival. His book is the second shortest in the Old Testament, so he was definitely a concise writer. He ministered during the reign of King Darius I (522–486 B.C.), and was probably about 80 years old when he wrote this book.

In 520 B.C., Haggai addressed his words to the people in Judah and Jerusalem who had returned from exile. He urged them to get their act together, to set their priorities straight, and to rebuild the temple (see Haggai 1:1-11). Then, he said, God would bring true blessing back upon them.

The problem was that when the people first returned from exile in 538 B.C. as a result of King Cyrus's decree, they made a good start in beginning to rebuild the temple, but now apathy had set in and the whole project had stagnated (Ezra 4:4-5). The people were too busy building their own homes to pay much attention to the temple. Haggai was one of the prophets chosen by God to get the people on their feet again and finish the task. Toward this end, Haggai preached a series of short fiery sermonettes.

The people needed encouragement because they had a defeated state of mind. While they were excited to be home again, they were also despondent over the ruination of their city. They were especially despondent over the fact that it was their own unfaithfulness that had brought about the ruination of the city. Haggai sought to help them overcome this defeated state of mind and move on to obedience and service to God.

The rebuilding of the temple was important not only because it was the religious center of Jewish life, but also because it represented the presence of the one true God among the Israelites before a watching pagan world. For the temple not to be rebuilt might give the impression to pagan nations that the true God was no longer interested in Israel, and no longer paying attention to the covenants He had made with His people. The temple was finally rebuilt during the years 520 to 515 B.C.

One key reference to the end times is found in Haggai 2:6, where we read "Thus says the LORD of hosts: Yet once more, in a little while, I will shake the heavens and the earth and the sea and the dry land." Such cosmic disturbances will be fulfilled in the end times in connection with the Tribulation period and the second coming of Christ (see Matthew 24:29-30).

Harlot, Great

See *Great Prostitute.*

Healing of Nations

At the end of the book of Revelation, we read of the wonders of the New Jerusalem, the eternal capital city of heaven in which believers will dwell for all eternity. Two fascinating components of the eternal city are the river of the water of life and the tree of life. According to Revelation 22:2, the New Jerusalem will have "the tree of life with its twelve kinds of fruit, yielding its fruit each month. The leaves of the tree were for the healing of the nations."

The Greek word for "healing" in Revelation 22:2 is *therapeia,* from which the English word *therapeutic* is derived, almost directly transliterated from the Greek. Rather than specifically meaning "healing," it should be understood as "health-giving." In other words, the leaves of the tree promote the enjoyment of life and a sense of well-being in the New Jerusalem, and are not for correcting ills which do not exist. There will be only perpetual health in the eternal state.

Hearts Failing

One interesting and understandable prophecy of the end times is that the hearts of human beings will fail for fear. The key reference to this is Luke 21:25-26: "There will be signs in sun, moon and stars. On the earth, nations will be in anguish and perplexity at the roaring and tossing of the sea. Men will faint from terror, apprehensive of what is coming on the world, for the heavenly bodies will be shaken."

Apparently it is the terror of cosmic disturbances that will cause great emotional distress about what is happening and *will yet* happen. It will be more than people can endure, and there will be great panic.

Heaven

Heaven is the place where God and the angels live, and is the destiny of all believers in Jesus Christ. There are a number of ways the "highest" heaven is described in the Bible. Each of the descriptions reveals something new, something exciting, about our future abode.

The city of glory. In Revelation 21 we find a description of a city of great glory, which is likely what Jesus was referring to during His earthly ministry when He told the disciples: "In my Father's house are many rooms; if it were not so, I would have told you. I am going there to prepare a place for you. And if I go and prepare a place for you, I will come back and take you to be with me that you also may be where I am" (John 14:2,3). Christ has personally prepared this glorious abode for His followers (compare with John 1:3; Colossians 1:16).

Presented to our amazed gaze in Revelation 21 is a scene of such transcendent splendor that the human mind can scarcely take it in. This is a scene of ecstatic joy and fellowship of sinless angels and redeemed glorified human beings. The voice of the One identified as the Alpha and the Omega, the beginning and the end, utters a climactic declaration: "Behold, I am making all things new" (Revelation 21:5). Certainly the actual splendor of heaven far exceeds anything that we have yet experienced. As the apostle Paul said, "No eye has seen, no ear has heard, no mind has conceived what God has prepared for those who love him" (1 Corinthians 2:9).

The heavenly country. Hebrews 11 is the Faith Hall of Fame in the Bible. In this pivotal chapter, we read of the eternal perspective of many of the great faith warriors in biblical times. All of them were looking forward to living in the heavenly country (Hebrews 11:13-15). These great warriors of the faith were not satisfied with mere earthly things. They looked forward to "a better country"—heaven.

The holy city. In Revelation 21:1-2 we find heaven described as "the Holy City." This is a fitting description. Indeed, in this city there will be no sin or unrighteousness of any kind.

The home of righteousness. Second Peter 3:13 tells us that "in keeping with his promise we are looking forward to a new heaven and a new earth, the home of righteousness." What a perfect environment this will be to live in.

The kingdom of light. Colossians 1:12 refers to heaven as "the kingdom of light." Christ, of course, is the light of the world (John 8:12). The eternal kingdom thus takes on the character of the King. Christ the "Light of the world" rules over the "kingdom of light."

The paradise of God. The word paradise literally means "garden of pleasure" or "garden of delight." Revelation 2:7 makes reference to heaven as the "paradise of God." The apostle Paul in 2 Corinthians 12:4 said he was "caught up to paradise" and "heard inexpressible things, things that man is not permitted to tell." Apparently this paradise of God is so resplendently glorious, so ineffable, so wondrous, that Paul was forbidden to say anything about it to those still in the earthly realm.

The New Jerusalem. The New Jerusalem, the eternal city, is said to measure approximately 1,500 miles by 1,500 miles by 1,500 miles. The eternal city is so huge that it would measure approximately the distance between the Mississippi River and the Atlantic Ocean. It is tall enough that from the earth's surface it would reach about one-twentieth of the way to the moon.

The eternal city could either be cube-shaped or pyramid-shaped. It may be preferable to consider it shaped as a pyramid, for this would explain how the river of the water of life can flow down its sides as pictured in Revelation 22:1-2.

Heavens, Three

The Scriptures make reference to the "third heaven"—which is the ineffable and glorious dwelling place of God in all His glory

(2 Corinthians 12:2). It is elsewhere called the "heaven of heavens" and the "highest heaven" (1 Kings 8:27; 2 Chronicles 2:6).

If God's abode is called the "third" heaven, then what is the first and the second heaven? Scripture gives us the answer. The first heaven is that of the earth's atmosphere (Job 35:5). The second heaven is that of the stellar universe (Genesis 1:17; Deuteronomy 17:3).

H

Hebrews

The book of Hebrews describes itself as a "word of exhortation," not as a letter (Hebrews 13:22). The exhortation draws heavily on the Old Testament, and urges Hebrew Christians to remain steadfast in their commitment to Christ and His cause. It was probably written about A.D. 68.

This book is, in one way, a New Testament commentary on the Old Testament and its relationship to Jesus Christ. It teaches that the offering of sacrifices and the various priestly activities were mere types that pointed to Christ, the once-for-all sacrifice for sin, the true Priest, the one Mediator between God and man (see Hebrews 7–9). Hebrews may be considered a grand portrait of Christ with the Old Testament as its background.

Bible scholars are not sure who wrote this theological book. Though a number of hypotheses have been suggested through the centuries, perhaps only three are worthy of mention: the apostle Paul, Apollos, and Barnabas. Regardless of who actually wrote the epistle, at least four things are certain: 1) The author and his readers were known to each other (Hebrews 6:9; 13:18,19,23,24); 2) Timothy was known to both (13:23); 3) The writer was quite familiar with the Old Testament, including the Levitical system of sacrifices; and 4) he writes in polished Greek, indicating a high level of education.

Whatever is known today of the original readers of Hebrews is derived from the epistle itself. The earliest manuscripts have the simple title, "To the Hebrews." This group was apparently a single congregation of Hebrew Christians living somewhere in the Roman world (Hebrews 1:1; 13:23-24). Scholars have suggested various hypotheses as to where they may have lived, including Jerusalem, Alexandria, Caesarea, Ephesus, the city of Rome, and Antioch in Syria. But there is no hard proof for any of these localities.

The author of Hebrews makes it clear that this group of Jewish believers was going through a severe period of persecution (Hebrews 10:32-34). The general tenor and content of the epistle indicate that this persecution was likely religious in nature.

For a Jew to become a believer in Jesus Christ in the first century required a great sacrifice. Such a believer was immediately branded as an apostate and a blemish to the Jewish nation. He was considered "unclean" in the strongest possible sense. Defecting Jews were immediately expelled from the synagogue; their children were denied the privilege of attending school at the synagogue; they lost their jobs in any geographical areas controlled by the Jews; in short, they lost everything of earthly value to them. Furthermore, the high priest of the Jewish nation had the authority to throw such troublesome Jews into jail (see Hebrews 10:33-34). It was circumstances such as these that apparently caused many of these Hebrew believers to wane in their commitment to Christ.

At first, these Jewish Christians joyfully accepted persecution (Hebrews 10:34). But after a while, it apparently became too much for them to bear and their endurance weakened (10:35-36). The warning passages in this epistle seem to indicate that these believers had degenerated in their faith and had become settled in a state of spiritual retrogression.

While they certainly never entertained thoughts of actually renouncing Jesus Christ, they nevertheless expressed the desire to drift back into the outward observances of Judaism—including rituals, ceremonies, and sacrifices. They apparently reasoned that if they took part in such Jewish rituals, the Jewish leaders might be satisfied and leave them alone.

However, the book makes clear that Jesus is the ultimate fulfillment of the Old Testament, and Jesus is greater than all Old Testament institutions (Hebrews 1:5–7:28). Hence, to step back into Judaism in whatever form is unacceptable. The author of Hebrews calls his readers to move on to maturity in the Christian faith (6:1).

There are several important references in Hebrews to end-time events. Hebrews 2:5, for example, tells us, "It is not to angels that he [God] subjected the world to come, about which we are speaking." This is apparently a reference to the future millennial kingdom, which will not be ruled by angels but by the divine Messiah, Jesus Christ, and redeemed Christians (see Revelation 20:6).

Hebrews 9:27 informs us that "man is destined to die once, and after that to face judgment." Both Christians and unbelievers will be judged, Christians at the Judgment Seat of Christ (1 Corinthians 3:1-10; 2 Corinthians 5:10) and unbelievers at the Great White Throne judgment (Revelation 20:11-13).

Hebrews 11:16 informs us that as far as the biblical saints are concerned, "they desire a better country, that is, a heavenly one. Therefore God is not ashamed to be called their God, for he has prepared for them a city" (NASB). Christians are merely "pilgrims passing through" earthly life on the way to the heavenly city, the New Jerusalem.

Finally, in Hebrews 12:26, God promises: "Yet once more I will shake not only the earth, but also the heavens" (NASB). This no doubt refers to the judgments that will fall on humankind during the future Tribulation, including earthquakes (Revelation 6:12; 8:5; 11:13,19; 16:18), prior to the second coming of Jesus Christ.

Hell

The Scriptures assure us that hell is a real place. But hell was not part of God's original creation, which He called "good" (Genesis 1). Hell was created later to accommodate the banishment of Satan and his fallen angels who rebelled against God (Matthew 25:41). Human beings who reject Christ will join Satan and his fallen angels in this infernal place of suffering.

In the Old Testament, the word *hell* sometimes translated the

Hebrew word *Sheol.* The term *Sheol* can have different meanings in different contexts. Sometimes the word means "grave." Other times it refers to the place of departed people in contrast to the state of living people. The Old Testament portrays Sheol as a place of horror (Psalm 30:9), weeping (Isaiah 38:3), and punishment (Job 24:19).

When we get to the New Testament, we find that a number of words relate to the doctrine of hell. It would seem that Hades is the New Testament counterpart to Sheol in the Old Testament. The rich man, during the intermediate state, endured great suffering in Hades (Luke 16:19-31).

Hades, however, is a temporary abode and will one day be cast into the lake of fire. In the future, the wicked evildoers in Hades will be raised from the dead and judged at the Great White Throne judgment. They will then be cast into the lake of fire, which will be their permanent place of suffering throughout all eternity.

Another word related to the concept of hell is Gehenna (Matthew 10:28; 2 Kings 23:10). This word has an interesting history. For several generations in ancient Israel, atrocities were committed in the Valley of Ben Hinnom—atrocities that included human sacrifices, even the sacrifice of children (2 Chronicles 28:3; 33:6; Jeremiah 32:35). These unfortunate victims were sacrificed to the false Moabite god Molech. Jeremiah appropriately called this valley a "valley of slaughter" (Jeremiah 7:31-34).

Eventually the valley came to be used as a public rubbish dump into which all the filth in Jerusalem was poured. Not only garbage but also the bodies of dead animals and the corpses of criminals were thrown on the heap where they—like everything else in the dump—would perpetually burn. The valley was a place where the fires never stopped burning. And there was always a good meal for a hungry worm.

This place was originally called (in the Hebrew) *Ge ben hinnom* (the valley of the son of Hinnom). It was eventually shortened to the name *Ge-Hinnom.* The Greek translation of this Hebrew phrase is *Gehenna.* It became an appropriate and graphic term for the reality of hell. Jesus Himself used the word eleven times in reference to the eternal place of suffering of unredeemed humanity.

A final word related to hell is *Tartaros* (2 Peter 2:4). This word occurs only one time in the Bible, and refers to a place where certain fallen angels (demons) are confined. Most fallen angels are free to roam the earth, doing their destructive damage wherever they find opportunity. But these imprisoned fallen angels are not free to roam, apparently because they committed an especially heinous sin against God in the past.

The Scriptures use a variety of words to describe the horrors of hell—including fiery furnace (Matthew 13:42), unquenchable fire (Mark 9:47), the fiery lake of burning sulfur (Revelation 19:20), the lake of fire (Revelation 20:15), eternal fire (Matthew 18:8), eternal punishment (Matthew 25:46), destruction (Matthew 7:13), everlasting destruction (2 Thessalonians 1:8-9), the place of weeping and gnashing of teeth (Matthew 13:42), and the second death (Revelation 20:14). The horror of hell is inconceivable to the human mind.

Hell, Degrees of Punishment in

Scripture reveals that there are degrees of punishment in hell (see Matthew 10:15; 16:27; Luke 12:47-48; Revelation 20:12-13; 22:12). This means that an Adolf Hitler, for example, will suffer eternally much more than a Christ-rejecting moralist. The degree of punishment will be commensurate with one's sin against the light which one has received.

Hermeneutics of Biblical Prophecy

Following are some basic principles for interpreting biblical prophecy. These are standard hermeneutic principles accepted by the best of interpreters.

When the plain sense makes good sense, seek no other sense. A plain reading of Genesis indicates that when God created Adam in His own rational image, He gave Adam the gift of intelligible speech. This enabled him to communicate objectively with his creator, and with other human beings, via sharable linguistic symbols called words (Genesis 1:26; 11:1,7). Scripture shows that God sovereignly chose to use human language as a medium of revelational communication, often through the "Thus saith the LORD" (KJV) pronouncements of the prophets (Isaiah 7:7; 10:24; 22:15; 28:16; 30:15; 49:22; 51:22; 52:4).

If the primary purpose of God's originating of language was to make it possible for Him to communicate with human beings, as well as to enable human beings to communicate with each other, then it must follow that He would ordinarily use language and expect man to use it in its normal and plain sense. This view of language is a prerequisite to understanding not only God's spoken word but His written word (Scripture) as well. This is why we emphasize: When the plain, literal sense of Scripture makes good sense, seek no other sense.

Submit all "preunderstandings" to Scripture. Theological "preunderstandings"—doctrinal opinions we have previously formed—should not bias our interpretation of Scripture. Of course, all interpreters are influenced to some degree by personal, theological, denominational, and political prejudices. None of us approaches Scripture in a "chemically pure" state. For this reason, preunderstandings must be *in harmony with Scripture* and *subject to correction by it.* Only those preunderstandings that are compatible with Scripture are legitimate. We must allow our presuppositions and preunderstandings to be modified or even completely reshaped by the text itself.

Pay close attention to the context. Each statement in Scripture must be taken in its proper context. Every word in the Bible is part of a sentence; every sentence is part of a paragraph; every paragraph is part of a book; and every book is part of the whole of Scripture. The interpretation of a specific passage must not contradict the total teaching of Scripture on a point. Individual verses do not exist as isolated fragments, but as parts of a whole. The exposition of these verses, therefore, must involve exhibiting them in right relation both to the whole and to each other. Scripture interprets Scripture.

Make a correct genre judgment. The Bible contains a variety of literary genres, each of which has certain peculiar characteristics that must be recognized in order to interpret the text properly. Biblical genres include the historical (for example, Acts), the dramatic epic (Job), poetry (Psalms), wise sayings (Proverbs), and apocalyptic writings (Revelation). An incorrect genre judgment will lead one far astray in interpreting Scripture. A parable, for example, should not be treated as history, nor should poetry (which contain many symbols) be treated as straightforward narrative. A case in point would be how the Psalms refer to God as a Rock (Psalm 18:2; 19:14). This should be understood not literally but as a symbol of God's sturdiness: God is our rock-solid foundation. The Psalms often use such metaphors.

The wise interpreter allows his knowledge of genres to control how he approaches each individual biblical text. In this way, he can accurately determine what the biblical author was intending to communicate to the reader.

Even though the Bible contains a variety of literary genres and many figures of speech, the biblical authors *most often* employed literal statements to convey their ideas. Where they use a literal means to express their ideas, the Bible student must employ a corresponding means to explain these ideas—namely, a literal approach. A literal method of interpreting Scripture gives to each word in the text the same basic meaning it would have in normal, ordinary, customary usage—whether employed in writing, speaking, or thinking. Without such a method, communication between God and man would be impossible.

Consult history and culture. The interpreter of Scripture must seek to step out of his Western mindset and into an ancient Jewish mindset, paying special attention to such things as Jewish marriage rites, burial rites, family practices, farm practices, business practices, the monetary system, methods of warfare, slavery, the treatment of captives, the use of covenants, and religious practices. Armed with such detailed historical information, interpreting the Bible correctly becomes a much easier task because we better understand the world of the biblical writers. So, for example, a thorough historical understanding of the Jewish belief in the land promises made to Abraham, Isaac, and Jacob (Genesis 15:18-21; 26:3-4; 28:13-14) helps us better appreciate why Jews believe the land of Israel is their land.

Recognize that a literal approach allows for figures of speech. There are figures of speech in the Bible, but what is understood to be a figure of speech and what is taken literally should be based on the biblical text itself—such as when Jesus used obviously figurative parables to express spiritual truth. In other words, we should watch for textual clues for the existence of metaphors and figures of speech, and when we come across such a figure of speech, we must use our hermeneutic skills to ascertain the literal truth being taught by the figure of speech.

Hinderer

In 2 Thessalonians 2:7 we read of someone who restrains the "mystery of lawlessness" (lawlessness which will come to a climax in the future Tribulation period under the Antichrist, who fully embodies lawlessness, as energized by Satan): "The mystery of lawlessness is already at work; only he who now restrains it will do so until he is out of the way" (NASB).

Who is this restrainer? There are some who interpret the restrainer as human government. In this view, the Antichrist will one day overthrow human government so that he can work his will in the world. Here's a problem with this view: Are human beings (who make up human government) strong enough to stand against the Antichrist, who is energized by Satan? Moreover, Scripture reveals that not all human governments restrain sin; some actually encourage it.

Others (perhaps the majority) interpret the restrainer as being the Holy Spirit who indwells the church. Only God the Holy Spirit has sufficient power to engage in this restraining (see 1 John 4:4). In this view, the "restrainer" will be taken "out of the way" at the future rapture—that glorious event in which the dead in Christ are raised from the dead and living Christians are instantly translated into their resurrection bodies, and both groups are caught up to meet Christ in the air (1 Thessalonians 4:13-17). Pretribulationists believe this event will take place prior to the beginning of the Tribulation.

Historicist View of Revelation

The historicist approach to interpreting the book of Revelation holds that the book supplies a prophetic overview of the entire panoramic sweep of church history, from the first century to the second coming of Christ. This view is in contrast to 1) the futurist approach, which holds that most of the events described in Revelation will take place in the end times, just prior to the second coming of Jesus Christ; 2) the preterist approach, which sees most of the prophecies as having already been fulfilled in A.D. 70; and 3) the idealist approach, which holds that Revelation is primarily a symbolic description of the ongoing battle between God and the devil, between good and evil.

The historicist approach emerged in the fourth century when some interpreters saw parallels between current events and biblical prophecy. Later, Joachim of Fiore (A.D. 1135–1202) developed the approach by dividing history into three ages. The Reformers were attracted to historicism, viewing the pope as the Antichrist.

Holy City

In Revelation 21:1-2 we find the New Jerusalem—the capital city of heaven—described as "the holy city" (see also verse 10; 22:19). This is a fitting description. Indeed, in this city there will be no sin or unrighteousness of any kind. Only the pure of heart will dwell there.

This does not mean believers must personally attain moral perfection in order to dwell there. Those of us who believe in Christ have been given the very righteousness of Christ (Romans 4:11,22-24). Because of what Christ accomplished for us at the cross by taking our sins upon Himself (2 Corinthians 5:21), we have been made holy (Hebrews 10:14). Hence, we will have the privilege of living for all eternity in the holy city.

It is interesting to observe that in biblical times the term "holy city" was another name for earthly Jerusalem (Nehemiah 11:1; Daniel 9:24). However, in Revelation 11:8 it is compared to evil Sodom, because of the evil events that will then be transpiring in the city (perversion).

Holy Spirit and Prophecy

The Holy Spirit has a significant role in end-time events. Among the more significant ministries and activities are:

- The Holy Spirit will bring the church to completion. The church is formed as the Holy Spirit continues to baptize new believers into the body of Christ (Acts 2:1-4). Once the future rapture of the church occurs (1 Thessalonians 4:13-17), the church will have been completed.
- The Holy Spirit will be removed as the restrainer of sin (and restrainer of the sinful Antichrist) just prior to the Tribulation period (2 Thessalonians 2:6-8). This removal of restraint will occur when the church (as indwelt by the Holy Spirit) is raptured (1 Thessalonians 4:13-17). (See *Hinderer*.)
- During the Tribulation, the Holy Spirit will continue to be active in bringing salvation to many—both Jews and Gentiles (see Matthew 25:1-13,31-46; compare with Revelation 7:4-8).
- During the Tribulation, the Holy Spirit will empower God's servants for ministry (see Revelation 7:3-8; 11:3-12; compare with Zechariah 4:6; 2 Corinthians 3:5).
- During the future 1,000-year millennial kingdom, Christ in His rule will be anointed and energized by the Holy Spirit. Isaiah 11:1-2 speaks of this reality: "There shall come forth a shoot from the stump of Jesse, and a branch from his roots shall bear fruit. And the Spirit of the LORD shall rest upon him, the Spirit of wisdom and understanding,

the Spirit of counsel and might, the Spirit of knowledge and the fear of the LORD."

- All believers will be indwelt by the Holy Spirit. This is promised in the new covenant (Jeremiah 31:31-37), a covenant that has relevance not just for today but also for the future millennial kingdom.

Truly the role of the Holy Spirit in prophetic issues is broad and comprehensive.

Horns

A horn on an animal is used by that animal as a weapon (see Genesis 22:13; Psalm 69:31). For this reason, in Bible times the horn eventually came to be seen as a symbol of power and might. As an extension of this symbol, horns were sometimes used as emblems of dominion, representing kingdoms and kings, as is the case in the books of Daniel and Revelation (see Daniel 7–8; Revelation 12:13; 13:1,11; 17:3-16).

Horses

Horses are often mentioned in biblical prophecies of the end times. Famous examples include the four horsemen of the apocalypse who ride four different color horses, symbolizing different seal judgments that will fall upon humankind during the future Tribulation (Revelation 6). The rider of the white horse is the Antichrist, villain-supreme of the Tribulation (verse 2). The red horse represents bloodshed, and killing with the sword, and war (verses 3-4). The black horse symbolizes famine and subsequent death (verses 5-6). The pale horse is named Death, and is connected to the death of one-fourth of earth's population (verses 7-8). (See *Four Horsemen of the Apocalypse.*)

Not all horses in the book of Revelation, however, represent judgments. We are told in Revelation 19:11 that the second coming will feature Jesus Christ returning on a white horse.

Hour of Testing

In Revelation 3:10 we find words of Jesus that are often taken as a reference to the rapture of the church: "Because you have kept the word of My perseverance, I will keep you from the hour of testing, that hour which is coming on the whole world, to try those who dwell on the earth."

Posttribulationists interpret this verse as saying that believers will be "kept through" Satan's wrath during the Tribulation. Pretribulationists respond, however, that the Greek text does not say believers will be kept *through* the Tribulation (Greek: *dia,* "through"). Rather, the verse indicates believers will be saved "out of" or "from" (Greek: *ek*) the actual time (hour) of the Tribulation. This trial is specifically for those who "dwell on the earth"—that is, those who make this earth their home, "people of the world."

Pretribulationism is consistent with the fact that no Old Testament passage on the Tribulation mentions the church (Deuteronomy 4:29,30; Jeremiah 30:4-11; Daniel 8:24-27; 12:1,2), just as no New Testament passage on the Tribulation mentions the church (Matthew 13:30,39-42,48-50; 24:15-31; 1 Thessalonians 1:9,10; 5:4-9; 2 Thessalonians 2:1-11; Revelation 4–18). Pretribulationism is also consistent with God's promise to deliver the church from the "wrath to come" (1 Thessalonians 1:10 NASB; 5:9).

Idealist View of Revelation

The idealist approach to interpreting the book of Revelation holds that the book is primarily a symbolic description of the ongoing battle between God and the devil, between good and evil. This view is in contrast to 1) the futurist approach, which holds that most of the events described in Revelation will take place in the end times, just prior to the second coming of Christ; 2) the preterist approach, which sees most of the prophecies as having already been fulfilled in A.D. 70; and 3) the historicist view, which holds that Revelation supplies a prophetic overview of the entire panoramic sweep of church history, from the first century to the second coming of Christ.

Image of the Beast

In Daniel 11:31 we read of the Antichrist: "His armed forces will rise up to desecrate the temple fortress and will abolish the daily sacrifice. Then they will set up the abomination that causes desolation." We find further clarity on this "abomination that causes desolation" in the New Testament. This abomination will take place at the midpoint during the future Tribulation period when the Antichrist—the "man of sin" (2 Thessalonians 2:3 KJV)—sets up an image of himself inside the Jewish temple (see Daniel 9:27; Matthew 24:15). This will utterly desecrate the temple, making it abominable, and therefore desolate. The Antichrist—the world dictator—will then demand that the world worship and pay idolatrous homage to him. Any who refuse will be persecuted and even martyred.

Such an abomination took place once before in 168 B.C. At that time, Antiochus Epiphanes sacrificed a pig, an unclean animal, on an altar erected to Zeus in the temple at Jerusalem. Antiochus Epiphanes was thus a prototype of the future Antichrist.

Some Bible expositors—particularly of the amillennial and preterist persuasions—see the abomination of desolation in Matthew 24:15 as having already been fulfilled when Titus and his Roman warriors overran Jerusalem and destroyed the Jewish temple in A.D. 70. However, Paul's prophetic discussion of this event in 2 Thessalonians 2 would seem to demand a fulfillment in the future Tribulation when the Antichrist will seek to take God's place in the Temple and make people bow down and worship him (see verses 3-4).

See *Abomination of Desolation.*

See *Olivet discourse.*

Imminency

The term *imminent* literally means "ready to take place" or "impending." The New Testament teaches that the rapture is imminent—that is, there is nothing that must be prophetically fulfilled before the rapture occurs (see 1 Corinthians 1:7; 16:22; Philippians 3:20; 4:5; 1 Thessalonians 1:10; Titus 2:13; Hebrews 9:28; James 5:7-9; 1 Peter 1:13; Jude 21). The rapture is a *signless* event that can occur *at any moment.* This is in contrast to the second coming of Christ, which is preceded by many events in the seven-year Tribulation period (see Revelation 4–18).

Imminency is certainly implied in the apostle Paul's words in Romans 13:11-12: "The hour has come for you to wake up from your slumber, because *our salvation is nearer to us now than when we first believed.* The night is far gone; the day is at hand. So then let us cast off the works of darkness and put on the armor of light" (emphasis added). The word *salvation* in this context must be eschatological, referring to the rapture, for this "salvation" is a specific future event referenced by Paul. At the end of each day, the Christian is that much closer to the time when the rapture may occur.

Imminency is also implied in James 5:7-9:

> Be patient, then, brothers, until the coming of the Lord. See how the farmer waits for the land to yield its valuable crop and how patient he is for the autumn and spring rains. You too, be patient. Don't grumble against each other, brothers, so that you may not be judged; behold, *the Judge is standing at the door* (emphasis added).

Of course, imminency only makes sense within the theology of pretribulationism. In midtribulationism, the rapture is at least three-and-a-half years into the Tribulation. In posttribulationism, the rapture follows the Tribulation. Hence, imminency is impossible in these systems.

The fact that the rapture is a signless event, and could occur at any moment, ought to spur the Christian to live in purity and righteousness (see Titus 2:13-14). How blessed it will be for the Christian to be living in righteousness at that moment. How embarrassing it will be for the Christian to be engaged in sin at that moment.

Immortality versus Conditional Immortality (Annihilationism)

See *Annihilationism.*

Inerrancy of Scripture

The reason the Bible is inerrant is clear: 1) The Bible is the Word of God; 2) God cannot err; 3) therefore, the Bible cannot err. The Bible is clear about both premises, and the conclusion logically follows from them:

1. *The Bible is the Word of God.*
    - Matthew 4:4: "It is written: 'Man does not live on bread alone, but on every word that comes from the mouth of God.'"
    - 2 Peter 1:21: "Prophecy never had its origin in the will of man, but men spoke from God as they were carried along by the Holy Spirit."
2. *God cannot err.*
    - Hebrews 6:18: "It is impossible for God to lie."
    - Romans 3:4: "Let God be true, and every man a liar."
    - John 17:17: Jesus said to the Father, "Your word is truth."
3. *From this, it follows that the Bible cannot err.*

We can rest assured, then, that biblical prophecy is inerrant!

Inspiration of Scripture

The Bible is not the product of man but is rather God-inspired (2 Timothy 3:16-17). Inspiration does not mean the biblical writer just felt enthusiastic, like the composer of "The Star-Spangled Banner." Nor does it mean the writings are necessarily inspiring to read, like an uplifting poem. The biblical Greek word for inspiration literally means "God-breathed." Because Scripture is breathed out by God—because it *originates* from Him—it is true and inerrant.

Biblical inspiration may be defined as God's superintending of the human authors so that, using their own individual personalities and even their writing styles, they composed and recorded without error His revelation to humankind in the words of the original autographs. In other words, the original documents of the Bible were written by men, who, though permitted to exercise their own personalities and literary talents, wrote under the control and guidance of the Holy Spirit, the result being a perfect and errorless recording of the exact message God desired to give to humankind. Hence, the writers of Scripture were not mere writing machines. God did not use them like keys on a typewriter to mechanically reproduce His message. Nor did He dictate the words, page by page. The biblical evidence makes it clear that each writer had a style of his own. (Isaiah had a powerful literary style; Jeremiah had a mournful tone; Luke's style had medical overtones; and John was very simple in his approach.) The Holy Spirit infallibly worked through each of these writers, through their individual styles, to inerrantly communicate His message to humankind.

Second Peter 1:21 provides a key insight regarding the human-divine interchange in the process of inspiration. This verse informs us that "prophecy [or Scripture] never had its origin in the will of man, but men spoke from God as they were carried along by the Holy Spirit." The phrase *carried along* in this verse literally means "forcefully borne along." Even though human beings were used in the process of writing down God's Word, they were all literally "borne along" by the Holy Spirit. The human wills of the authors were not the originators of God's message. God did not permit the will of sinful human beings to misdirect or erroneously record His message. Put another way, God *moved* and the prophet *mouthed* these revelational truths. Indeed, God *revealed* and man *recorded* His Word to humankind.

Interestingly, the Greek word for "carried along" in 2 Peter 1:21 is the same as that found in Acts 27:15-17. In this passage the experienced sailors could not navigate the ship because the wind was so strong. The ship was being driven, directed, and carried along by the wind. This is similar to the Spirit's driving, directing, and carrying the human authors of the Bible as He wished. The word is a strong one, indicating the Spirit's complete superintendence of the human authors. Just as the sailors were active on the ship (though the wind, not the sailors, ultimately controlled the ship's movement), so the human authors were active in writing as the Spirit directed. This assures us that biblical prophecy truly did derive from God, and not mere human beings.

Intermediate State

The state of our existence between physical death and the future resurrection is properly called the "intermediate state." It is an *in-between* state—that is, it is the state of our existence in-between the time our mortal bodies die and the time we receive resurrection bodies in the future (see Revelation 6:9-11).

The intermediate state, then, is a *disembodied* state. It is a state in which one's physical body is in the grave while one's spirit or soul is either in heaven with Christ or in a place of great suffering apart from Christ (see 2 Corinthians 5:8; Philippians 1:21-23; Luke 16:19-31). One's destiny in the intermediate state depends wholly upon whether one has placed faith in Christ during one's earthly existence (Acts 16:31).

Man has both a material part and an immaterial part. Man's material part is his body. Man's immaterial part is his soul or spirit (these terms are used interchangeably in Scripture). At the moment of death, man's immaterial part departs or separates from his material part (Genesis 35:18). (The Greek word for death literally means "separation.") So, at death man becomes disembodied when his or her spirit or soul departs from the physical body.

There are many verses in Scripture that speak of the "departure" of the spirit at death. The preacher tells us that at the moment of death "the spirit returns to God who gave it" (Ecclesiastes 12:7). At the moment of Jesus' death, He prayed to the Father: "Into your hands I commit my spirit" (Luke 23:46). When Stephen was dying after being stoned, he prayed, "Lord Jesus, receive my spirit" (Acts 7:59).

This separation of the spirit from the physical body, however, is only a temporary situation. Scriptures reveals there is a day coming in which God will reunite each person's soul or spirit to his or her resurrection body (1 Thessalonians 4:13-17). When that day finally arrives, human beings will never again be in a situation where they are disembodied. They will live forever in their resurrection bodies.

Resurrected believers will live forever in the immediate presence of God (Revelation 21). Resurrected unbelievers will spend eternity in a place of great suffering called the lake of fire (20:15).

Intermediate State, Conscious Awareness in

Some have wrongly concluded that at the moment of death, consciousness vanishes. They think the soul "sleeps." This is not the view of Scripture, however. Indeed, the Scriptures never speak of the soul sleeping, but rather speak of the body sleeping. This is because the body takes on the appearance of sleep at the moment of death.

In Scripture, man's soul or spirit is always portrayed as being fully conscious in the intermediate state. Perhaps this is nowhere better illustrated than in Jesus' parable of the rich man, Lazarus, and Abraham, all three of whom are portrayed as consciously interacting with each other in the intermediate state (Luke 16:19-31). This is also seen to be true of Christian martyrs whose bodies are dead but whose souls consciously interact (speak) with God (Revelation 6:9-11).

Another passage that clearly indicates conscious existence in the intermediate state is Matthew 17:1-4. In this passage Jesus, along with Peter, James, and John, are portrayed as being on a high mountain. Jesus was then transfigured before them, and His face became as bright as the sun. At that moment, both Moses and Elijah—whose time on earth had long passed—supernaturally appeared to Jesus from the intermediate state and spoke with Him. Moses and Elijah appeared and they were fully conscious and carried on a conversation with Jesus.

So it is with all of us who die. We are fully conscious and we can converse with others who are with us.

Interpretation, Method of

See *Hermeneutics of Biblical Prophecy.*

Iraq

Ezekiel 38:1-6 speaks of a northern coalition of nations that will one day invade Israel. These nations include Russia, Iran, Sudan, Turkey, Libya, Kazakhstan, Kyrgyzstan, Uzbekistan, Turkmenistan, Tajikistan, Armenia, and possibly northern Afghanistan. One is naturally curious as to why Iraq is not mentioned as a part of the invading coalition. Certainly today's Iraq would dearly love to see Israel annihilated. So why no mention?

There are several possible answers. First, it is not beyond the realm of possibility that Iraq will indeed be a part of this invading coalition. In addition to the specific nations mentioned in Ezekiel 38, we find the phrase "many peoples with you" (verses 6,9,15 NASB; see also verse 22). It may be that Iraq is a part of the "many peoples."

Another possible scenario is that Iraq will not be a part of this Islamic invading coalition because a rebuilt Babylon (capital of Iraq) will be the headquarters of the Antichrist during the Tribulation period (Revelation 17–18). Scripture reveals that the Antichrist will sign a seven-year peace pact with Israel (Daniel 9:27), and this will actually constitute the beginning of the Tribulation period. If the Ezekiel invasion takes place in the first half of the Tribulation, Iraq could not possibly be a part of the invading force simply because Iraq, with its capital in Babylon, will be controlled by the Antichrist, who signed the peace pact with Israel. In fact, it may be that the nations of Ezekiel 38:1-6 launch an invasion into Israel in defiance of the Antichrist. In any event, God utterly destroys the invaders (Ezekiel 39).

Isaiah

Isaiah is considered the greatest of the Old Testament prophets. Some have even called him the "prince" of Old Testament prophets.

Certainly his book is a prince-sized book, being the third longest in the Bible. Only Jeremiah and the Psalms exceed it in length.

The New Testament authors quote from Isaiah quite often (21 times). This shows they thought it was a very important book. Jesus thought it was important too. He even inaugurated His public ministry with a quotation from Isaiah (Luke 4:17-21).

Isaiah's name means "the Lord saves." His name is appropriate, for salvation was an important part of his message to the people of Judah. Of course, salvation and judgment often go together in the Bible. If a person refuses to be saved and turns away from God, then he must suffer the consequences in judgment. Isaiah combines these themes in his book.

Isaiah was born and reared in Jerusalem in days of great prosperity. It would seem his family was an affluent one. He was also apparently highly educated and very intelligent.

According to Jewish tradition, Isaiah's father Amoz was a brother of King Amaziah. This would make Isaiah a first cousin to King Uzziah and a grandson of King Joash. Isaiah had many opportunities to fellowship with royalty. He even gave advice on foreign affairs to King Hezekiah.

Isaiah received his call from God in the year of King Uzziah's death (740 B.C.). His ministry continued through the reign of Hezekiah, who died in 687 B.C. This means Isaiah's ministry spanned about half a century. He wrote his book between 740 and 680 B.C.

The book of Isaiah is one of the best-loved prophetic books in the Old Testament. The primary reason for this is that it contains more references to the person and work of Jesus Christ than any other book in the Old Testament. John 12:41, for example, says that Isaiah "saw Jesus' glory and spoke about him."

Isaiah is often referred to as "the Messianic prophet." He predicted the Messiah's virgin birth (7:14), His deity and kingdom (9:1-7), His righteous reign (11:2-5), His vicarious suffering and death (52:13–53:12), and much more. No wonder the great composer Handel based so much of his musical masterpiece, "The Messiah," on the book of Isaiah.

Aside from speaking about Christ, Isaiah preached about God's righteousness (Isaiah 5:16; 11:4; 42:6,21; 51:6), warned about judgment for sin (13–23), and proclaimed God's love and forgiveness (54:10; 55:3; 63:9). He also prophesied the glory that awaits those who remain faithful to God (2–4; 62–63). One thing that stands out in this book is God's tremendous power, majesty, glory, and sovereignty (44–45). Despite the greatness of the nations on the earth, they are as nothing before God Almighty (40:15).

As would be expected, the book of Isaiah has a number of passages that deal with the end times. For example, Isaiah 24:1-23 deals with the judgments of the Tribulation period. Isaiah 25:1-12 speaks of the triumphs of the millennial kingdom. Isaiah 34:1-17 addresses Armageddon and its judgments. Isaiah 35:1-10 provides further insights on the blessings of the millennial kingdom, while Isaiah 56:1-8 speaks of millennial blessings extended to the Gentiles. Isaiah 60:1-22 speaks of the glory of Israel in the millennial kingdom. Clearly, the book of Isaiah is rich in insights regarding the prophetic future.

Israel, Rebirth of

When the modern state of Israel was born in 1948 as a self-governing nation, it represented the beginnings of an actual fulfillment of specific Bible prophecies about an international regathering of the Jews in unbelief before the judgment of the Tribulation. This regathering was to take place after centuries of exile in various nations around the world.

In Ezekiel 36:10 God promised, "I will multiply the number of people upon you, even the whole house of Israel. The towns will be inhabited and the ruins rebuilt." God promised, "I will take you out of the nations; I will gather you from all the countries and bring you back into your own land" (36:24). Israel would again be prosperous, for God "will increase the fruit of the trees and the crops of the field, so that you will no longer suffer disgrace among the nations because of famine" (36:30).

In the vision of dry bones in Ezekiel 37, the Lord is miraculously portrayed as bringing the bones back together into a skeleton, and the skeleton becomes wrapped in muscles and tendons and flesh, and God then breathes life into the body. There is no doubt that this chapter is speaking about Israel, for we read that "these bones are the whole house of Israel" (verse 11). Hence, this chapter portrays Israel as becoming a living, breathing nation, brought back from the dead, as it were.

1948 is therefore a year to remember. In A.D. 70, Titus and his Roman warriors trampled on and destroyed Jerusalem, definitively and quite thoroughly ending Israel as a political entity (see Luke 21:20). Since then, the Jews have been dispersed worldwide for many centuries. In the year 1940, no one could have guessed that within a decade Israel would be a nation again. And yet, it happened. Israel achieved statehood in 1948, and the Jews have been returning to their homeland ever since.

Israel at this time still remains in unbelief. But there is a day in the future, according to Joel 2:28-29, in which there will be a spiritual awakening in Israel. It would seem that Armageddon will be the historical context in which Israel finally becomes converted (Zechariah 12:2–13:1). The restoration of Israel will include the confession of Israel's national sin (Leviticus 26:40-42; Jeremiah 3:11-18; Hosea 5:15), following which Israel will be saved, thereby fulfilling Paul's prophecy in Romans 11:25-27. In dire threat at Armageddon, Israel will plead for their newly found Messiah to return and deliver them. They will "mourn for Him, as one mourns for an only son" (Zechariah 12:10 NASB; Matthew 23:37-39; see also Isaiah 53:1-9), at which point their deliverance will surely come (see Romans 10:13-14). Israel's leaders will have finally realized the reason why the Tribulation has fallen on them—perhaps due to the Holy Spirit's enlightenment of their understanding of Scripture, or the testimony of the 144,000

Jewish evangelists, or perhaps the testimony of the two prophetic witnesses. Later, in the millennial kingdom, Israel will experience a full possession of the promised land and the reestablishment of the Davidic throne. It will be a time of physical and spiritual blessing, the basis of which is the new covenant (Jeremiah 31:31-34).

See *Regathering of Jews to Homeland, Necessity of.*

J

Jacob's Trouble, Time of

In Jeremiah 30:7 the Tribulation period is referred to as the "time of Jacob's trouble." The Tribulation will be a time of judgment—a time of unprecedented trouble and distress—on Messiah-rejecting Israel as a national entity. The precise details of this distress may be found in Revelation 6–18.

Jeremiah

The book of Jeremiah was written by a prophet of the same name between 627 and 570 B.C. His name literally means "Jehovah throws," a term referring to the laying of a foundation. Certainly Jeremiah's words, like any prophet's words, were foundational for the people.

Jeremiah was born into a priestly family, and was called from birth to be a spokesman for God (Jeremiah 1:5). He was from the small village of Anathoth (1:1). He began his ministry in Judah during the reign of Josiah (640–609 B.C.), and continued through the reigns of four other kings: Johoahaz (609 B.C.), Johoiakim (609–598 B.C.), Jehoiachin (598–597 B.C.), and Zedekiah (597–586 B.C.). He prophesied during the same general time as the prophets Habakkuk, Zephaniah, and Ezekiel.

The difficult thing for Jeremiah was that he was given a harsh message to deliver to the people, and he expressed inadequacy in fulfilling the prophetic task to which he was assigned (Jeremiah 1:6-10). For decades he warned the Israelites of an impending judgment that was coming, but he was virtually ignored (2–35). Nobody would listen. The people continued in such horrible sins as flagrant idol worship, adultery, injustice, tyranny against the helpless, dishonesty, and more. Such sins were causing Jeremiah's people to rush toward judgment. And because Jeremiah pointed toward a coming judgment, his life was often endangered by political and religious leaders (36–38).

The judgment that finally came upon the people of God was the Babylonian exile (Jeremiah 39–45). Jerusalem and its temple were destroyed in 587 B.C., and the Babylonians took all the people captive. Though Jeremiah as a prophet had to speak forth about this coming judgment, he was nevertheless mournful and grieved at what he saw coming upon his nation.

A number of verses in Jeremiah have relevance for end times prophecy. In Jeremiah 30:7, for example, the Tribulation period is referred to as the "time of Jacob's trouble." The Tribulation will be a time of judgment on Messiah-rejecting Israel.

Jeremiah 30:8 then makes reference to "that day," which alludes to the day of the Lord. This day will see the restoration of Israel under the divine Messiah, Jesus Christ.

Later in Jeremiah, we are told that all believers will be indwelt by the Holy Spirit. This is promised in the new covenant (Jeremiah 31:31-37), a covenant that has relevance not just for today but also for those who live in the future 1,000-year millennial kingdom over which Christ will rule.

Jerusalem

The city of Jerusalem is famous worldwide in view of the fact that it was the scene of Jesus' arrest, trial, crucifixion, and resurrection.

The city itself rests in the Judean hills, at about 2,640 feet above sea level. During the time of Jesus, the city was probably home to about a quarter of a million people.

In Jewish thinking in biblical times, no city could possibly compare with Jerusalem. People from all around would go to Jerusalem for the three major festivals and to pay the annual temple tax. Jerusalem was the geographical heart of the Jewish religion. Jesus Himself made a number of visits to Jerusalem (Luke 2:22-51; 10:38-42; 13:34).

Historically, king David of Israel captured the city in the tenth century B.C. During the reign of his son Solomon, Jerusalem became the center of religious life with the magnificent temple that was built there.

As prophesied by Jesus, Jerusalem and the temple built by Herod were utterly destroyed in A.D. 70 by Rome (Matthew 24:2). This definitively and quite thoroughly ended Israel as a political entity (Luke 21:20). Since then, the Jews have been dispersed worldwide for many centuries. In 1948, however, Israel again became a nation against all odds. Then, in 1967, Israel captured Jerusalem and the West Bank during the Six-Day War. Jews have been streaming back to the holy land ever since. All this is in fulfillment of scriptural prophecies that Israel would become a nation again after a long and worldwide dispersion (see Ezekiel 36–37).

It is ironic that Jerusalem literally means "city of peace." For a long time now, there has been anything but peace in Jerusalem. This is primarily due to external threats from Muslim nations. Of great relevance to the study of end times events is the scriptural prediction that Israel will one day be invaded by a northern military coalition made up of Russia, Iran, Sudan, Turkey, Libya, and some other Muslim nations (see Ezekiel 38:1-6). God Himself will destroy the invading nations (see Ezekiel 39).

Scripture reveals that the Jewish temple will be rebuilt in Jerusalem in the end times (see Matthew 24:1-2,15,27-31; Daniel 9:26-27; 11:31). In the middle of the Tribulation period, the Antichrist will set himself up as God, put an image of himself in the Jewish temple (thereby causing the abomination of desolation), and the False Prophet will seek to force all people to worship the Antichrist (see 2 Thessalonians 2:1-4).

Scripture also reveals that Armageddon will take place north of Jerusalem. In fact, the word Armageddon literally means "Mount of Megiddo," and refers to a location about 60 miles north of Jerusalem. This is the location of Barak's battle with the Canaanites (Judges 4) and Gideon's battle with the Midianites (Judges 7). This will be the site for the final horrific battles of humankind just prior to the second coming (Revelation 16:16).

Jerusalem will be restored to glory during the future millennial kingdom, over which Christ will rule. Scripture even reveals that there will be a millennial temple (Ezekiel 40–48).

Meanwhile, however, Jerusalem will continue to be a sore spot in the world. As we read in Zechariah 12:2-3: "Behold, I am about to make Jerusalem a cup that causes reeling to all the peoples around...It will come about in that day that I will make Jerusalem a heavy stone for all the peoples...And all the nations of the earth will be gathered against it" (NASB).

Jerusalem, New

See *New Jerusalem.*

Jesus Christ in Biblical Prophecy

The word *Messiah* comes from the Hebrew term *mashiach,* which means "anointed one." The Greek parallel to this term is *christos,* often translated as "Christ." The terms are equated, for in John 1:41, Andrew said to Peter, "'We have found the Messiah' (that is, the Christ)."

The New Testament is clear that Jesus is the promised divine Messiah. Recall that when the angel announced the birth of Jesus to the shepherds in the field, he identified Jesus this way: "Today in the town of David a Savior has been born to you; he is Christ the Lord" (Luke

2:11). Later, Simeon, who was filled with the Holy Spirit, recognized the babe Jesus as Christ, in fulfillment of God's promise to him that "he would not die before he had seen the Lord's Christ" (Luke 2:26).

Hundreds of messianic prophecies in the Old Testament point to a single Messiah or Christ—Jesus Christ. For example, Isaiah predicted the Messiah's virgin birth (Isaiah 7:14), His deity and kingdom (9:1-7), His reign of righteousness (11:2-5), His vicarious suffering and death on the cross (52:13–53:12), and much more. It is only logical to conclude that if these hundreds of Old Testament messianic prophecies were written hundreds of years before they occurred, and if they could never have been foreseen and depended upon factors outside human control for their fulfillment, and if all of these prophecies perfectly fit the person and life of Jesus Christ, then Jesus had to be the Messiah.

Just as prophecies of Christ's first coming were literally fulfilled, so the prophecies of His second coming (and events related to it) will be literally fulfilled as well. Moreover, Jesus is at the very heart of biblical prophecy pertaining to the end times. For example:

- It is Jesus who comes to snatch Christians off the earth at the rapture, prior to the Tribulation (see 1 Thessalonians 4:13-17).
- It is Jesus who is (obviously) the central figure at the second coming (Revelation 19:11-16).
- It is Jesus who judges Christians at the Judgment Seat of Christ (1 Corinthians 3:10-15; 2 Corinthians 5:10).
- It is Jesus who judges the nations at the Judgment of the nations, following the Tribulation period and prior to the millennial kingdom (Matthew 25:31-46).
- It is Jesus who reigns during the 1,000-year millennial kingdom (Revelation 20:1-4).
- It is Jesus who judges the wicked at the Great White Throne judgment (Revelation 20:11-13).

- Jesus as God dwells with His people forever in the eternal state (Philippians 1:23).

Jewish Temple, Rebuilding

There is substantial Scriptural evidence for the rebuilding of the Jewish temple in the end times. First of all, a key prerequisite to the rebuilding of the temple—Israel back in her homeland as a nation—has been a reality since 1948. Moreover, the Jews have been streaming back to the holy land from around the world ever since (see Ezekiel 36-37).

That the temple must be rebuilt by the middle of the seven-year Tribulation is clear from the fact that Jesus, in His discourse on the Mount of Olives, warned of a catastrophic event that assumes the existence of the temple: "When you see the abomination of desolation spoken of by the prophet Daniel, standing in the holy place (let the reader understand), then those who are in Judea must flee to the mountains" (Matthew 24:15-16 NASB). This "abomination of desolation" refers to a desecration of the Jewish temple by the Antichrist.

It is significant that Jesus says this, because just previously (in verses 1-2), Jesus positively affirmed that the great Temple built by Herod (the Jewish temple of Jesus' day) would be utterly destroyed: "Truly I say to you, not one stone here will be left upon another, which will not be torn down" (NASB). This prophecy was literally fulfilled in A.D. 70 when Titus and his Roman warriors overran Jerusalem and the Jewish temple.

The only conclusion that can be reached is that though the temple of Jesus' day would be destroyed, the abomination of desolation would occur in a yet-future temple. This latter temple would be built by the middle of the Tribulation period (see also Daniel 9:27; 12:11).

Even today there are reports that various individuals and groups have been working behind the scenes to prepare various materials for the future temple, including priestly robes, temple tapestries, and worship utensils. These items are being prefabricated so that when the temple is finally rebuilt, everything will be ready for it. I reiterate that the temple does not need to be rebuilt *until* the middle of the Tribulation period. Hence, the fact that many items are *already* being prefabricated is all the more exciting to many prophecy enthusiasts.

Jews

The term *Jew* comes from the Hebrew word, *Yehudi,* which originally referred to a descendant of Judah (2 Kings 16:6). Sometime following the Babylonian captivity, however, the word came to refer to all Hebrews, the descendants of Abraham, all those of the country of Judah (2 Chronicles 32:18; Jeremiah 32:12; 34:9; 38:19). In New Testament times, the term likewise referred to Israelites in general (as opposed to Gentiles—Galatians 2:14; Titus 1:14).

Judaism, which derives from the Greek word *Ioudaismos,* refers to the religion of the Jews (Galatians 1:13-14). Jews believe that the entirety of God's Word is communicated in the Old Testament, and they give special attention to the Torah, God's Law, found in the first five books of the Old Testament. Their primary confession of faith is the Shema, which affirms that Yahweh is the one true God (Deuteronomy 6:4).

Of great significance to the study of biblical prophecy, the church and Israel (the Jews) continue to be distinct in the New Testament. For example, we are instructed in 1 Corinthians 10:32, "Do not cause anyone to stumble, whether Jews, Greeks [Gentiles] or the church of God" (insert added). Moreover, Israel and the church are seen as distinct throughout the book of Acts, with the word "Israel" being used 20 times and the word "church" 19 times. We are also told in Romans 9–11 that God still has a plan for Israel. This ultimately means that there is no basis for saying that the church fulfills all the prophecies and promises made to Israel.

See *Replacement Theology.*

Joel

This book was written by Joel, son of Pethuel, in about 835 B.C. (Joel 1:1). Joel's name means "The Lord is God."

A devastating swarm of locusts had just ripped through the land of Judah, resulting in famine. This black cloud of devouring insects struck like a firestorm. As these consuming locusts ate up the agricultural produce and caused the light of the sun to be hidden and darkened, Joel saw in this catastrophe a little foretaste of the day of judgment that was surely coming upon God's people (Joel 1:15–2:11). In fact, Joel indicated that as bad as the locust plague was, it would pale by comparison to God's day of judgment. He therefore called the people to repentance (2:12-17). The reality is, Joel said, that God cannot ignore sin. Blessing can only follow obedience.

Joel provides us with a number of end time prophecies. For example, he cites God as saying: "I restore the fortunes of Judah and Jerusalem" (3:1), a promise that will be fulfilled at the second coming of Christ, at which time Israel will be regathered to Palestine (see Matthew 24:31).

Joel 3:2 again cites God: "I will gather all nations and bring them down to the Valley of Jehoshaphat. There I will enter into judgment against them..." This will also take place at the second coming of Christ, when Christ will divinely judge the Gentile nations regarding their treatment of Israel (see Matthew 25:40,45).

Finally, in Joel 3:9-17 we find a description of the campaign of Armageddon (compare with Revelation 16:14). Verse 18 makes reference to the day of Messiah's reign in His earthly millennial kingdom. Then, through verse 21, we find God's affirmation that Israel will be pardoned by God for her sins—something that will take place in close proximity to the second coming (see Zechariah 12:10-11; Romans 11:25-26).

John, Gospel of

John was, by trade, a fisherman. He was sometimes called a "son of thunder" by Jesus—perhaps because of a feisty nature (Mark 3:17). John was very close to Jesus, and is identified as the "disciple whom Jesus loved" (John 13:23). So close was John to Jesus that John was with Mary at the foot of the cross when Jesus was crucified, and Jesus entrusted the care of His mother to John before He died (John 19:26-27). Besides his Gospel, John also wrote 1, 2, and 3 John and the book of Revelation.

John's Gospel was likely written around A.D. 90. Its purpose was to set forth Jesus as the Savior and Redeemer of the world by presenting convincing proofs of His deity, humanity, and Messiahship. The Gospel has the evangelistic aim of persuading men to trust in Christ, the divine Messiah (see John 20:31). It is interesting to observe that the word "believe" occurs about a hundred times in this Gospel (more than any other Gospel).

A large portion of John's Gospel deals with the doctrine of God. In fact, over half the Gospel deals with truths relating to the Father, Son, and Holy Spirit. This is significant in light of John's evangelistic aim. In a cultural atmosphere where there were many cults, false religions, and divergent philosophical schools of thought, it is easy to see why John went to such extremes to prove the existence of the one true God.

An important concept in John's Gospel is that Jesus reveals the Father to the world. Jesus was the supreme revelation of God. For instance, John 1:18 says, "No one has ever seen God, but God the One and Only, who is at the Father's side, has made him known." In John 14:9, Jesus said, "Anyone who has seen me has seen the Father."

In demonstrating the true identity of Jesus as the divine Messiah, John used a number of revealing titles of Christ. Jesus is called "the Lord" (4:1 NASB; 6:23; 11:2; 20:20; 21:12), "Son of God" (1:49; 5:25; 10:33; 11:4,27), "Son of Man" (3:14-15; 5:27; 6:27,62), "Teacher" or "Rabbi" (1:38,49; 3:2; 4:31; 6:25; 9:2; 11:8; 20:16), "King" (1:49; 12:13; 18:33,37), and "Christ" or "Messiah" (1:41; 4:25-26; 11:27). Most of these titles point to the deity of Christ. John also demonstrated that

Jesus has the attributes of deity, including omniscience (4:29), omnipresence (14:23), and preexistence (1:1; 8:58; 17:5). The miracles He performed further demonstrate His divine identity (for example, see John 2:23; 5:1-15).

While John fully established Jesus' deity, he also demonstrated that in the Incarnation, Jesus was fully human (John 1:14). Indeed, He had a human body (19:40), a human soul (12:27), and a human spirit (11:33; 13:21). Jesus also manifested human characteristics, such as becoming thirsty (19:28-30) and getting tired (4:6).

In sum, Jesus in the Incarnation was fully God and fully man. Such is the perfect Redeemer of humankind that John speaks of in his Gospel. Jesus came "down from heaven" (6:41), and was born of Mary, who was "the mother of Jesus" (2:1 NASB). This is crucial to John's message of salvation, for in order for God to save man, He Himself must become a man and die as a substitutionary sacrifice for the sins of man (John 1:29,36).

John also provides insights on some end times prophetic events. For example, in John 5:28-29 Jesus affirmed that "an hour is coming, in which all who are in the tombs will hear his voice, and will come forth; those who did the good deeds to a resurrection of life, those who committed the evil deeds to a resurrection of judgment." Here Jesus makes reference to the resurrection of both believers (which takes place in a number of stages, the first being the rapture—see 1 Thessalonians 4:13-17) and unbelievers at the end of the millennial kingdom (Revelation 20:11-15).

Jesus also revealed to His followers that He was going to prepare a place for them: "Let not your hearts be troubled. Believe in God; believe also in me. In my Father's house are many rooms. If it were not so, would I have told you that I go to prepare a place for you? And if I go and prepare a place for you, I will come again and will take you to myself, that where I am you may be also" (John 14:1-3 ESV). The place Jesus is preparing for us is the New Jerusalem, the capital city of heaven where the saints of all ages will dwell forever (see Revelation 21).

Judgment of Fallen Angels

Fallen angels are destined for judgment and doom. Jesus makes specific reference to "the eternal fire" that was "prepared for the devil and his angels" (Matthew 25:41). The eternal fire—also known as the lake of fire, or hell—is the ultimate destiny of all fallen angels.

Some angels are apparently already confined, awaiting their future judgment. Jude 6 informs us that "the angels who did not stay within their own position of authority, but left their proper dwelling, he has kept in eternal chains under gloomy darkness until the judgment of the great day." Likewise, we are told that "God did not spare angels when they sinned, but cast them into hell and committed them to chains of gloomy darkness to be kept until the judgment" (2 Peter 2:4). Other fallen angels are still free to roam the earth, harassing followers of Christ.

Following the millennial kingdom, Satan will finally be cast into the lake of fire: "The devil, who had deceived them, was thrown into the lake of burning sulfur, where the beast and the false prophet had been thrown. They will be tormented day and night for ever and ever" (Revelation 20:10).

What we learn from the above passages is that even though Satan and his fallen angels are presently active in our world, they are destined for eternal suffering. While the execution of these judgments is not yet enacted, the judgments have been pronounced and it's just a matter of time before Satan's final doom is brought about, along with his fallen angelic followers.

Judgment of Israel

After the Tribulation period, but prior to the millennial kingdom, there will be a judgment of both the Gentile nations (Matthew 25:31-46) as well as Jewish survivors. Those who are recognized as believers in Jesus among those who participate in these judgments will be invited into Christ's millennial kingdom.

The Judgment of the Jews is described in Ezekiel 20:34-38. According to this passage:

- The judgment will take place after the Lord has gathered the Israelites from all around the earth to Palestine.
- Christ will purge out the rebels—those who have refused to turn to Him for salvation.
- Believers from among this group will enter in Christ's millennial kingdom where they will then enjoy the blessings of the new covenant (verse 37; see also Jeremiah 31:31).
- These saved Jews are not yet given resurrection bodies. They will enter the kingdom in their mortal bodies and continue to have babies throughout the millennium (just as their Gentile counterparts will—Matthew 25:46). Though longevity will characterize the millennial kingdom, both mortal Jews and Gentiles will continue to age and die. They will be resurrected at the end of the millennium.

Judgment of the Nations

Within premillennial eschatology, Matthew 25:31-46 is properly interpreted as the judgment of the nations. The nations are comprised of the sheep and the goats, representing the saved and the lost among the Gentiles. According to Matthew 25:32, they are intermingled and require separation by a special judgment. This judgment follows the second coming of Christ, since it occurs "when the Son of Man comes in his glory, and all the angels with him" (Matthew 25:31).

Some interpreters have argued that this judgment is the same as the Great White Throne judgment in Revelation 20:11-13. However, a comparison of the judgment in Matthew with the one in Revelation makes this view unlikely:

Different time. The judgment of the nations occurs at the second coming of Christ (Matthew 25:31); the Great White Throne judgment occurs following the millennial kingdom (Revelation 20:11-12).

Different scene. The judgment of the nations occurs on earth (Matthew 25:31-33); the Great White Throne judgment occurs (obviously) at the Great White Throne (Revelation 20:11).

Different subjects. At the judgment of the nations, three groups of people are mentioned: the sheep, the goats, and the brothers (Matthew 25:32,40). The Great White Throne judgment involves the unsaved dead (Revelation 20:12).

Different basis. The basis of judgment at the judgment of the nations is how Christ's "brothers" were treated (Matthew 25:40); the basis of judgment at the Great White Throne judgment is their works (Revelation 20:12).

Different result. The result of the judgment of the nations is twofold: the righteous enter into the kingdom; the unrighteous are cast into the lake of fire. The result of the Great White Throne judgment is that the wicked dead are cast into the lake of fire (the righteous are not mentioned).

Resurrection. No resurrection is mentioned in connection with the judgment of the nations. However, a resurrection does take place in connection with the Great White Throne judgment (Revelation 20:13).

Clearly, a plain reading of the text indicates that these judgments are not the same. The judgment of the nations deals with the Gentile nations, and takes place following the second coming of Christ.

Judgment Seat of Christ

All believers will one day stand before the Judgment Seat of Christ (*Bema*) (Romans 14:8-10; 1 Corinthians 3:11-15; 9:24-27). At that time each believer's life will be examined in regard to deeds done while in the body. Personal motives and intents of the heart will also be weighed.

The idea of a "Judgment Seat" relates to the athletic games of Paul's day. After the games concluded, a dignitary took his seat on an elevated throne in the arena. One by one the winning athletes came up to the throne to receive a reward—usually a wreath of leaves, a victor's crown. In the case of Christians, each of us will stand before Christ the Judge and receive (or lose) rewards.

Christ's judgment of us will not be in a corporate setting—like a big class being praised or scolded by a teacher. Rather it will be individual and personal. "We will all stand before God's judgment seat" (Romans 14:10). Each of us will be judged on an individual basis.

This judgment has nothing to do with whether or not the Christian will remain saved. Those who have placed faith in Christ are saved, and nothing threatens that. Believers are eternally secure in their salvation (John 10:28-30; Romans 8:29-39; Ephesians 1:13; 4:30; Hebrews 7:25). This judgment rather has to do with the reception or loss of rewards.

Scripture indicates that this judgment will take place immediately after the rapture and Christ takes the saints back to heaven. No Bible verse explicitly states this. But a number of factors lead us to this conclusion.

For one thing, many scholars believe that the twenty-four elders in heaven that are mentioned in Revelation 4:1,10 represent believers—and they are portrayed as already having their crowns in heaven at the very start of the Tribulation period. Moreover, when the "bride of Christ" (the corporate body of Christians) returns to earth with Christ at the second coming, the bride is "clothed with righteous deeds"—implying that she has already passed through the judgment (Revelation 19:8).

It seems to be the testimony of Scripture that some believers at the Judgment may have a sense of deprivation and suffer some degree of forfeiture and shame. Indeed, certain rewards may be forfeited that otherwise might have been received, and this will involve a sense of loss. Second John 8 thus warns us, "Watch out that you do not lose what you have worked for, but that you may be rewarded fully" (compare with 1 John 2:28).

We must keep all this in perspective, however. Christ's coming for us at the rapture and the prospect of living eternally with Him is something that should give each of us joy. And our joy will last for all eternity.

The scope of the judgment includes actions. The Christian's judgment will focus on his personal stewardship of the gifts, talents, opportunities, and responsibilities given to him in this life. The very character of each Christian's life and service will be utterly laid bare under the unerring and omniscient vision of Christ, whose "eyes were like blazing fire" (Revelation 1:14).

Numerous Scripture verses reveal that each of our actions will be judged before the Lord. The psalmist said to the Lord, "Surely you will reward each person according to what he has done" (Psalm 62:12; see also Matthew 16:27). In Ephesians 6:8 we read that the Lord "will reward everyone for whatever good he does, whether he is slave or free."

The scope of the judgment includes thoughts. At the Judgment Seat of Christ, it won't just be our actions that will come under scrutiny. Also scrutinized will be our thoughts. In Jeremiah 17:10 God said, "I the LORD search the heart and examine the mind, to reward a man according to his conduct, according to what his deeds deserve." The Lord "will bring to light what is hidden in darkness and will expose the motives of men's hearts" (1 Corinthians 4:5). The Lord is the One "who searches hearts and minds" (Revelation 2:23).

The scope of the judgment includes words. Finally, the scope of the believer's judgment will include all the words he has spoken. Christ once said that "men will have to give account on the day of judgment for every careless word they have spoken" (Matthew 12:35-37). This is an important aspect of judgment, for tremendous damage can be done through the human tongue (see James 3:1-12).

Rewards and crowns. What kinds of rewards will believers receive at the Judgment Seat of Christ? Scripture often speaks of them in terms of crowns that we wear. In fact, there are a number of different crowns that symbolize the various spheres of achievement and award in the Christian life.

The *crown of life* is given to those who persevere under trial, and especially to those who suffer to the point of death (James 1:12; Revelation

2:10). The *crown of glory* is given to those who faithfully and sacrificially minister God's Word to the flock (1 Peter 5:4). The *crown incorruptible* is given to those who win the race of temperance and self-control (1 Corinthians 9:25). The *crown of righteousness* is given to those who long for the second coming of Christ (2 Timothy 4:8).

It is highly revealing that in Revelation 4:10 we find believers casting their crowns before the throne of God in an act of worship and adoration. This teaches us something very important. Apparently the crowns (as rewards) are bestowed on us not for our own glory but ultimately for the glory of God. We are told elsewhere in Scripture that believers are redeemed in order to bring glory to God (1 Corinthians 6:20). It would seem that the act of placing our crowns before the throne of God is an illustration of this.

Here's something else to think about: The greater reward or crown one has received, the greater capacity one has to bring glory to the Creator. The lesser reward or crown one has received, the lesser is his capacity to bring glory to the Creator. Because of the different rewards handed out at the Judgment Seat of Christ, believers will have differing capacities to bring glory to God.

Still, we shouldn't take this to mean that certain believers will have a sense of loss throughout eternity. After all, each believer will be glorifying God to the fullness of his capacity in the next life. Each one of us, then, will be able to "declare the praises of him who called [us] out of darkness into his wonderful light" (1 Peter 2:9).

K

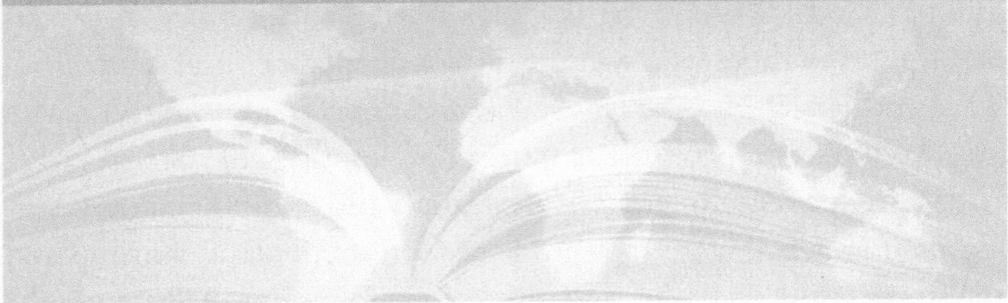

Keys of Death and of Hades

In the New Testament a *key* always implies authority to open a door and give entrance to a place or realm. When Jesus affirms in Revelation 1:18, "I hold the keys of death and Hades," He is thereby implying that He—as God—has the authority to grant entrance and exit from those realms (see also John 5:21-26; 1 Corinthians 15:54-57; Hebrews 2:14; Revelation 20:12-14). The Lord Jesus decides who lives, who dies, and when.

Kingdom of God

The terms "kingdom of God" and "kingdom of heaven" are essentially interchangeable terms in the Bible. The Gospels of Mark, Luke, and John use the term "kingdom of God" (for example, Mark 1:15; Luke 9:2). Matthew, however, uses "kingdom of heaven" some 34 times but "kingdom of God" only four times. The apparent reason Matthew did this is that he was a Jew writing to Jews. He was showing sensitivity to the Jewish preference of avoiding using God's name when possible to ensure one was not using it in vain (in violation of the third of the Ten Commandments—Exodus 20:7). The other Gospel writers were not writing to a Jewish audience, and hence used the term "kingdom of God."

There are two primary senses in which "kingdom of God" and "kingdom of heaven" are used in Scripture: a *present* sense and a *future* sense. The present sense involves the idea that God spiritually rules over His people who have been delivered from the kingdom of darkness and transferred to the kingdom of Jesus Christ (Colossians 1:13). The *kingdom* of God arrived in New Testament times because the *King* (Jesus) had arrived (see Matthew 5:3; 8:12; 12:28; 19:24; 21:31; 21:43; 25:34; Luke 12:32; John 3:3,5; 18:36; Romans 14:17, Colossians 1:13; James 2:5; 2 Peter 1:11; Revelation 12:10). Of course, we might more broadly make reference to God's *eternal* kingdom or rule, for God's rule over the entire universe is truly timeless, universal, and providential.

The future (or temporal) aspect of the kingdom relates to the future millennial reign of Jesus Christ on earth. Following the second coming, Christ will institute a kingdom of perfect peace and righteousness on earth that will last for 1,000 years (Revelation 20:1-6). After this reign of true peace, the eternal state begins (Revelation 21–22). This kingdom is prophesied many times in the Old Testament (for example, Isaiah 65:17–66:24; Zechariah 14:9-17).

Kingdom Parables

See *Parables of the Kingdom.*

King, Messianic

The kingship of Jesus Christ is a common theme in Scripture, in both the Old and New Testaments. Genesis 49:10, for example, prophesied that the Messiah would come from the tribe of Judah and reign as a king. The Davidic covenant in 2 Samuel 7:16 promised a Messiah who would have a dynasty, a people over whom He would rule, and an eternal throne. In Psalm 2:6, God the Father is portrayed announcing the installation of God the Son as King in Jerusalem. Psalm 110 affirms that the Messiah will subjugate His enemies and rule over them. Daniel 7:13-14 tells us that the Messiah-King will have an everlasting dominion. These and many other Old Testament passages point to Christ's role as sovereign King.

When we get to the New Testament, we find that before Jesus was even born, an angel appeared to Mary and informed her: "You will be with child and give birth to a son...The Lord God will give him the throne of his father David, and he will reign over the house of Jacob forever; his kingdom will never end" (Luke 1:31-33).

After Jesus was born in Bethlehem, some Magi from the east came to Jerusalem and asked, "Where is the one who has been born king of the Jews? We saw his star in the east and have come to worship him" (Matthew 2:2). When they found Jesus, they bowed down and worshiped Him, even though He was just a babe (verse 11).

During His three-year ministry, Jesus proclaimed the good news of the kingdom to thousands of people (for example, Matthew 9:35). Certainly the kingdom was at the very core of His teachings.

The book of Revelation tells us that when Christ physically comes again, He will come as King of kings and Lord of lords (Revelation 19:16). Christ will then rule on the throne of David in Jerusalem throughout the millennial kingdom, in fulfillment of the Davidic covenant (2 Samuel 7:16; Luke 1:32-33).

King of kings and Lord of lords

When Jesus comes again, He will come as the King of kings and Lord of lords (Revelation 19:16). This title means that Jesus is the One who is absolutely supreme over all earthly rulers (1 Timothy 6:15; see also Deuteronomy 10:17; Psalm 136:3). When He comes, there will be many crowns on His head—crowns that represent total sovereignty. His eyes will be like blazing fire (Revelation 19:11-16). No one will be in a position to challenge His kingly authority.

Following the second coming, Christ will institute a kingdom of perfect peace and righteousness on earth that will last for 1,000 years. After this reign of true peace, the eternal state begins (Revelation 20:1-7; see also Isaiah 65:17-25; Ezekiel 37:21-28; Zechariah 8:1-17).

Knowledge Increased

The prophet Daniel was instructed, "Close up and seal the words of the scroll until the time of the end. Many will go here and there to increase knowledge" (Daniel 12:4). This verse seems to indicate that it would not be until much of human history had unfolded that the words of Daniel's prophecy would become more understood. In the end times, an increased understanding of what Daniel wrote would emerge. Indeed, people will "go here and there" in search of understanding. Note that this phrase is often used in reference to the movement of a person who is intently searching for something.

The term "time of the end" in this verse would seem to point to the future seven-year Tribulation period—the seventieth week (see Daniel 11:35,40). Apparently, what Daniel wrote will not be fully understood until that time. During Daniel's seventieth week, people will "go here and there" in search of prophetic understanding, so they can understand what is happening around them.

Even in Daniel's own day, however, his words would have brought comfort to the then-living Jewish people, for they indicate that God will ultimately deliver Israel from Gentile domination.

L

Lake of Fire

The lake of fire will be the eternal abode of Satan, the Antichrist, the false prophet, and unbelievers throughout history (Revelation 19:20; 20:10-15). All residents will be tormented day and night forever and ever. It is eternal.

Jesus often referred to the eternal destiny of the wicked as "eternal fire." Following His second coming, when He separates the sheep (believers) from the goats (unbelievers), Jesus will say to the goats: "Depart from me, you who are cursed, into the eternal fire prepared for the devil and his angels" (Matthew 25:41). This eternal fire is part and parcel of the lake of fire.

Scripture also refers to the destiny of the wicked as the "fiery furnace." Jesus said that at the end of the age the holy angels will gather all evildoers and "throw them into the fiery furnace, where there will be weeping and gnashing of teeth" (Matthew 13:42). "Weeping" carries the idea of wailing as an outward expression of deep grief. This weeping will be caused by the environment, the company, the remorse and guilt, and the shame that afflicts all who are in hell.

What precisely is the "fire" of hell? Some believe it is literal. And, indeed, that may very well be the case. Others believe "fire" is a metaphorical way of expressing the great wrath of God. Scripture tells us: "The Lord your God is a consuming fire, a jealous God" (Deuteronomy 4:24). "God is a consuming fire" (Hebrews 12:29). "His wrath is poured out like fire" (Nahum 1:6). "Who can stand when he appears? For he will be like a refiner's fire..." (Malachi 3:2). God said, "My wrath will break out and burn like fire because of the evil you have done—burn with no one to quench it" (Jeremiah 4:4). How awful is the fiery wrath of God!

Lamb of God

A type is an Old Testament institution, event, person, object, or ceremony that has reality and purpose in biblical history, but which also—by divine design—foreshadows something yet to be revealed. The Passover lamb in the Old Testament (Exodus 12:21) was a "type" of Christ, who is Himself the Lamb of God (John 1:29,36).

An understanding of the Passover lamb in the Old Testament provides significant insight on the concept of substitution, a theological concept directly related to Christ's role as Lamb of God. The Old Testament reveals that the sacrificial lamb had to be "unblemished" (Exodus 12:5; Leviticus 4:3,23,32). At the time of the sacrifice, a hand would be laid on the unblemished sacrificial animal to symbolize a transfer of guilt (Leviticus 4:4,24,33). Notice that the sacrificial lamb did not thereby actually become sinful by nature; rather, sin was *imputed* to the animal and the animal acted as a sacrificial substitute. In like manner, Christ the Lamb of God was utterly unblemished (1 Peter 1:19), but our sin was imputed to Him and He was our sacrificial substitute on the cross of Calvary. Simply because our sin was imputed to Him does not mean He changed in nature or actually became sinful.

Scripture reveals that Christ's death, as the Lamb of God, was "for" (Greek: *huper*) us in the sense that it was *on our behalf* (2 Corinthians 5:21). The word is used in this same *on-behalf-of* sense elsewhere in Scripture. Jesus at the Last Supper said: "This is my body which is given *for* you" (Luke 22:19, emphasis added here and in the verses that follow). Likewise, in John 10:15 Jesus affirmed, "I lay down my life *for* the sheep." Paul thus exults that "God demonstrates his own love for us in this: While we were still sinners, Christ died *for* us" (Romans 5:8; see also Galatians 3:13; 1 Timothy 2:6; Hebrews 2:9). Jesus "gave himself *for* us to redeem us..." (Titus 2:14), "the just *for* the unjust, so that he might bring us to God" (1 Peter 3:18; see also 2:21). The idea of substitution richly permeates these verses relating to Christ's role as the Lamb of God.

A strong emphasis in the New Testament, in agreement with the Old Testament concept of sacrifice, is that the Lamb of God was absolutely sinless. The writer of Hebrews affirmed that "we do not have a high priest who cannot sympathize with our weaknesses, but One who has been tempted in all things as we are, yet without sin" (Hebrews 4:15). Jesus was "holy, innocent, [and] undefiled" (Hebrews 7:26). He "committed no sin, nor was any deceit found in his mouth" (1 Peter 2:22). Jesus' betrayer was remorseful, saying, "I have sinned by betraying innocent blood" (Matthew 27:4). A hardened Roman soldier cried out, "Certainly this man was innocent" (Luke 23:47). The apostle Peter thus affirmed that we are redeemed not "with perishable things like silver or gold...but with precious blood, as of a lamb unblemished and spotless, the blood of Christ" (1 Peter 1:18-19). John said, "You know that he appeared in order to take away sins; and in him there is no sin" (1 John 3:5).

Perusing these various verses about Jesus and His role as the Lamb of God, we may conclude that Jesus was always without sin *actually,* but at the cross He was made to be sin for us *judicially.* While Jesus never committed a sin *personally,* He was made to be sin for us *substitutionally.* Just as the righteousness that is imputed to Christians in justification is extrinsic to them, so the sin that was imputed to Christ on the cross was extrinsic to Him, and never in any sense contaminated His essential nature. An innocent person was punished voluntarily *as if* guilty, that the guilty person (you and I) might be gratuitously rewarded *as if* innocent.

In a nutshell, the whole redemptive plan involving Jesus as Lamb of God is one of substitution—and without such substitution there can be no salvation. It was by His utterly selfless sacrificial death on the cross that our sinless Savior—the unblemished Lamb of God—paid the penalty for our sins and thereby canceled the debt of sin against us, thus wondrously making possible our reconciliation with God.

Now the worshipful words that are among the opening verses of the book of Revelation make fullest sense: "To Him who loves us and released us from our sins by His blood...to Him be the glory and the dominion forever and ever" (Revelation 1:5-6 NASB; see also 5:6,8,12,13; 6:1,16; 7:10,14,17; 8:1; 12:11; 14:4,10; 17:14; 19:7,9; 21:9,14,22,23,27).

Lampstands

In the book of Revelation, the apostle John says he saw "seven golden lampstands," and "among the lampstands someone 'like a son of man,' dressed in a robe reaching down to his feet and with a golden sash around his chest" (Revelation 1:12-13). Jesus Himself was in the midst of the seven lampstands, for He "walks among" them (2:1).

Jesus reveals that "the seven lampstands are the seven churches" (1:20) that are discussed in Revelation 2–3: the churches of Ephesus, Smyrna, Pergamum, Thyatira, Sardis, Philadelphia, and Laodicea. The churches are no doubt symbolized as lampstands because they are intended to be the bearer of God's light in this dark world (compare with Matthew 5:16). As Jesus reveals in Revelation 2–3, however, they do not always succeed and are often in need of correction.

Land Promises to Israel

Abraham's name literally means "father of a multitude." He lived around 2000 B.C., originating from the city of Ur, in Mesopotamia, on the River Euphrates. He was apparently a very wealthy and powerful man.

God called Abraham to leave Ur and go to a new land—the land of Canaan (Genesis 11:31), which God was giving to Abraham and his descendants (12:1-3). Abraham left with his wife, Sarah, and his nephew, Lot. Upon arriving in Canaan, his first act was to construct an altar and worship God. This was typical of Abraham; God is of first importance.

God made a pivotal covenant with Abraham around 2100 B.C. In this covenant, God promised Abraham a son, and that his descendants would be as numerous as the stars in the sky (Genesis 12:1-3; 13:14-17). The promise may have seemed unbelievable to Abraham since his wife was childless (11:30). Yet Abraham did not doubt God; he knew God would faithfully give what He had promised. God reaffirmed the covenant in Genesis 15, perhaps to emphasize to Abraham that even in his advanced age, the promise would come to pass. Abraham was also promised that he would be personally blessed, that his name would become great, that those who bless him would be blessed and those who curse him would be cursed, and that all the families of the earth would be blessed through his posterity.

At one point, an impatient Sarah suggested that their heir might be procured through their Egyptian handmaiden, Hagar. Ishmael was thus born to Abraham, through Hagar, when he was 86 years old. But Ishmael was not the child of promise. In God's perfect timing, God's promise to Abraham and Sarah of bearing a son was fulfilled when they were very old (Abraham was 100 years old, Sarah was 90), far beyond normal childbearing age (Genesis 17:17; 21:5). Their son was named Isaac. As promised, the entire Jewish nation eventually developed from his line. Isaac means "laughter," and is fitting because it points to the joy derived from this child of promise. Recall that when Abraham and Sarah heard they would have a son in their old age, they laughed (see Genesis 17:17-19; 18:9-15).

Isaac's significance is found in the fact that he would carry on the covenant first given to his father Abraham. The New Testament calls him a child of promise (Galatians 4:22-23), and he was a man of good character. He was a man who trusted in God (Genesis 22:6,9), practiced regular prayer (Genesis 26:25; Hebrews 11:11-17), and sought peace (Genesis 26:20-22).

In a famous episode in the Bible, Abraham's faith was stretched when he was commanded by God to sacrifice his beloved son of promise, Isaac, which command he obeyed without hesitation. In his heart, Abraham believed God would provide a substitute lamb for the burnt offering (Genesis 22:8). God, of course, intervened before his son was actually sacrificed, but the episode served to demonstrate the tremendous faith Abraham had in God. In God's providence, Isaac indeed was the son of promise.

God made specific land promises to Abraham. We read in Genesis 15:18-21: "On that day the LORD made a covenant with Abram and said, 'To your descendants I give this land, from the river of Egypt to the great river, the Euphrates—the land of the Kenites, Kenizzites, Kadmonites, Hittites, Perizzites, Rephaites, Amorites, Canaanites, Girgashites and Jebusites.'"

The land promises made to Abraham were then passed down through Isaac's line. Indeed, in Genesis 26:3-4 we read the Lord's very words to Isaac: "Stay in this land for a while, and I will be with you and will bless you. For to you and your descendants I will give all these lands and will confirm the oath I swore to your father Abraham. I will make your descendants as numerous as the stars in the sky and will give them all these lands, and through your offspring all nations on earth will be blessed."

The land promises then passed from Isaac to Jacob (not to Esau). The Lord said to Jacob, "I am the LORD, the God of your father Abraham and the God of Isaac. I will give you and your descendants the land on which you are lying. Your descendants will be like the dust of the earth, and you will spread out to the west and to the east, to the north and to the south. All peoples on earth will be blessed through you and your offspring" (Genesis 28:13-14).

This distinct family line through which God's covenant promises were to be fulfilled is affirmed later in the Bible. For example, in Psalm

105:8-11, we read, "He remembers his covenant forever, the word he commanded, for a thousand generations, the covenant he made with Abraham, the oath he swore to Isaac. He confirmed it to Jacob as a decree, to Israel as an everlasting covenant: 'To you I will give the land of Canaan as the portion you will inherit.'"

Clearly, then, the land promises made by God and recorded in the Bible are for the descendants of Abraham, Isaac, and Jacob—*the Jews.* From a biblical perspective, there is virtually no question about God's intended recipients of the land.

Laodicea

Laodicea is the seventh church among the seven churches addressed in Revelation 2–3. This was a wealthy and commercially successful city that was east of Ephesus, west of Colossae. It had three primary industries: banking, wool, and medicine. Because of an inadequate water supply in the city, an underground aqueduct was built in which water was piped in from hot springs south of the city, becoming lukewarm in transit to Laodicea. There is no historical record that this church had even been visited by the apostle Paul, but he does express concern for it (see Colossians 2:1-2; 4:16).

Jesus warned this church that it was neither cold nor hot (Revelation 3:15), and that therefore He would spit it out of His mouth—by which He probably meant discipline (verse 16). Church members, thinking they were rich, were actually wretched and poor (verse 17). They were apparently blind to their true spiritual condition. Jesus informed them that He disciplines whom He loves, and urged them to repent (verse 19). He expressed His desire to fellowship with the repentant church: "Here I am! I stand at the door and knock. If anyone hears my voice and opens the door, I will come in and eat with him, and he with me" (verse 20). Those who get their act together, and do as Jesus asks, are promised that they will be able to sit with Jesus on His throne (verse 21).

Last Days/Latter Days

A number of New Testament passages use the terms "last days," "last times," and "last time" to refer to the present church age in which we now live. For example, the writer of Hebrews says, "God, after He spoke long ago to the fathers in the prophets in many portions and in many ways, in these last days has spoken to us in His Son" (Hebrews 1:1-2). We also see this in 1 Peter 1:20, where we are told that Christ, in the incarnation, "has appeared in these last times for the sake of you." Theologians believe such references refer to the current church age, which began in New Testament times. This means that we today are living in the "last days," in the sense defined in these New Testament verses, since the entire church age is a part of the "last days."

However, it is critical to recognize that there is a distinction between how the term "last days" is used in the New Testament in reference to the church and how the term is used in the Old Testament in reference to Israel. The Old Testament use of the term "last days" (and similar terms) refers to the time leading up to the coming of the Messiah to set up His millennial kingdom on earth. Among the many verses that substantiate this is Deuteronomy 4:30, where we read: "When you are in distress and all these things have come upon you, in the latter days, you will return to the Lord your God and obey him." The Hebrew word translated "distress" can also be translated as "tribulation." Contextually, then, this verse equates the future Tribulation with the "latter days." The Old Testament usage of such terms as *latter days, last days, latter years, end of time,* and *end of the age* all refer to a time when Israel is in her time of tribulation. Deuteronomy 4:30 will find its ultimate fulfillment in the final restoration of Israel which will take place at the second coming of Jesus Christ.

Taking all the biblical data into account, it would seem that in regard to Israel, "last days" probably embraces a seven-to-ten-year period, which would span the time from the rapture through the end of the Tribulation and include the "glorious appearing" of Jesus Christ. (It could be up to ten years because there could be a few years between the rapture and the beginning of the Tribulation, which starts with the signing of the covenant between the Antichrist and Israel [Daniel 9:27].)

Last Hour

In 1 John 2:18, the apostle John warned, "Children, it is the last hour, and as you have heard that antichrist is coming, so now many antichrists have come. Therefore we know that it is the last hour." Contextually, many scholars suggest that the entire time span between the first and second comings constitute the last hour (see 1 Timothy 4:1; James 5:3; 1 Peter 4:7; 2 Peter 3:3; Jude 18). During this time span, various aspects of "antichrist" are manifest.

The actual term "antichrist" is a compound word composed of two Greek words. "Anti" means "instead of" or "against" or "opposed to." Hence, the term literally means "instead of Christ" or "against Christ" or "opposed to Christ."

In his epistles and the book of Revelation, John helps us to understand the broader concept of the term "antichrist." For example, he makes reference to the "spirit of antichrist," by which he means demonic spirits who promulgate anti-Christian teachings (1 John 4:3; see also 1 Timothy 4:1).

He also speaks of "antichrists" (plural), by which he means individuals (false teachers) throughout church history who have taught anti-Christian doctrines, such as a denial of the incarnation of Jesus Christ (1 John 2:19-23; 2 John 7). Such individuals may be considered wolves in sheep's clothing, purveying damning lies (see Ephesians 5:11).

Finally, there is a single individual known as the Antichrist who is yet to come, and will emerge into power during the future Tribulation period (see Daniel 8:9-11; 11:31-38; 12:11; Matthew 24:15; 2 Thessalonians 2:1-12; Revelation 13:1-5; 19:20; 20:10). This individual will be the embodiment of all that is anti-God and anti-Christian.

Having said all this, the main point John is making in 1 John 2:18 is that because antichrists are now on the scene, teaching their false doctrines, this is a clear indication that we are now in the "last hour."

Last Trumpet

In 1 Corinthians 15:51-52, the apostle Paul speaks about the rapture: "Listen, I tell you a mystery: We will not all sleep, but we will all be changed—in a flash, in the twinkling of an eye, at the last trumpet. For the trumpet will sound, and the dead will be raised imperishable, and we will be changed."

In Old Testament times, a trumpet was used to signal the appearance of God (see Exodus 19:16). In 1 Corinthians 15 this trumpet blast is said to be "last" because this appearance of God *will never cease.* From that point forward, Christians will never again be apart from God.

Midtribulationists often argue that because the rapture occurs at the last trumpet (1 Corinthians 15:51-52; 1 Thessalonians 4:16-17), and because the seventh trumpet sounds in the middle of the Tribulation (Revelation 11:15-19), then the rapture must occur during the middle of the Tribulation. Pretribulationists respond, however, that the seventh trumpet relates to the infliction of judgment, whereas the last trumpet deals with the rapture. These are obviously two different trumpets related to two different events.

Lawless One

See *Man of Sin.*

Lion of the Tribe of Judah

In Revelation 5:2 the question is asked, "Who is worthy to open the book and break its seals?" (NASB). This has reference to the seal judgments unleashed during the Tribulation period. In verse 5, the good news comes that there is one who is worthy to open the scroll—"The Lion of the tribe of Judah, the Root of David, has triumphed. He is able to open the scroll and its seven seals."

The tribe of Judah is the kingly tribe (see Genesis 49:9). The term *lion* symbolizes dignity, nobility, sovereignty, strength, courage, fierceness, and victory. Hence, this term points to the Messiah who is from the kingly tribe of Judah, and is himself characterized by dignity, nobility, sovereignty, strength, courage, fierceness, and victory.

He is also said to be from "the Root of David" (Revelation 5:5). Jesus, the Messiah, is the promised One who fulfills the Davidic covenant (2 Samuel 7:12; Isaiah 11:1,10). In keeping with this, Matthew's Gospel was written to Jews and was intended to convince Jews that Jesus was indeed the divine Messiah, which is the reason he first proves Jesus is a descendant of David (see Matthew 1:1).

In view of such facts, John is assured, Jesus the divine Messiah is competent and worthy to open the seven seals.

Literal Interpretation and Prophecy

The word *literal* as used in hermeneutics (the science of interpretation) comes from the Latin *sensus literalis,* meaning the "literal sense" of the text, as opposed to a nonliteral or allegorical sense of it. It refers to the understanding of a text which any person of normal intelligence would get, without using any special keys or codes.

Another way to describe the literal meaning of Scripture is that it embraces the normal, everyday, common understanding of the terms. Words are given the meaning which they normally have in common communication. It is the basic, normal, or plain way of interpreting a passage.

The literal method does not eliminate figures of speech. When the Bible speaks of the eye, arms, or wings of God (Psalm 34:15; Isaiah 51:9; Psalm 91:4), these should not be taken as true literally. God does not really have these physical features since He is pure Spirit (John 4:24). Likewise, He cannot literally be a rock (Psalm 42:9), which is material. But we would not know what *is not* literally true of God unless we first know what *is* literally true. For example, if it were not literally true that God is pure Spirit and infinite, then we would not be able to say that certain things attributed to God elsewhere in the Bible are not literally true such as materiality and finitude. For example, when Jesus said "I am the true vine" (John 15:1), the literal method of interpretation does not take this as physically true. What He said is literally true (namely, that believers derive their spiritual life from Christ our vine), but it is not true literally that Jesus is a physical vine. It is important to understand all this, for apocalyptic literature (such as the book of Revelation) makes heavy use of figures of speech.

Of course, it is sometimes difficult to determine when a passage should not be taken literally. Certain guidelines are helpful in making this determination. Briefly put, a text should be taken figuratively 1) when it is obviously figurative, as when Jesus said He was a door (John 10:9 NASB); 2) when the text itself authorizes the figurative sense, as when Paul said he was speaking allegorically (Galatians 4:24); or 3) when a literal interpretation would contradict other truths inside or outside the Bible, as when the Bible speaks of the "four corners of the earth" (Revelation 7:1). In short, as the dictum puts it, "When the literal sense makes good sense, seek no other sense, lest it result in nonsense." Likewise, when the literal sense *does not* make good sense—such as the claim that God is a pure Spirit and yet has eyes, ears, and arms—then we should seek some other sense lest it result in nonsense.

The literal method does not eliminate the use of symbols. In reality, the Bible is filled with symbols. But each symbol is emblematic of something literal. For example, the book of Revelation contains many symbols which represent literal things. John said the "seven stars" in Christ's right hand were "the seven angels [messengers] to the seven churches" (Revelation 1:20), "the seven lampstands" were "the seven churches" (1:20), the "golden bowls full of incense" were "the prayers of the saints" (5:8), and "waters" were "peoples, multitudes, nations and languages" (17:15). Clearly, then, each symbol represents something literal. There are often textual clues that point us to the literal truth found in a symbol—either in the immediate context, or in the broader context of the whole of Scripture.

The literal method does not eliminate the use of parables. Jesus often used parables that are not to be taken literally. Yet, there is always a literal point that each parable conveys. That Jesus wanted His parables to be clear to those who were receptive is evident in the fact that He carefully interpreted two of them for the disciples—the parables of the Sower (Matthew 13:3-9) and the Tares (13:24-30). He did this not only so there would be no uncertainty as to their meaning, but to guide believers as to the proper method to use in interpreting the other parables. The fact that Christ did not interpret His subsequent parables indicates that He fully expected believers to understand the literal truths intended by His parables by following the methodology He illustrated for them.

Reasons for a literal approach to interpretation. There are many reasons for adopting a literal interpretation of Scripture (including prophecy): 1) It is the normal approach in all languages. 2) The greater part of the Bible makes sense when taken literally. 3) It will take the secondary meaning when demanded. 4) All secondary meanings actually depend on the literal meaning. 5) It is the only sane and safe check on the subjectively-prone imagination of man. 6) It is the only approach in line with the nature of inspiration (Scripture is "God-breathed").

Biblical confirmation of a literal interpretation. There are numerous confirmations of the literal method of interpretation found in the Bible. Following are some representative examples:

1. Later biblical texts take earlier ones as literal. For example, the creation events in Genesis 1–2 are taken literally by later books (for example, Exodus 20:10-11). This is likewise the case regarding the creation of Adam and Eve (Matthew 19:6; 1 Timothy 2:13), the Fall of Adam and his resulting death (Romans 5:12,14), Noah's flood (Matthew 24:38), and the accounts of Jonah (Matthew 12:40-42), Moses (1 Corinthians 10:2-4,11) and numerous other historical figures.

2. Prophecies about the Messiah were literally fulfilled. Over a hundred predictions about the Messiah were literally fulfilled in Jesus' first coming, including that He would be 1) from the seed of a woman (Genesis 3:15); 2) the offspring of Abraham (Genesis 12:3); 3) from the tribe of Judah (Genesis 49:10); 4) the son of David (Jeremiah 23:5-6); 5) conceived of a virgin (Isaiah 7:14); 6) born in Bethlehem (Micah 5:2); 7) heralded as God (Isaiah 40:3); 8) hailed as King (Zechariah 9:9); 9) the One suffering for our sins (Isaiah 53); 10) the One being pierced in His side (Zechariah 12:10); 11) the One dying about A.D. 33 (Daniel 9:24-25); and 12) the One rising from the dead (Psalm 2,16).
3. By specifically indicating within the text the presence of "parables" (see Matthew 13:3) or an "allegory" (Galatians 4:24), the Bible thereby indicates that the ordinary meaning is a literal one.
4. By giving the interpretation of a parable, Jesus revealed that there is a literal meaning behind them (Matthew 13:18-23).
5. By rebuking those who did not interpret the resurrection literally, Jesus indicated the literal interpretation of the Old Testament was the correct one (Matthew 22:29-32; see also Psalm 2,16).
6. By interpreting prophecy literally (Luke 4:16-21), Jesus indicated His acceptance of the literal interpretation of the Old Testament.

Little Horn

Horns in biblical times were sometimes used as emblems of dominion, representing kingdoms and kings, as is the case in the books of Daniel and Revelation (see Daniel 7–8; Revelation 12:3; 13:1,11; 17:3-16). Daniel 7:3-8 makes specific reference to four beasts—representing kingdoms—that play an important role in biblical prophecy. The first three of these are Babylon (verse 4), Medo-Persia (verse 5), and Greece (verse 6). It is the fourth kingdom that has relevance for our discussion of the "little horn."

In Daniel 7:7, Daniel makes reference to the fourth beast—a mongrel beast composed of parts of a lion, bear, and leopard that was more terrifying and powerful than the three preceding beasts. The wild imagery in this verse refers to the Roman Empire. The text indicates that while Rome fell apart (in the fifth century A.D.), it will be revived in the end times, apparently comprised of ten nations ruled by ten kings (or ten horns). However, an eleventh horn—a little horn (the Antichrist)—seems to emerge from insignificance to absolute control and dominance over this revived empire. As a ruler, he starts out small, but becomes the greatest of all (see verse 20; 2 Thessalonians 2:3-10; Revelation 13:1-10).

Little Scroll

In Revelation 10 we read of an angel who came down from heaven and "had a little scroll open in his hand" (verses 1-2). John was told to obtain the scroll from the angel (verse 8) and was instructed, "Take it and eat it. It will turn your stomach sour, but in your mouth it will be sweet as honey" (verse 9). John responded quickly: "I took the little scroll from the angel's hand and ate it. It tasted as sweet as honey in my mouth, but when I had eaten it, my stomach turned sour" (verse 10).

The symbolism in this passage indicates that the truths being communicated to John—with promises and prophecies, anticipating God's glory and ultimate victory—were certainly sweet to believers (see Psalm 19:9-10). However, they were also utterly bitter to unbelievers because of the judgment and wrath of God poured out upon them (compare with Ezekiel 2:8–3:3).

M

Magog

Magog, mentioned in the Table of Nations in Genesis 10:2, is one of the nations in the end-times northern military coalition that will launch an invasion into Israel (Ezekiel 38:1-6). It probably constitutes the geographical area in the southern portion of the former Soviet Union. Many scholars take Magog to generally refer to the mountainous area near the Black and Caspian Seas, the former domain of the Scythians. More specifically, it likely refers to the area that is today occupied by the former southern Soviet republics of Kazakhstan, Kyrgyzstan, Uzbekistan, Turkmenistan, Tajikistan, and possibly even northern parts of modern Afghanistan. Significantly, this entire area is Muslim-dominated, with more than enough religious motivation to move against Israel.

Malachi

The book of Malachi was written by a prophet of the same name between 433 and 400 B.C. The word Malachi means "my messenger" or "the Lord's messenger," a good name for a prophet of God. His is the last book in the Old Testament.

Malachi's ministry took place following the rebuilding of the Jewish temple (515 B.C.). The people had returned to their homeland from exile, but this had not translated into a desire to walk closely with God. They practiced empty rituals without attaching any real meaning to them.

Malachi begins his book by assuring the people of God's constant and unchanging love for them (Malachi 1:1-5). This was necessary because the people were so disillusioned. They were complacent and had lost national pride. Poverty was widespread, there was drought, famine, and ruined crops, and the people had been brutalized by foreign powers. Past promises of restoration had not yet come to pass, and hence the people were discouraged. They were even wondering whether the prophets of the past had gotten things right. They began to wonder if God cared for them anymore. Spiritual lethargy was at an all-time high. So God assured them through Malachi that, indeed, His love for them is unending.

To compound the problem, however, the people in their discouragement were not living as they should before a holy God. They were living in deep sin. There was social corruption, temple worship was a sham, and priests were ignoring their duties (see Malachi 1:6–2:16). Hence, Malachi utters not only words of God's love, but words of stern warning. He spoke forceful and indicting words designed to move the people to faithfulness to the covenant God had established with them. If they continued to live like they were, more judgment was surely on the horizon. Repentance was therefore in order!

Malachi sets forth a number of end-time prophecies worthy of note. For example, in Malachi 3:2-4, the prophet makes reference to the judgment that will take place at the second coming of Christ (see also Joel 2:11; Amos 5:18; Luke 21:36; Revelation 19:11-21).

Malachi 4:1 then makes reference to the day of the Lord. "The day is coming," the prophet says, when God will bring punishment to the wicked and deliverance to the godly (see also Isaiah 13:6; Joel 2:11,31; Zephaniah 1:14-18).

Finally, in Malachi 4:2, we find reference to the millennial kingdom. The reference to the "sun of righteousness" refers to the righteousness that will be displayed throughout the earth during this kingdom. Just as the sun sends its light rays everywhere, so righteousness will be pervasive during the kingdom.

Man of Sin

In 2 Thessalonians 2:3, the apostle Paul speaks of the Antichrist as the "man of sin" (KJV), or "man of lawlessness" (ESV). (Note that sin *is* lawlessness—see 1 John 3:4.) Though sin and lawlessness are already at work in our own day (2 Thessalonians 2:7), Paul says a day is coming in which a specific individual will come into power in the future Tribulation period who will be the embodiment of sin and lawlessness (compare with 1 John 2:18; Revelation 11:7; 13:1-10). This lawless one will lead the entire world into rebellion against God (2 Thessalonians 2:10). He will even exalt himself and oppose God by moving into the Jewish temple, declaring himself God, and demanding to be worshiped as God.

Mansions, Heavenly

In John 14:1-3, we read Jesus' comforting words to His followers regarding His preparing a place for them in heaven, and coming again to get them. Following is the King James Version rendering:

> Let not your heart be troubled: ye believe in God, believe also in me. In my Father's house are many mansions: if it were not so, I would have told you. I go to prepare a place for you. And if I go and prepare a place for you, I will come again, and receive you unto myself; that where I am, there ye may be also.

Based on this rendering, many Christians have concluded that each of us has a mansion awaiting us in heaven. A number of unbiblical songs have also promoted this idea. However, this is not an accurate rendering from the original Greek. The Greek word carries the idea, "dwelling places, abodes, rooms, apartments." All these "rooms" are in the Father's large house. The English Standard Version is representative of translations that are more accurate here:

> Let not your hearts be troubled. Believe in God; believe also in me. In my Father's house are many rooms. If it were not so, would I have told you that I go to prepare a place for you? And if I go and prepare a place for you, I will come again and will take you to myself, that where I am you may be also.

Another unbiblical idea that has emerged based on the King James rendering of this verse is that committed and faithful Christians will have large mansions to live in, whereas unfaithful Christians will have to make do with little shacks. The truth is, John 14:1-3 reveals that Jesus Himself is preparing a place for each of us in the Father's house, and *every room* will be a wonderful abode. The fact that we will be "under one roof" with God indicates that we will have great intimacy with Him throughout all eternity.

Maranatha

The Aramaic term *maranatha* is an expression found at the end of the apostle Paul's first letter to the Corinthians: "If anyone does not love the Lord, he is to be accursed. Maranatha" (1 Corinthians 16:22 NASB; see also Revelation 22:20). The term literally means, "our Lord, come." Some Bible translations actually render the term this way. For example, the English Standard Version reads: "If anyone has no love for the Lord, let him be accursed. Our Lord, come!"

Since the word is related in the same verse to a curse, some biblical scholars believe the verse communicates the idea, "The Lord is coming soon, and He will render judgment against those who do not love Him" (compare with Philippians 4:5; James 5:8-9).

Mark of the Beast

The book of Revelation reveals that the False Prophet will seek to force human beings to worship the Antichrist, the man of sin. He "causes all, the small and the great, and the rich and the poor, and the free and the slave, to be marked on the right hand or the forehead, so that no one can buy or sell unless he has the mark, that is, the name of the beast or the number of its name" (Revelation 13:16-17). This "squeeze play"—demanding the mark of the beast on people—will effectively force them to make a choice: either worship the Antichrist or starve (with no ability to buy or sell).

What is the mark that will be placed on human beings? Apparently human beings in that day will somehow be branded, just as animals today are branded (and as slaves were once branded by their slave-owners). We cannot be absolutely certain how the number 666 relates to this personage or the mark. However, in some way that is presently unknown to us, this number will be a crucial part of his identification.

It is sobering to realize that receiving this mark of the beast is apparently an unpardonable sin (Revelation 14:9-10). The decision to receive the mark is an irreversible decision. Once made, there is no turning back.

See *666*.

Marriage Supper of the Lamb

The marriage supper of the Lamb is an event that will be magnificent. Jesus is the bridegroom, while the church is the bride of Christ. We read in Revelation 19:7-9:

> Let us rejoice and exult and give him the glory, for the marriage of the Lamb has come, and his Bride has made herself ready; it was granted her to clothe herself with fine linen, bright and pure—for the fine linen is the righteous deeds of the saints. And the angel said to me, "Write this: Blessed are

> those who are invited to the marriage supper of the Lamb." And he said to me, "These are the true words of God."

The backdrop to this imagery is rooted in Hebrew weddings. There were three phases: 1) the marriage was legally consummated by the parents of the bride and groom; 2) the bridegroom came to claim his bride; and 3) there was a marriage supper, which was a feast lasting several days.

All three of these phases are seen in Christ's relationship to the church, or bride of Christ: 1) As individuals living during the Church Age come to salvation, they become a part of the Bride of Christ (or the church); 2) the Bridegroom (Jesus Christ) comes to claim His bride at the rapture, at which time He takes His bride to heaven, the Father's house (John 14:1-3), with the actual marriage taking place in heaven some time after the rapture, prior to the second coming (Revelation 19:11-16); and 3) the marriage supper of the Lamb, which apparently takes place on earth at the beginning of the millennial kingdom. That this will be an earthly feast celebrated in the millennial kingdom seems to correspond to the illustrations of weddings in Scripture (see Matthew 22:1-14; 25:1-13). Guests at the marriage supper apparently include those who become believers during the Tribulation period, and are thus invited into the millennial kingdom (Matthew 25:46).

Martyrdom During Tribulation

The martyrdom of God's people will be commonplace during the future seven-year Tribulation period. For example, in Revelation 6:9-11 we read the words of John:

> I saw under the altar the souls of those who had been slain because of the word of God and the testimony they had maintained. They called out in a loud voice, "How long, Sovereign Lord, holy and true, until you judge the inhabitants of earth and avenge our blood?" Then each of them was

given a white robe, and they were told to wait a little longer, until the number of their fellow servants and brothers who were to be killed as they had been was completed.

Some of these martyred "fellow servants" are mentioned in Revelation 7:9-17. As well, the two witnesses of Revelation 11—witnesses who will have the same miraculous powers as Moses and Elijah—will experience martyrdom. These two, however, will be raised from the dead after three days, and then ascend into heaven (verses 8-12).

Matthew

The Gospel of Matthew was written by Matthew, son of Alphaeus, between 50 and 60 A.D., prior to the destruction of the Jewish temple by the Romans. By trade, Matthew had the unpopular job of being a tax collector. When Jesus called Matthew (also called Levi) to follow Him, he left everything in obedience to the call (Matthew 9:9; Mark 2:14; Luke 5:27-28). Perhaps his immediate decision to follow Jesus was motivated by previously hearing Jesus speak on several occasions. Matthew's name means "gift of the Lord." He was selected by Jesus to be one of the twelve disciples.

Matthew, himself a Jew, wrote this Gospel to convince Jewish readers that Jesus is the promised Messiah. It contains about 130 Old Testament citations and allusions, more than any other Gospel (for example, 2:17-18; 4:13-15; 13:35; 21:4-5; 27:9-10). Matthew's genealogy of Jesus is particularly relevant in this regard. Since Matthew's Gospel was written to Jews, he needed to prove to Jews that Jesus was the fulfillment of the Abrahamic covenant (Genesis 12:1-3) and the Davidic covenant (2 Samuel 7:12-14). By tracing Jesus' lineage to Abraham and David in the opening genealogy, Matthew accomplished this end.

Though Matthew was writing to convince the Jews that Jesus was the divine Messiah, he does not confine the good news to his own people, the Jews. Indeed, he emphasizes that the gospel is for all people.

Any who respond to Jesus by faith can become a part of the family of God (Matthew 28:19).

There is a great deal of prophetic significance in Matthew's Gospel, particularly in the Olivet discourse of Jesus (Matthew 24–25). For example, in Matthew 24:34 Jesus said, "I tell you the truth, this generation will certainly not pass away until all these things have happened." What "generation" will not pass away before "all these things have happened"? Christ is apparently saying that those people who witness the signs stated earlier in Matthew 24—the abomination of desolation (verse 15), the great Tribulation such as has never been seen before (verse 21), and the sign of the Son of Man in heaven (verse 30)—will see the coming of Jesus Christ within that very generation. Since it was common knowledge among the Jews that the future Tribulation period would last only seven years (Daniel 9:24-27), it is obvious that those living at the beginning of this time would likely live to see the second coming seven years later (except for those who lose their lives during this tumultuous time).

Jesus' parable of the ten virgins also carries prophetic significance (Matthew 25:1-13). In this parable, Jesus compared the kingdom of heaven to ten virgins who went out to meet the bridegroom (Matthew 25:1). Five of the virgins were foolish and five of them were wise. The foolish virgins did not take oil for their lamps (verse 3) while the wise virgins did (verse 4). All the virgins subsequently went to sleep while waiting for the bridegroom (verse 5).

When the bridegroom arrived they all began to trim their lamps, but the foolish virgins did not have any oil (Matthew 25:6-8). While the foolish virgins were away buying oil, the door to the wedding feast was shut after the wise virgins had entered (verses 9-10). When the foolish virgins returned, they begged to be let into the feast but they were told that they were not known (verses 11-12).

The main point of the parable seems to be that only those who are watchful for the kingdom of God and alert for the coming of the Son of Man (that is, *believers*) will be able to enter it (Matthew 25:13).

Contextually, this refers to true believers who are living during the future Tribulation period, prior to the second coming of Christ. His coming will be sudden, when it is not expected. Believers are those who anticipate Jesus' coming and seek to be prepared for it, living their lives accordingly. Jesus' return will terminate the opportunity for people to "prepare themselves" (trust in Jesus) to enter His kingdom. Only those who are previously prepared (saved, by trusting in Christ) will be permitted to enter. No unprepared (unsaved) person will be permitted to enter.

Jesus also speaks of the importance of feeding and clothing His "brothers" in Matthew 25:35-40. In this passage, Jesus said the following:

> For I was hungry and you gave me something to eat, I was thirsty and you gave me something to drink, I was a stranger and you invited me in, I needed clothes and you clothed me, I was sick and you looked after me, I was in prison and you came to visit me. Then the righteous will answer him, "Lord, when did we see you hungry and feed you, or thirsty and give you something to drink? When did we see you a stranger and invite you in, or needing clothes and clothe you? When did we see you sick or in prison and go to visit you?" The King will reply, "I tell you the truth, whatever you did for one of the least of these brothers of mine, you did for me."

M

Many expositors have noted that these verses deal with the situation on earth immediately following the second coming of Christ (see verse 31). After His second coming, Christ gathers all people and separates the "sheep" from the "goats" based on how they treated the "brothers." Who are the brothers? Many expositors believe they are the 144,000 Jews mentioned in Revelation 7 and 14 who will apparently be engaged in evangelism all over the earth during the Tribulation period. The "sheep" are believers who give evidence of their faith by treating the 144,000 brothers kindly by giving them drink, and food, and clothing, and such. Only believers will be aware of God's teaching from the Bible regarding these 144,000 Jewish evangelists, and they show the reality of their faith by the way they treat the brothers. The "goats," by contrast, give evidence that they are not believers because they give no evidence of faith in their lives.

Contextually, then, Matthew 25:31-46 is dealing with a very specific context (the Tribulation period), and should not be taken to be a general description of what God requires for a person to be saved. Since Scripture interprets Scripture, we conclude that one is saved by faith in Christ (Ephesians 2:8-9), and this faith gives evidence of itself in many ways (James 2:14-17), including treating people (such as the brothers in the Tribulation period) kindly.

Meshech and Tubal

Meshech and Tubal are among the nations that make up the northern military coalition that will launch an end-times invasion into Israel (Ezekiel 38:1-6). In years past, popular treatments on Bible prophecy have interpreted Meshech and Tubal (verse 2) to be Moscow and Tobolsk, based primarily on the similarity of the pronunciation of the terms. This is the way C.I. Scofield took it in his popular Scofield Study Bible. In fact, he indicated that "all agree" on this identification.

Biblically, Meshech and Tubal were the sixth and fifth sons of Japheth, the son of Noah (Genesis 10:2). All things considered, it would seem that Meshech and Tubal—often mentioned together in Scripture—refer to the geographical territory to the south of the Black and Caspian Seas of Ezekiel's day, which is today modern Turkey, though there may be some overlap with some neighboring countries. This is evident in that Meshech and Tubal are apparently the same as the Mushki and Tabal of the Assyrians, and the Moschi and Tibareni of the Greeks, who inhabited the territory that constitutes modern Turkey. This is confirmed by the ancient historian Herodotus.

Messiah

The word *Messiah* comes from the Hebrew term *mashiach,* which means "the anointed one." The Greek parallel to this term is *christos* ("Christ"), for in John 1:41 Andrew affirms that "the Messiah" is "the Christ."

The New Testament confirms that Jesus is the promised divine Messiah. When the angel announced the birth of Jesus to the shepherds in the field, he identified Jesus this way: "Today in the town of David a Savior has been born to you; he is Christ the Lord" (Luke 2:11). Later, Simeon, who was filled with the Holy Spirit, recognized the babe Jesus as the Christ, in fulfillment of God's promise to him that "he would not die before he had seen the Lord's Christ" (Luke 2:26).

Hundreds of messianic prophecies in the Old Testament point to a single Messiah or Christ—Jesus Christ. For example, Isaiah predicted the Messiah's virgin birth (Isaiah 7:14), His deity and kingdom (9:1-7), His reign of righteousness (11:2-5), His vicarious suffering and death on the cross (52:13–53:12), and much more. It is only logical to conclude that if these hundreds of Old Testament messianic prophecies were written hundreds of years before they occurred, and if they could never have been foreseen and depended upon factors outside human control for their fulfillment, and if all of these prophecies perfectly fit the person and life of Jesus Christ, then Jesus had to be the Messiah.

Certainly others recognized that Jesus was the Christ or the prophesied Messiah. Peter recognized Jesus as being the Christ (Matthew 16:16), as did Martha (John 11:25-27). Further, Jesus made His identity *as* the Christ the primary issue of faith. This is seen on two different occasions in the New Testament (Matthew 16:13-20; John 11:25-27). Jesus often warned that others would come falsely claiming to be the Christ (Matthew 24:4,5,23,24).

It is significant that after Jesus was arrested, He stood before Caiaphas the high priest, who demanded: "Tell us if you are the Christ, the Son of God." Jesus answered forthrightly, "Yes, it is as you say" (Matthew

26:63-64). For giving that answer, He paid with His life. But as promised, the divine Messiah resurrected from the dead (John 2:19-21).

Messianic Prophecies

From the book of Genesis to the book of Malachi, the Old Testament abounds with anticipations of the coming Messiah. Numerous predictions—fulfilled to the "crossing of the t" and the "dotting of the i" in the New Testament—relate to His birth, life, ministry, death, resurrection, and glory.

Some liberal scholars have attempted to argue that these prophecies were made after Jesus lived, not before. They have suggested that the books of the Old Testament were written close to the time of Christ and that the messianic prophecies were merely Christian inventions. But to make this type of claim is to completely ignore the historical evidence. Even the most liberal critics admit that the prophetic books were completed some 400 years before Christ, and the book of Daniel by about 167 B.C. Though the evidence is strong that the majority of these books actually date much earlier, the reality is that it is just as difficult to predict an event 200 years in advance as it is to predict 750 years in advance. Either way requires God's divine omniscience.

God's ability to foretell future events is one thing that separates Him from all the false gods. Addressing the polytheism of Isaiah's time, God said:

- "Who then is like me? Let him proclaim it. Let him declare and lay out before me what has happened since I established my ancient people, and what is yet to come—yes, let him foretell what will come" (Isaiah 44:7).
- "Do not tremble, do not be afraid. Did I not proclaim this and foretell it long ago? You are my witnesses. Is there any God besides me? No, there is no other Rock; I know not one" (Isaiah 44:8).
- "Who foretold this long ago, who declared it from the

distant past? Was it not I, the LORD? And there is no God apart from me" (Isaiah 45:21).

- "I foretold the former things long ago, my mouth announced them and I made them known; then suddenly I acted, and they came to pass...Therefore I told you these things long ago; before they happened I announced them to you so that you could not say, 'My idols did them; my wooden image and metal god ordained them'" (Isaiah 48:3,5).

Of course, anyone can make predictions—that is easy. But having them fulfilled is another story altogether. The more statements you make about the future and the greater the detail, the better the chances are that you will be proven wrong. But God was never wrong; all the messianic prophecies in the Old Testament were fulfilled specifically and precisely in the person of Jesus Christ.

Jesus often indicated to listeners that He was the specific fulfillment of messianic prophecy. For example, He made the following comments on different occasions:

- "Do not think that I have come to abolish the Law or the Prophets; I have not come to abolish them but to fulfill them" (Matthew 5:17).
- "But this has all taken place that the writings of the prophets might be fulfilled" (Matthew 26:56).
- "And beginning with Moses and all the Prophets, he explained to them what was said in all the Scriptures concerning himself" (Luke 24:27).
- "This is what I told you while I was still with you: Everything must be fulfilled that is written about me in the Law of Moses, the Prophets and the Psalms" (Luke 24:44).
- "You diligently study the Scriptures because you think that by them you possess eternal life. These are the Scriptures that testify about me, yet you refuse to come to me to have life" (John 5:39-40).

- "If you believed Moses, you would believe me, for he wrote about me..." (John 5:46-47).
- "Then he rolled up the scroll, gave it back to the attendant and sat down. The eyes of everyone in the synagogue were fastened on him, and he began by saying to them, 'Today this scripture is fulfilled in your hearing'" (Luke 4:20-21).

The chart below lists some of the more important messianic prophecies that were directly fulfilled by Jesus Christ.

M

Messianic Prophecies Fulfilled by Jesus Christ

Topic	Old Testament Prophecy	New Testament Fulfillment in Christ
Seed of woman	Genesis 3:15	Galatians 4:4
Line of Abraham	Genesis 12:2	Matthew 1:1
Line of Jacob	Numbers 24:17	Luke 3:23,34
Line of Judah	Genesis 49:10	Matthew 1:2
Line of Jesse	Isaiah 11:1	Luke 3:23,32
Line of David	2 Samuel 7:12-16	Matthew 1:1
Virgin Birth	Isaiah 7:14	Matthew 1:23
Birthplace: Bethlehem	Micah 5:2	Matthew 2:6
Forerunner: John	Isaiah 40:3; Malachi 3:1	Matthew 3:3
Escape into Egypt	Hosea 11:1	Matthew 2:14
Herod kills children	Jeremiah 31:15	Matthew 2:16
King	Zechariah 9:9	Matthew 21:5
Prophet	Deuteronomy 18:15-18	Acts 3:22-23
Priest	Psalm 110:4	Hebrews 5:6-10
Judge	Isaiah 33:22	John 5:30
Called "Lord"	Psalm 110:1	Luke 2:11
Called "Immanuel"	Isaiah 7:14	Matthew 1:23

Anointed by Holy Spirit	Isaiah 11:2	Matthew 3:16-17
Zeal for God	Psalm 69:9	John 2:15-17
Ministry in Galilee	Isaiah 9:1-2	Matthew 4:12-16
Ministry of miracles	Isaiah 35:5-6	Matthew 9:35
Forsaken by the Father	Psalm 22:1	Matthew 27:46
Ridiculed	Psalm 22:7-8	Matthew 27:39,43
Stumbling stone to Jews	Psalm 118:22	1 Peter 2:7-8
Rejected by own people	Isaiah 53:3	John 7:5,48
Light to Gentiles	Isaiah 60:3	Acts 13:47-48
Taught parables	Psalm 78:2	Matthew 13:34
Cleansed the temple	Malachi 3:1	Matthew 21:12
Betrayed for 30 shekels	Zechariah 11:12	Matthew 26:15
Forsaken by disciples	Zechariah 13:7	Mark 14:50
Silent before accusers	Isaiah 53:7	Matthew 27:12-19
Hands and feet pierced	Psalm 22:16	John 20:25
Heart broken	Psalm 22:14	John 19:34
Crucified with sinners	Isaiah 53:12	Matthew 27:38
No bones broken	Psalm 22:17	John 19:33-36
Soldiers gambled	Psalm 22:18	John 19:24
Suffered thirst on cross	Psalm 69:21	John 19:28
Vinegar offered	Psalm 69:21	Matthew 27:34
Christ's prayer	Psalm 22:24	Matthew 26:39
Disfigured	Isaiah 52:14	John 19:1
Scourging and death	Isaiah 53:5	John 19:1,18
His "forsaken" cry	Psalm 22:1	Matthew 27:46
Committed self to God	Psalm 31:5	Luke 23:46
Rich man's tomb	Isaiah 53:9	Matthew 27:57-60
Resurrection	Psalm 16:10; 22:21	Matthew 28:6
Ascension	Psalm 68:18	Luke 24:50-53
Right hand of God	Psalm 110:1	Hebrews 1:3

The evidence is substantial and it is massive. Jesus is the fulfillment of virtually hundreds of messianic prophecies. Critics may continue to make their claims against the biblical account, but they have an uphill battle against the incumbent.

Messianic Psalms

"Messianic psalms" are psalms that contain prophecies regarding the coming Messiah. There are two categories: *Suffering Messiah Psalms* relate specifically to the Messiah's suffering on behalf of sinners (see, for example, Psalm 16; 22; 40). *Royal Psalms,* by contrast, point to the Messiah as King, particularly in His kingly role in the millennial kingdom and throughout eternity (see, for example, Psalm 2; 45; 72; 110).

Micah

The book of Micah was written by a prophet of the same name in about 700 B.C. The name Micah means "Who is like the Lord?" He was a contemporary of fellow prophets Amos, Hosea, and Isaiah in the eighth century B.C., and carried on his ministry during the reigns of kings Jotham, Ahaz, and Hezekiah. He preached to Samaria and Jerusalem.

Micah was a simple farmer whose prophetic message was rooted in the injustices and exploitation he had witnessed. His primary message was that those who were rightly related to God should be interested in social justice and reach out to help the poor and disenchanted. But instead of this, those who claimed to be right with God in his day continued to ignore social injustices and, indeed, they exploited the poor. Micah indicted Samaria and Jerusalem, as well as the leaders and people of Israel and Judah. He communicated that God hates injustice. God's desire for people is this: "To act justly and to love mercy and to walk humbly with your God" (Micah 6:8).

Micah thundered a stern message that things would not be allowed to continue the way they were going. Judgment would fall—a judgment so severe, Micah said, that even Jerusalem's temple would be destroyed. Bad times were coming! Following this judgment, however, Micah said God would restore His people and bring about a kingdom of peace (see Micah 5:2).

Midtribulationism

Midtribulationism—the view that Christ will rapture the church in the middle of the Tribulation period—has been taught by such proponents as Gleason Archer (A.D. 1916–2004), J. Oliver Buswell (1895–1977), and Merrill Tenney (1904–1985). The two witnesses of Revelation 11, who are caught up to heaven in the middle of the Tribulation, are believed to be representative of the church. Pretribulationists respond, however, that there is virtually no indication in the context that these witnesses represent the church.

Proponents of midtribulationism argue that the church will be delivered from wrath (1 Thessalonians 5:9), which, they say, is in the second half of the Tribulation, but not from Tribulation in the first half. Pretribulationists point out, however, that since the entire Tribulation period is characterized by wrath (Zephaniah 1:15,18; 1 Thessalonians 1:10; Revelation 6:17; 14:7,10; 19:2), it makes more sense to say the church is delivered from the entire seven-year period (Revelation 3:10).

Proponents also argue that because the rapture occurs at the last trumpet (1 Thessalonians 4:16-17), and because the seventh trumpet sounds in the middle of the Tribulation (Revelation 11:15-19), then the rapture must occur during the middle of the Tribulation. Pretribulationists respond, however, that the seventh trumpet sounds at the end of the Tribulation (see Revelation 11:15). Besides, the seventh trumpet is unrelated to the rapture but rather deals with judgment.

Millennial Kingdom

Following the second coming of Christ, Jesus will personally set up His kingdom on earth. In theological circles, this is known as the millennial kingdom (see Revelation 20:2-7; see also Psalm 2:6-9; Isaiah 65:18-23; Jeremiah 31:12-14,31-37; Ezekiel 34:25-29; 37:1-13; 40–48; Daniel 2:35; 7:13-14; Joel 2:21-27; Amos 9:13-14; Micah 4:1-7; Zephaniah 3:9-20).

The millennial kingdom is an issue of great debate among Christians. The debate is largely rooted in what hermeneutic approach one uses in interpreting the prophetic texts involved. Those who take an allegorical approach will generally uphold amillennialism or postmillennialism. Those who take a literal approach will embrace premillennialism. For more on all this…

See *Premillennialism.*
See *Amillennialism.*
See *Postmillennialism.*

Millennial Temple and Sacrifices

Ezekiel 40–48 speaks of a millennial temple (see also Joel 3:18; Isaiah 2:3; 60:13) and millennial animal sacrifices (see also Isaiah 56:7; 60:7; Jeremiah 33:17-18; Zechariah 14:19-21). Scholars have differed over the question whether these prophecies should be taken literally or in some figurative sense.

Some interpret the chapters symbolically, saying that the temple is somehow representative of the church. The problem is, those who see it as representative of the church do not agree among themselves what the symbol is supposed to say about the church.

Because the text reads quite literally, providing precise dimensions, specifications, and instructions (just as specific as those for the Tabernacle and the Temple of Solomon), it seems best to take the passage literally—that is, there will in fact be a millennial temple and millennial animal sacrifices. In view of the fact that Ezekiel was told to "declare all that you see to the house of Israel," it seems impossible to conclude that this is supposed to symbolize the future church.

The dimensions provided for this temple make it significantly larger than any other temple built in Israel's history (Solomon's temple, the postexilic temple, and the Tribulation temple). This large temple will apparently be a symbol of God's presence among His people during the millennium (see Ezekiel 37:26-27). Apparently, the restoration of Israel as a nation will also entail a restoration of God's presence (and glory) reentering the temple and being with His people in a visible sense.

The temple will be built at the beginning of the messianic kingdom (Ezekiel 37:26-28) by Christ (Zechariah 6:12-13), redeemed Jews (Ezekiel 43:10-11), and representatives from the Gentile nations (Zechariah 6:15; Haggai 2:7). Of great interest is the fact that even redeemed Gentiles will be included in worship in this millennial temple (see Isaiah 60:6; Zephaniah 3:10; Zechariah 2:11). The worship of Jesus Christ in the future temple is a key aspect of divine revelation on this subject (see Jeremiah 33:15-22; Ezekiel 40–48; Zechariah 14:16-21).

A key exegetical problem relates to the sacrifices that will be offered in this temple. The problem is, Christ's once-for-all sacrifice has taken away sin, and has caused the Mosaic Law of sacrifices to be abolished (see Hebrews 7–10). Why, then, is the sacrificial system predicted here?

First, let us observe that Israel and the church are not only distinct today (1 Corinthians 10:32; Romans 9–11), they will also be distinct in the millennial kingdom. We might surmise, then, that temple activities in the millennium relate primarily to Israel (though redeemed Gentiles can also participate), and not to the church (see Isaiah 60–61). This being the case, some Bible expositors have surmised that the millennial sacrifices will be a kind of Jewish memorial of the awful price Christ—the Lamb of God (now living in their midst)—had to pay for the salvation of these believing-but-as-of-yet-glorified Jews. (They are in their mortal bodies, having entered into the millennial kingdom following the Tribulation, which they survived.) All this will allegedly function much like the Lord's Supper does today, as a memorial ritual (1 Corinthians 11:25-26).

The problem with this viewpoint is that Ezekiel says the sacrifices are "to make atonement" (Ezekiel 45:15,17,20). Hence, the "memorial" viewpoint seems to fall short of explaining these sacrifices.

Other interpreters believe they have found a solution in the idea that the purpose of the sacrifices in the millennial temple is to remove ceremonial uncleanness and prevent defilement from polluting the purity of the temple environment. According to this view, such will be necessary because Yahweh will again be dwelling on the earth in the midst of sinful (and therefore unclean) *mortal* people. (Remember, these people survive the Tribulation period, and enter the millennial kingdom in their mortal bodies—still retaining their sin natures, even though redeemed by Christ as believers.) The sacrifices will remove any ceremonial uncleanness.

Seen in this light, the sacrifices cannot be seen as a return to the Mosaic law. The law has forever been done away with through Jesus Christ (Romans 6:14-15; 7:1-6; 1 Corinthians 9:20-21; 2 Corinthians 3:7-11; Galatians 4:1-7; 5:18; Hebrews 8:13; 10:1-14).

Moon

See *Cosmic Disturbances.*

Mount of Megiddo

The word Armageddon literally means "Mount of Megiddo," and refers to a location about 60 miles north of Jerusalem. This is the location of Barak's battle with the Canaanites (Judges 4) and Gideon's battle with the Midianites (Judges 7). This will be the site for the final horrific battles of humankind just prior to the second coming (Revelation 16:16).

Napoleon is reported to have once commented that this site is perhaps the greatest battlefield he had ever witnessed. Of course, the battles Napoleon fought will dim in comparison to Armageddon. So horrible will Armageddon be that no one would survive if it were not for Christ coming again (Matthew 24:22). Scripture reveals that God

Himself will destroy the armies of the Antichrist and false prophet in the "battle on the great day of God Almighty" (Revelation 16:14). This will occur when He shall gather them "at the place that in Hebrew is called Armageddon" (Revelation 16:16).

Mount of Olives

The Mount of Olives—a high hill to the east of Jerusalem—is so-called because the mount was, in ancient times, apparently covered with dense olive groves. Zechariah 14:4 tells us that at the second coming of Christ, the Messiah's "feet shall stand on the Mount of Olives that lies before Jerusalem on the east, and the Mount of Olives shall be split in two from east to west by a very wide valley, so that one half of the Mount shall move northward, and the other half southward." Jesus returns to the same mountain from which He ascended from earth (see Acts 1:10-11).

Mysteries

A mystery in the biblical sense is a truth that cannot be discerned simply by human investigation, but requires special revelation from God. Generally, this word refers to a truth that was unknown to people living in Old Testament times, but is now revealed to humankind by God (Matthew 13:17; Colossians 1:26).

This is illustrated in a key verse about the rapture of the church, 1 Corinthians 15:51-55:

> Behold! I tell you a mystery. We shall not all sleep, but we shall all be changed, in a moment, in the twinkling of an eye, at the last trumpet. For the trumpet will sound, and the dead will be raised imperishable, and we shall be changed. For this perishable body must put on the imperishable, and this mortal body must put on immortality. When the perishable puts on the imperishable, and the mortal puts on immortality, then shall come to pass the saying that

> is written: "Death is swallowed up in victory." "O death, where is your victory? O death, where is your sting?"

The rapture of the church was categorized as a mystery because it had never been revealed in Old Testament times, but was now being revealed. It was new prophetic revelation from God.

N

Nahum

The book of Nahum was written by a prophet of the same name in about 650 B.C. Aside from the fact that he was a prophet of God, and that he was a contemporary of Zephaniah, Jeremiah, and Habakkuk, we know little of his life. History is not even clear as to where he came from. But the important thing was the message he preached.

Nahum's ministry took place toward the end of Josiah's reign. His book describes the fall and destruction of Nineveh, the Assyrian capital, in graphic language. About a hundred years previously, the Ninevites had repented under the preaching of Jonah. But now Nineveh had returned in full force to idolatry, paganism, and brutality (Nahum 3:1-4). Nineveh pridefully believed in its own intrinsic power, and failed to recognize that the only true ultimate power in the universe is that of the one true God.

Nahum thus prophesied that even though the Assyrians might seem invincible, their days were numbered, for judgment was rapidly approaching. Nineveh is pictured as a prostitute that had hurt others, and must now be punished as a prostitute. Just as Nahum prophesied, Assyria was utterly destroyed in 612 B.C.

New Covenant

The new covenant was an unconditional covenant God made with humankind in which He promised to provide for forgiveness of sin, based entirely on the sacrificial death and resurrection of Jesus Christ (Jeremiah 31:31-34). Under the old covenant, worshipers never enjoyed a sense of total forgiveness. Under the new covenant, however, Christ our High Priest made provisions for such forgiveness. When Jesus ate the Passover meal with the disciples in the Upper Room, He spoke of the cup as "the new covenant in My blood" (Luke 22:20 NASB; see also 1 Corinthians 11:25). Jesus has done all that is necessary for the forgiveness of sins by His once-for-all sacrifice on the cross (2 Corinthians 5:21). This new covenant is the basis for our relationship with God in the New Testament.

New Heaven and a New Earth

In the Garden of Eden where Adam and Eve sinned against God, a curse was placed upon the earth by God (Genesis 3:17-18; see also Romans 8:20). Hence, before the eternal kingdom can be made manifest, God must deal with this cursed earth. Indeed, the earth—along with the first and second heavens (the earth's atmosphere and the stellar universe)—must be renewed. The old must make room for the new.

The Scriptures often speak of the passing of the old heaven and earth. For example, in the book of Revelation we read, "Then I saw a new heaven and a new earth, for the first heaven and the first earth had passed away, and there was no longer any sea...He who was seated on the throne said, 'I am making everything new!'" (21:1,5). The Greek word used to designate the newness of the cosmos is *kainos*. This word means "new in nature" or "new in quality." Hence, the phrase "new heavens and a new earth" refers not to a cosmos that is totally other than the present cosmos. Rather, the new cosmos will stand in continuity with the present cosmos, but it will be utterly renewed and renovated.

In keeping with this, Matthew 19:28 speaks of "the regeneration." Acts 3:21 speaks of the "restoration of all things " (NASB). The new earth, being a renewed and an eternal earth, will be adapted to the vast moral and physical changes which the eternal state necessitates. The new heavens and the new earth will be brought into blessed conformity with all that God is—in a state of fixed bliss and absolute perfection. The new earth will actually be a part of heaven itself. Perhaps the best aspects of the new heavens and new earth are that Satan and all sinners will be quarantined away from it (Revelation 20:10), there will no longer be any death, crying, or pain (Revelation 21:1), there will no longer be any curse (Revelation 22:3), and believers will behold God face to face (Revelation 22:4). What a wonder it will be.

New Jerusalem

Perhaps the most elaborate description of the heavenly city contained in the Bible is Revelation 21 where we read of the New Jerusalem. The city measures approximately 1,500 miles by 1,500 miles by 1,500 miles (Revelation 21:5 NASB). The eternal city is so huge that it would measure approximately the distance between the Mississippi River and the Atlantic Ocean. It is tall enough that from the earth's surface it would reach about one-twentieth of the way to the moon.

The eternal city could either be cube-shaped or pyramid-shaped. It may be preferable to consider it shaped as a pyramid, for this would explain how the river of the water of life can flow down its sides as pictured in Revelation 22:1-2.

As we read of John's description of the New Jerusalem, we find a whole series of contrasts with the earth. For example, earthly cities are dark at night, but the New Jerusalem is always lighted (Revelation 22:5). Whereas earthly cities succumb to disease, there is only healing in the New Jerusalem (22:2). While earthly cities suffer drought, there is an endless flow in the river of life (22:1-2).

Revelation 21:12 tells us that the New Jerusalem has "a great, high wall with twelve gates, and with twelve angels at the gates. On the gates were written the names of the twelve tribes of Israel." Moreover, we are told, "the wall of the city had twelve foundations, and on them were the names of the twelve apostles of the Lamb" (Revelation 21:14).

Perhaps the angels are at each of the twelve gates not only as guardians but also in view of their role as ministering spirits to the heirs of salvation (Hebrews 1:14). Perhaps the names of the twelve tribes of Israel are written on the gates to remind us that "salvation is from the Jews" (John 4:22). And perhaps the names of the apostles appear on the foundations to remind us that the church was built upon these men of God (Ephesians 2:20).

The "river of the water of life" has intrigued Bible interpreters since the first century. In Revelation 22:1, we read, "Then the angel showed me the river of the water of life, as clear as crystal, flowing from the throne of God and of the Lamb down the middle of the great street of the city."

Perhaps one of the best explanations is that this pure river of life, though it may be a real and material river, is nevertheless symbolic of the abundance of spiritual life that will characterize those who are living in the eternal city. The stream seems to symbolize the perpetual outflow of spiritual blessing to all the redeemed of all ages, now basking in the full glow of eternal life. What spiritual blessedness there will be in the eternal state.

Newspaper Exegesis

Current events must never be the means of interpreting the prophetic Scriptures, but rather the prophetic Scriptures must interpret current events. To illustrate, when it is stated that certain events transpiring in our world today—such as the political alliances emerging between Russia, Iran, and other Muslim nations—seem to be setting the stage for the fulfillment of the end-time prophecies described in Ezekiel 38–39, it is not because sensational headlines from the newspaper have been found and then forced into Ezekiel's prophecies as the definitive fulfillment of these prophecies. Rather, it is because the Scriptures reveal specific details about this end-times invasion into Israel that we can accurately "discern the times," something Christ clearly desires of us (Matthew 16:1-3; Luke 21:29-33). Properly discerning the times involves measuring current events against what the Bible reveals in order to give thoughtful consideration as to whether there is a legitimate correlation. If we conclude there is, we can rejoice in God's sovereign control of human history while at the same time resist the temptation to set dates, recognizing that this is something God forbids (Acts 1:7). All the while, we avoid sensationalism, recognizing that Christ calls His followers to live soberly and alertly as they await His coming (Mark 13:32-37).

Nicolaitans

The Nicolaitans, who followed Nicolas—some believe he was a deacon who apostatized—were a sect that emerged during the apostolic period that were anti-law (antinomian), being open to license in Christian conduct, including "free love" and sex. They also ate food that had been sacrificed to idols and engaged in idolatrous worship (compare with 2 Peter 2:15; Jude 11). They denied that God was the Creator of the world, and hence felt no obligation to obey a Creator-God.

Church Father Ignatius (c. A.D. 110) spoke of the Nicolaitans as "lovers of pleasure" (*Epistle of Ignatius to the Trallians,* chapter 11), and defines the term: "A Nicolaitan...a corrupter of his own flesh" (*Epistle of Ignatius to the Philadelphians,* chapter 6). Irenaeus (c. A.D. 180) likewise commented: "They live lives of unrestrained indulgence" (*Against Heresies,* I.26.3).

This sect is mentioned twice in the book of Revelation (2:6,15). Christians at the church of Ephesus were commended by the Lord for their stand against the Nicolaitans.

Noah, Days of

In the Olivet discourse, where Jesus speaks of the prophetic future, He affirmed: "As it was in the days of Noah, so it will be at the coming of the Son of Man" (Matthew 24:37; see also Luke 17:26). The analogy is a good one, for the days of Noah were times of carousing and unpreparedness, as people will be prior to the second coming of Christ. Just as it was in the days of Noah, people living in the days prior to the second coming will be engaged in life as usual, having no concept that a judgment is imminent, sensing no danger. Just as Noah had warned the people of his day and was ignored (2 Peter 2:5), so Christian leaders today warn of the prophetic future and are ignored by the world.

Northern Confederacy, End-Times Invasion into Israel

Ezekiel 38:1-6 speaks of the northern military coalition that will one day invade Israel. The invading nations include:

- *Rosh,* which likely refers to modern Russia, to the uttermost north of Israel.
- *Magog,* which refers to the geographical area in the southern portion of the former Soviet Union—probably including the former southern Soviet republics of Kazakhstan, Kyrgyzstan, Uzbekistan, Turkmenistan, Tajikistan, and possibly even northern parts of modern Afghanistan.
- *Meshech and Tubal,* which refers to the geographical territory to the south of the Black and Caspian Seas of Ezekiel's day, which is today modern Turkey.
- *Persia,* which refers to modern Iran. Persia became Iran in 1935 and the Islamic Republic of Iran in 1979.
- *Ethiopia,* which refers to the geographical territory to the south of Egypt on the Nile River—what is today known as Sudan.

- *Put,* a land to the west of Egypt, which is modern-day Libya. The term may also include the modern-day countries of Algeria and Tunisia.
- *Gomer,* which apparently refers to part of the geographical territory in modern Turkey.
- *Beth-togarmah,* which also apparently refers to modern-day Turkey, though it may also include Azerbaijan and Armenia.

The unique alignment of nations as described in Ezekiel 38–39 has never occurred in the past, but is occurring in modern days, which would lend credence to the idea that Christians today are living in the end times. Note that an alliance between many of the nations mentioned in Ezekiel 38–39 may not necessarily have made good sense in Ezekiel's day (since some are not even located near each other), but it makes great sense in our day because the nations that make up the coalition are predominantly Muslim. That in itself is more than enough reason for them to unify in attacking Israel—especially given current Islamic hatred for Israel.

Note also that while Ezekiel wrote his book some 2,600 years ago (in Old Testament times), Islam did not come into being until the seventh century A.D. This means that at the time Ezekiel wrote his book, the conditions for the unification of these nations did not yet exist. Nevertheless, as a prophet of God, he set forth his divinely inspired prophecies, and in our day—with the existence of Islam—the prophecies make perfect sense, especially when measured against current events.

Nostradamus

Was Nostradamus a Christian prophet? By no means! Nostradamus was a sixteenth-century French astrologer and physician. If anything, he was an occultic prophet, not a biblical prophet. He relied quite heavily on horoscopes and other occult methods of divination.

His brand of prophecy thus stands condemned by Scripture (Deuteronomy 18:9-14).

Many of Nostradamus's predictions are esoteric, vague, and open-ended. This is why his predictions have been interpreted in so many different ways by Nostradamus enthusiasts. This is unlike the biblical prophecies, which are much more straightforward and precise. (Micah 5:2, for example, predicted the Messiah would be born in Bethlehem. Isaiah 7:14 predicted He would be born of a virgin.)

How do we account for the appearance of Nostradamus having predicted certain events accurately? There are a number of possible explanations. It may be that Satan inspired these predictions, and even though Satan is not omniscient (all-knowing) like God is, he is a good guesser. Or, it may be that Satan inspired Nostradamus to utter a prophecy and then Satan worked in the world in such a way to bring about some semblance of a fulfillment, thereby lending credence to Nostradamus as a "prophet." Perhaps Satan's goal was to use Nostradamus as a means of drawing other people into occultism. Clearly, though, he was not a biblical prophet.

Number of the Beast

See *666.*

Numbers in Prophecy

The study of numbers in the Bible requires a delicate balance. On the one hand, it does seem that some numbers carry symbolic significance in Scripture. Some scholars suggest, for example, that the number 40 may carry some spiritual significance in the purposes of God. For example, the flood of Noah's time lasted 40 days. Moses was on the mount of God for 40 days. The Israelites sojourned for 40 years in the wilderness. The temptation of Jesus lasted 40 days. On the other hand, there are plenty of references in Scripture to numbers that have no special significance. An example would be Numbers 7:85, where we find reference to "each silver dish weighing one hundred and thirty shekels and each bowl seventy, all the silver of the utensils was 2,400 shekels" (NASB).

There are multiple numbers mentioned in the book of Revelation, some of which hold symbolic significance and others that do not. An example of a number used in literal fashion might be Revelation 7:4-8, which makes reference to 144,000 Jews, with 12,000 from each of the twelve tribes. A number that may symbolize completeness is the number seven, for in the book of Revelation we read of seven churches (Revelation 1:9–3:22), seven seal judgments (6:1–8:1), seven trumpet judgments (8:2–11:19), seven bowl judgments (15–16), and the like. In the case of the judgments, the number seven may indicate fullness of judgment, or completeness of judgment.

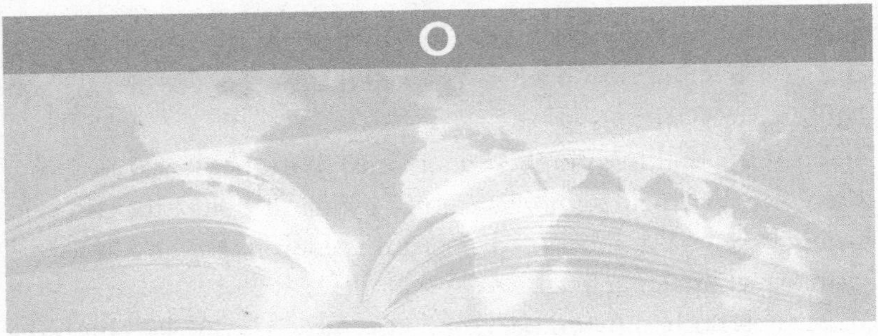

Obadiah

The book of Obadiah was written by a prophet of the same name between 848 and 841 B.C. Obadiah ministered during King Jororam's reign in Judah. His name means "servant of the Lord." Aside from these brief facts, we know little of this obscure prophet. He may have been a contemporary of Elijah and Elisha.

In his prophecies, Obadiah spoke of the coming downfall of Edom, an area directly southeast of the Dead Sea that is rich in mountainous terrain. The Edomites had invaded Judah when Jerusalem was being overrun and destroyed by the Babylonians in 587 B.C. Obadiah indicated that the Edomites would thus be destroyed. While Edom was to be destroyed, the Israelites would one day be restored to their land.

It is interesting to observe that the Edomites were descendants of Esau. As the biblical record indicates, Esau struggled with his brother Jacob even within their mother's womb (Genesis 25:22). Obadiah shows that the descendants of these brothers continued to struggle.

Obadiah includes a few references to end time events. For example, Obadiah 15 makes reference to the "day of the LORD," referring specifically to the time of Christ's second coming and the judgments on all the nations that accompany that event (see also Joel 3:2). Some expositors believe the "deliverers" mentioned in Obadiah 21 may refer to judges that will participate in ruling during Christ's 1,000-year millennial kingdom.

Olivet Discourse

Jesus, the divine Messiah, fulfilled the three primary offices of Prophet, Priest, and King. As a Prophet, Jesus gave major discourses such as the Upper Room discourse (John 14–16), the Olivet discourse (Matthew 24–25), in which Jesus speaks about the end times, and the Sermon on the Mount (Matthew 5–7).

The Olivet discourse is so-named because "Jesus was sitting on the Mount of Olives" when He delivered this discourse (Matthew 24:3). The disciples had come to Him and asked, "Tell us, when will these things be, and what will be the sign of your coming and of the close of the age?" The entire Olivet discourse should be viewed as a response to these questions of the disciples.

Highlights of Jesus' teaching in this discourse include His prediction of the destruction of the Jewish temple (Matthew 24:1-2), the signs of the end of the age, such as the appearance of false Christs, wars, earthquakes, famines, the abomination of desolation, and cosmic disturbances (verses 4-28), the sign of His coming (verses 29-31), how the end times will be much like the days of Noah (verses 36-39), parables that stress being ready when Christ returns (24:32-35,45-51; 25:1-13,14-30), and the judgment of the nations that will take place following the second coming (verses 31-46).

Some believe the entire Olivet discourse as well as the biblical prophecies in the book of Revelation (especially chapters 6–18) have already been fulfilled in the destruction of Jerusalem and the Jewish Temple in A.D. 70. This view is known as preterism (from the Latin *preter,* meaning past).

There are two forms of preterism: moderate (partial) preterism and extreme (full) preterism. Moderate preterism holds that while the literal resurrection and second coming are yet future, the other prophecies in Revelation and Matthew 24–25 have already been fulfilled when Jerusalem fell to Rome in A.D. 70. Extreme or full preterism goes so far as to say that all New Testament predictions were fulfilled in the past, including those of the resurrection and second coming. This latter view is heretical, denying two of the fundamentals of the faith: the physical resurrection and a literal second coming.

Preterists support their view by pointing to Matthew 24:34 in the Olivet discourse, where Jesus asserted: "This generation will not pass away until all these things take place" (NASB). This verse allegedly proves the prophecies would soon be fulfilled. Contrary to this view, Christ was simply saying that the generation alive when such events as the abomination of desolation (verse 15), the great Tribulation (verse 21), and the sign of the Son of Man in heaven (verse 30) begin to come to pass will *still* be alive when these prophetic judgments are completed. Another option is that the word *generation* here is to be taken in its secondary meaning of "race." Jesus' statement could mean that the Jewish race would not pass away until all things are fulfilled. Either way, the verse does not support preterism.

See *Preterism.*

One Hundred Forty-Four Thousand

See *144,000.*

Overcomers

In Revelation 2–3, we find Christ's words to the seven churches of Asia Minor. In each case, He speaks of blessing for those who are overcomers (see Revelation 2:7,11,17,26; 3:5,12,21).

There are at least three viewpoints on how to interpret "overcomers" in these verses. The first view acknowledges that according to John's own testimony, to be an *overcomer* is to be a Christian (see 1 John 5:5).

Hence, what is promised to the overcomers in Revelation should be a normal expectation for all true Christians. The failure of a person to overcome means that there was no true salvation in the first place in that person's life. Others rebut that the contexts of 1 John 5 and Revelation 2–3 are entirely different, and hence the "overcomer" in 1 John may have nothing to do with the "overcomer" in the book of Revelation.

A second view is that the promises made to believers in Revelation 2 and 3 are for those who are faithful and obedient. In this view, believers failing to overcome means there has been a loss of salvation among these believers. Other verses, however, seem to indicate that a true believer cannot lose his or her salvation (see Ephesians 1:13; 4:30; John 10:28-30; Romans 8:29-39; Hebrews 7:25).

A third view is that the promises in Revelation 2 and 3 are experienced by believers who are faithful and obedient, but those who fail to overcome suffer a loss of rewards, not salvation. This view recognizes that not all who claim to be Christian succeed in fulfilling the conditions for the promise that is made. Why warn Christians about these matters unless there was the possibility that some Christians might fail? Since these verses are intended to be motivational, it must be a possibility that some Christians will not succeed. Again, though, their loss is not salvation but only rewards (see 1 Corinthians 3:1-10; 2 Corinthians 5:10).

P

Parables of the Kingdom

Though Jesus' teachings take a variety of forms, a full third of them involve the use of parables. The word *parable* literally means "a placing alongside of" for the purpose of comparison. A parable is a teaching tool. Jesus would often tell a story from real life—involving, for example, a woman who lost a coin, or a shepherd watching over sheep, or a worker in a vineyard—and use that story to illustrate a spiritual truth. By taking such a story and "placing it alongside" a spiritual truth, the process of comparison helps us to understand Jesus' spiritual teaching more clearly.

A number of Jesus' parables teach important truths about the kingdom:

Matthew 13:31-32—The Parable of the Mustard Seed. In Matthew 13:31-32 Jesus said, "The kingdom of heaven is like a grain of mustard seed, which a man took and planted in his field. Though it is the smallest of all your seeds, yet when it grows, it is larger than all the garden plants and becomes a tree, so that the birds of the air come and perch in its branches."

In this parable, Jesus taught that the kingdom of heaven would have an almost imperceptible beginning—hardly even noticeable. But just as a small mustard seed can produce a large plant (it can grow up past 15 feet high), so the kingdom would start small but grow to be very large.

Matthew 13:33—The Parable of Yeast. In Matthew 13:33 Jesus said, "The kingdom of heaven is like yeast that a woman took and mixed into a large amount of flour until it worked through all the dough." Many expositors believe this means that just as yeast has a penetrating and permeational quality in baking recipes, so there would be a dynamic growth of the kingdom of God as a result of the penetrating power of the gospel of Christ and the supernatural work of the Holy Spirit.

Matthew 13:44-46—The Parables of the Hidden Treasure and a Pearl. In Matthew 13:44-46 Jesus said, "The kingdom of heaven is like treasure hidden in a field. When a man found it, he hid it again, and then in his joy went and sold all he had and bought that field. Again, the kingdom of heaven is like a merchant looking for fine pearls. When he found one of great value, he went away and sold everything he had and bought it." Here, Jesus was pointing to the incredible value of the kingdom of heaven. Those who truly see its importance will do anything within their power to possess it. They will allow nothing to stand in their way.

Matthew 13:47-50—The Parable of the Net. In Matthew 13:47-50 Jesus said, "Once again, the kingdom of heaven is like a net that was let down into the lake and caught all kinds of fish. When it was full, the fishermen pulled it up on the shore. They sat down and collected the good fish in baskets, but threw the bad away. This is how it will be at the end of the age. The angels will come out and separate the wicked from the righteous and throw them into the fiery furnace, where there will be weeping and gnashing of teeth." Up until the second coming, when judgment will take place, there will be both genuine Christians and phony (professing) Christians that coexist within the kingdom. At the end of the age, there will be a separation of the righteous from the unrighteous. The righteous (that is, true believers) will be invited into Christ's kingdom, while the unrighteous (professing believers who are really unbelievers) will be excluded from His kingdom and sent to a place of suffering (see Matthew 25:31-46).

Paradise of God

The word *paradise* literally means "garden of pleasure" or "garden of delight." Revelation 2:7 makes reference to heaven as the "paradise of God." The apostle Paul in 2 Corinthians 12:4 said he "was caught up to paradise" and "heard inexpressible things, things that man is not permitted to tell" (2 Corinthians 12:4).

Apparently this paradise of God is so resplendently glorious, so ineffable, so wondrous, that Paul was forbidden to say anything about it to those still in the earthly realm. But what Paul saw instilled in him an eternal perspective that enabled him to face the trials that lay ahead of him.

Parousia

A Greek term often used in connection with both the rapture and the second coming of Christ is *parousia.* Context is the key issue in determining which "coming" is in view.

This word has a number of nuances of meaning—including "present," "presence," "being physically present," "coming to a place," and "arriving." It often denotes both an arrival and a consequence "presence with."

For example, *parousia* is used to describe the physical coming and presence of Christ with His disciples on the Mount of Transfiguration (2 Peter 1:16). Likewise, the apostle Paul says in 1 Corinthians 16:17: "I rejoice over the *coming* of Stephanas and Fortunatus and Achaicus, because they have supplied what was lacking on your part" (NASB). Paul says in 2 Corinthians 7:6-7: "God, who comforts the depressed, comforted us by the *coming* of Titus..." In 2 Corinthians 10:10 Paul relays what some people had said about him: "His letters are weighty and strong, but his bodily *presence* is weak, and his speech of no account." Paul also tells the Philippians: "Therefore, my beloved, as you have always obeyed, so now, not only as in my *presence* but much more in my absence, work out your own salvation with fear and trembling." Such usage clearly establishes that *parousia* is often used to communicate the idea of physical presence.

Having said this, it is significant that the term is especially used in connection with the rapture and the second coming of Christ. In both cases Christ will be physically present—in the clouds at the rapture, and on earth at the second coming.

Partial Rapture View

This view, expressed in the writings of Witness Lee (1905–1997) of the Local Church movement, is based on the parable of the ten virgins—depicting five virgins being prepared and five unprepared (Matthew 25:1-13). This is interpreted to mean that only faithful and watchful Christians will be raptured. Unfaithful Christians will be "left behind" to suffer through the Tribulation.

Pretribulationists respond that this verse has nothing to do with the rapture. Those virgins who were "unprepared" apparently refer to people living during the Tribulation period who are unprepared for Christ's second coming (seven years after the rapture). Besides, Scripture indicates that if one is a believer, one is "saved" (John 3:16-17; Acts 16:31) and hence will participate in the rapture (1 Corinthians 15:51-52). Moreover, the Spirit's baptism places all believer's in Christ's body (1 Corinthians 12:13) and therefore all believers will be raptured (1 Thessalonians 4:16-17).

Patmos

Patmos is a mountainous, rocky desert island located on the Aegean Sea, about sixty square miles in size, and lies off the southwest coast of Asia Minor (what is today modern Turkey). On this desolate and barren island, people were banished and exiled for crimes committed on mainland Rome, generally being forced to engage in hard labor in mines.

The aged apostle John, as a punishment for sharing the good news of Jesus Christ with everyone he met, was exiled here by Domitian, the emperor of Rome. John was sent here to die of either old age or starvation.

Little did John know what God had in store for him on the seclusion of this tiny island. Somewhere around A.D. 90—some 60 years after Jesus had resurrected from the dead and ascended into heaven—John had the most sweeping and panoramic vision ever received by a saint of God. This vision is recorded in the book of Revelation.

Peace and Safety

In 1 Thessalonians 5:1-3, the apostle Paul provides instructions regarding the day of the Lord:

> Now concerning the times and the seasons, brothers, you have no need to have anything written to you. For you yourselves are fully aware that the day of the Lord will come like a thief in the night. While people are saying, "There is peace and security," then sudden destruction will come upon them as labor pains come upon a pregnant woman, and they will not escape (ESV).

A critical component of this prophecy is that in the end times people will think they are at peace and are secure. World conditions will appear to be calm. Apparently, this false sense of peace will come when the Antichrist signs a seven-year covenant with Israel (Daniel 9:27). People will think all is well, having no idea that judgment is about to fall.

This reminds one of Old Testament times when false prophets

would forecast an optimistic future, despite the sins of the people. Such prophets completely ignored the imminence of God's impending judgment (see Jeremiah 6:14; 8:11; 14:13,14; Lamentations 2:14; Ezekiel 13:10,16; Micah 3:5).

Notice that Paul did not include himself in this group of people that would suffer sudden calamity. Paul said, "While people are saying, 'There is peace and security,' then sudden destruction will come upon them." Paul will have been raptured as part of the church prior to the Tribulation, prior to the signing of the covenant (see 1 Thessalonians 4:13-17). The calamity described in 1 Thessalonians 5:1-3 is a *post-rapture* event.

Pergamum

Pergamum (also called Pergamos) is a city in northwest Asia Minor (modern-day Turkey). This city is the site of one of the seven churches mentioned in Revelation 2–3 (see 1:11; 2:12-17). The city featured large buildings and a library with over 200,000 items. At one time, Pergamum was the capital city of the Roman province of Asia.

In Revelation 2:13, the risen Christ affirmed to church members: "I know where you live—where Satan has his throne. Yet you remain true to my name. You did not renounce your faith in me, even in the days of Antipas, my faithful witness, who was put to death in your city—where Satan lives" (verse 13).

We know that Satan, a spirit-being, is not omnipresent (everywhere-present) like God is, and therefore must have local existence (he can only be in one place at a time). It may be that Satan, at the time Christ spoke these words, was localized in Pergamum.

Scholars have noted that Pergamum in ancient times was the official center of emperor worship in Asia. In fact, Pergamum was among the first cities of Asia to build a temple to a Roman emperor. Other scholars have noted that Pergamum was the city where the temple of Asclepius (a pagan god) was located. The symbol of this false god was a serpent (a term also used of Satan in Scripture—see Genesis 3:1).

There was also a giant altar of Zeus that overlooked Pergamum. With all the false religion in this city, it is not surprising to hear Jesus say that Satan has a throne there.

The citizens who lived within the walls of this city in biblical times were expected to fully participate in the civil (pagan) religion. To fail to do this would cause one to be suspected of disloyalty to the state. Christ thus commended the Christians in Pergamum for avoiding participation in such paganism and remaining committed to Him despite where they lived (Revelation 2:13).

Yet, Jesus also chastened this church, saying: "I have a few things against you, because you have there some who hold the teaching of Balaam," and "you also have some who in the same way hold the teaching of the Nicolaitans" (2:14-15 NASB). The teaching of Balaam lured believers away from the Lord and into idolatry and sexual immorality. The Nicolaitans were open to license in Christian conduct, including "free love" and sex. They also ate food that had been sacrificed to idols and engaged in idolatrous worship.

Persia

Persia is one of the nations in the northern military coalition that will launch an end-times invasion into Israel (Ezekiel 38:1-6). A look at an ancient map of Persia shows that this same territory is occupied by modern Iran. In fact, it was in 1935 that Persia became modern Iran. During the Iranian Revolution in 1979, the name changed to the Islamic Republic of Iran.

Peter, Eschatology of

The epistles of Peter contain a number of end time prophecies. For example, in 1 Peter 1:4 we are told that every believer can look forward to "an inheritance which is imperishable and undefiled and will not fade away, reserved in heaven for you" (NASB). Christians thus have a living hope that cannot be destroyed. Our glorious inheritance will be awaiting us upon our arrival in heaven.

In 1 Peter 4:7, we are informed that "the end of all things is at hand." Therefore, Christians ought to be self-controlled and sober-minded as they live day to day.

We are warned in 2 Peter 3:3-4 of the unbelief that will predominate on planet earth in proximity to the second coming of Christ. We are told that "scoffers will come in the last days with scoffing, following their own sinful desires" (verse 3 ESV). They will scoff by saying, "Where is the promise of his coming? For ever since the fathers fell asleep, all things are continuing as they were from the beginning of creation" (verse 4). Christians will be mocked for their beliefs!

Peter affirmed that "the heavens and earth that now exist are stored up for fire, being kept until the day of judgment and destruction of the ungodly" (2 Peter 3:7). Verse 10 then states that "the day of the Lord will come like a thief, and then the heavens will pass away with a roar, and the heavenly bodies will be burned up and dissolved, and the earth and the works that are done on it will be exposed" (ESV).

Since these things will occur, Peter said, we ought to allow our prophetic views to influence the way we live as Christians—that is, we ought to live in holiness and godliness (2 Peter 3:11).

Peter likewise said that we are presently awaiting the new heavens and a new earth, in which righteousness dwells (2 Peter 3:13). We should therefore seek to be without spot or blemish (verse 14).

Philadelphia

Philadelphia—a term literally meaning "brotherly love"—was a city in Lydia, located in western Asia Minor, what is today modern-day Turkey. It is the site of one of the seven churches featured in the book of Revelation (Revelation 1:11). It was about 28 miles from the city of Sardis.

Philadelphia was a major player in the wine industry. Not surprisingly, its chief deity was the god of wine, Dionysus.

The church in this city was faithful to Christ. Christ affirmed to them, "You have kept my word and have not denied my name." Because of this faithfulness, Christ says: "I have placed before you an open door that no one can shut" (Revelation 3:8).

Jesus also promised this church: "I will also keep you from the hour of trial that is going to come upon the whole world to test those who live on the earth" (Revelation 3:10). Many pretribulationists believe this is a promise to Christians to deliver the church—via the rapture—from the wrath to come that will be made manifest in the future Tribulation.

Plagues and Pestilences

A plague is a disease or epidemic, or some other form of infliction, caused by God for the purpose of judgment. The Hebrew word for plague literally means "to strike" or "to smite."

There are many plagues mentioned throughout the Bible, but perhaps the most well-known are those that were inflicted by God through the hand of Moses on Pharaoh and the Egyptians. After Moses initially approached Pharaoh about releasing the Israelites from bondage, Pharaoh asked, "Who is the LORD, that I should obey Him and let Israel go?" (Exodus 5:2). To convince Pharaoh of God's identity and might, Moses (with God's power) smote the Egyptians with ten plagues, each of which grew progressively worse (see, for example, 7:14-25; 8:1-15; 9:1-7; 10:21-29).

Scripture reveals that there will be an outbreak of plagues in the end times as well (see Revelation 6:8; 9:18,20; 11:6; 15:1,6,8; 16:9,21; 18:4,8; 21:9; 22:18). It will be a horrific time to be on earth!

Postmillennialism

The postmillennial view, which takes a spiritual approach in interpreting biblical prophecy, teaches that through the church's progressive influence, the world will be Christianized before Christ returns. In postmillennialism, the millennium will basically involve a thousand years of peace and prosperity that precedes Christ's physical return. Famous proponents of this view include A.A. Hodge (A.D. 1823–1886), B.B. Warfield (1851–1921), A.H. Strong (1836–1921), Loraine Boettner (1932–2000), and R.J. Rushdooney (1916–2001).

Among the arguments claimed in favor of postmillennialism are: 1) A universal proclamation of the gospel is promised in Scripture (Matthew 28:18-20); 2) People from all nations will come to salvation (Revelation 7:9-10); 3) Christ's throne is in heaven, and it is from this throne—not a throne on earth—that He rules (see Psalm 47:2; 9:5); 4) Jesus' parable of the mustard seed indicates there will be a continual advance of Christianity in the world (Matthew 13:31-32); and 5) It is claimed that world conditions are improving morally, socially, and spiritually—all due to the church's influence.

Of course, many today would challenge some of these points. For example, it hardly seems that the world is getting better and better. Moreover, this view seems to contradict clear biblical passages which predict an apostasy in the end times prior to Christ's return (Matthew 24:3-14; Luke 18:8; 1 Timothy 4:1-5; 2 Timothy 3:1-7). (See *Apostasy* in this dictionary.)

Against postmillennialism, see *Apostasy, Literal Interpretation and Prophecy, Davidic Covenant,* and *Davidic Throne.*

Posttribulationism

This view, expressed in the writings of George Eldon Ladd and Robert Gundry (among others), is the view that Christ will rapture the church *after* the Tribulation at the second coming of Christ. This means the church will go through the time of judgment prophesied in the book of Revelation, but believers will allegedly be kept through Satan's wrath during the Tribulation (Revelation 3:10). Pretribulationists rebut, however, that Revelation 3:10 indicates believers will be saved "out of" (Greek: *ek*) the actual time of the Tribulation.

Posttribulationists argue that Revelation 20:4-6 proves that all believers will be resurrected at the end of the Tribulation. Pretribulationists rebut, however, that in context, only those believers who died during the Tribulation will be resurrected at this time (Revelation 20:4). Believers who live prior to the Tribulation will be resurrected earlier at the rapture (1 Thessalonians 4:13-17).

Posttribulationists note that "saints" are mentioned as being on earth during the Tribulation, and this must therefore mean the rapture has not yet occurred. Pretribulationists grant that there will be "saints" who live during the Tribulation period (for example, Revelation 6:9-11). But these people apparently become Christians sometime *after* the rapture.

Posttribulationists counter by citing Matthew 24:37-40 (see also Luke 17:34-35). In this passage, set in the context of the second coming, we are told that "two men will be in the field; one will be taken and the other left." Pretribulationists rebut, however, that the context indicates that those who are taken are taken not in the rapture but are taken *in judgment,* to be punished (see Luke 17:37).

Support for posttribulationism is bolstered by the claim that pretribulationism emerged late in church history, finding its origin in John Nelson Darby (A.D. 1800–1882), who allegedly got it from Edward Irving (1792–1834). Thus, the majority of church history knew nothing of this "novel" view. Pretribulationists rebut that the argument from church history involves the fallacy of chronological snobbery, wrongly arguing that truth is somehow determined by time. The fact is, some in the early church held to false doctrines, such as baptismal regeneration. Just because a doctrine is early does not mean it is correct. Conversely, just because a doctrine is late does not mean it is incorrect. Many believe that with the process of doctrinal development through the centuries, it makes sense that eschatology would become a focus later in church history. Besides, many throughout church history—as early as the first century—have held to the doctrine of the imminent return of Christ, a key feature of pretribulationism.

Pray for Jerusalem

In Psalm 122:6, believers are told, "Pray for the peace of Jerusalem" (Psalm 122:6). With Jerusalem increasingly becoming a sore spot in the world (Zechariah 12:2-3), this prayer has never been more important. One day, the prayers of Christians will be answered, for Israel will finally recognize her Messiah (Romans 9:3-4; 11:1). Redeemed Israel—finally at peace—will experience restoration and blessing in the millennial kingdom (compare with Romans 10:13-14).

Premillennialism

Premillennialism teaches that following the second coming, Christ will institute a kingdom of perfect peace and righteousness on earth that will last for one thousand years. Two forms of premillennialism have emerged. Dispensational premillennialism, championed by scholar John F. Walvoord (A.D. 1910–2002) among others, draws a distinction between the church and Israel, and holds that the millennium will be a time of fulfillment of unconditional promises made to Israel. Historic premillennialism, espoused by George Eldon Ladd (1911–1982) among others, more generally rests its case on a literal interpretation of Revelation 20:1-6.

Among the biblical arguments offered in favor of premillennialism are that this view: 1) Naturally emerges from a literal hermeneutic; 2) best explains the unconditional land promises made to Abraham and his descendants, which are yet to be fulfilled (Genesis 13:14-18); 3) makes the best sense of the unconditional Davidic covenant in regard to the throne promise (2 Samuel 7:12); 4) is most compatible with numerous Old Testament predictions about the coming messianic age; 5) is consistent with the Old Testament ending with an expectation of the messianic kingdom (for example, Isaiah 9:6; 16:5; Malachi 3:1); 6) best explains the scriptural teaching that Jesus and the apostles would reign on thrones in Jerusalem (Matthew 19:28; 25:31-34; Acts 1:6-7); and 7) is most consistent with the apostle Paul's promise that Israel will one day be restored (Romans 9:3-4; 11:1).

Many throughout church history have held to premillennialism, including church Fathers Justin Martyr (A.D. 100–165), Clement of Alexandria (150–215), and Tertullian (155–225). Augustine (354–430), early in his theological career, held to this view. Other theological luminaries who held to this view include John Nelson Darby (1800–1882), Griffith Thomas (1861–1924), Lewis Sperry Chafer (1871–1952), and James Montgomery Boice (1938–2000).

Preterism

The word "preterism" derives from the Latin *preter,* meaning "past." In this view, the biblical prophecies in the book of Revelation (especially chapters 6–18) and Matthew 24–25 (Christ's Olivet discourse) have already been fulfilled in the past. This approach to interpreting prophecy appeared in the early writings of Eusebius (263–339) in his *Ecclesiastical History.* Later writers who incorporated this approach include Hugo Grotius of Holland (ca. 1644), and, in modern times, David Chilton.

There are two forms of preterism: moderate (partial) preterism, and extreme (full) preterism. Moderate preterism is represented by modern writers such as R.C. Sproul, Hank Hanegraaff, and Gary DeMar. While they believe the literal resurrection and second coming are yet future, the other prophecies in Revelation and Matthew 24–25 have already been fulfilled when Jerusalem fell to Rome in A.D. 70. Extreme or full preterism goes so far as to say that all New Testament predictions were fulfilled in the past, including those of the resurrection and second coming. This latter view is heretical, denying two of the fundamentals of the faith: the physical resurrection and a literal second coming.

There is much current debate. For example, preterists point to Matthew 24:34 where Jesus asserted: "This generation will not pass away until all these things take place." This verse allegedly proves the prophecies would soon be fulfilled. Contrary to this view, many evangelicals believe Christ was simply saying that the generation alive when such events as the abomination of desolation (verse 15), the great Tribulation (verse 21), and the sign of the Son of Man in heaven (verse 30) begin to come to pass will still be alive when these prophetic judgments are completed. Other evangelicals believe the word generation here is to be taken in its secondary meaning of "race." Jesus' statement could mean that the Jewish race would not pass away until all things are fulfilled. Either way, it is argued, the verse does not support preterism.

Preterists also argue from Matthew 16:28 that Jesus said some of His followers "standing" there would not taste death until they saw Him return, "coming in His kingdom." Contrary to the preterist view, many evangelicals believe that when Jesus said this, He had in mind the transfiguration, which happened precisely one week later (Matthew 17:1-13). In this view, the transfiguration served as a preview of the kingdom in which the divine Messiah would appear in glory. Moreover, against the idea that this verse refers to A.D. 70 is the pivotal fact that some of the disciples "standing" there were no longer alive by A.D. 70 (all but John had been martyred by then). Still further, no astronomical events occurred in A.D. 70, such as the stars falling from heaven and the heavens being shaken (Matthew 24:29). And Jesus did not return "on the clouds of the sky, with power and great glory" (Matthew 24:30).

Preterists also point to verses which indicate that Jesus will come "soon" (Revelation 22:12,20), and that the events of which the book of Revelation speaks will be fulfilled "soon" (1:1; 22:6). Futurists point out, however, that the Greek word for "soon" often carries the meaning "swiftly, speedily, at a rapid rate." Hence, the term could simply indicate that when the predicted events first start to occur, they will progress swiftly, in rapid succession. Likewise, the word translated "soon" can simply mean "suddenly," not necessarily soon.

A favorite argument among preterists is that the book of Revelation was written prior to A.D. 70, and hence the book must have been fulfilled in A.D. 70 when Rome overran Jerusalem. Futurists point out, however, that some of the earliest church Fathers confirmed a late date, including Irenaeus (who knew Polycarp, John's disciple) who claimed the book was written at the close of the reign of Domitian (which took place from A.D. 81–96). Victorinus confirmed this date in the third century, as did Eusebius (263–340). Hence, since the book was written after A.D. 70, it could hardly have been referring to events that would be fulfilled in A.D. 70.

Against preterism, futurists note that key events described in the book of Revelation simply did not occur in A.D. 70. For example, in A.D. 70 "a third of mankind" was not killed, as predicted in Revelation 9:18. Nor has "every living creature in the sea died," as predicted in Revelation 16:3. In order to explain these texts, preterists must resort to an allegorical interpretation since they did not happen literally.

Pretribulationism

Pretribulationism is the view that Christ will rapture the entire church before any part of the Tribulation begins. This means the church will not go through the judgments prophesied in the book of Revelation (chapters 4–18).

In support of this view, Revelation 3:10 indicates that believers will be kept from the actual hour of testing that is coming on the whole world. Further, no Old Testament passage on the Tribulation mentions the church (Deuteronomy 4:29-30; Jeremiah 30:4-11; Daniel 8:24-27; 12:1-2), and no New Testament passage on the Tribulation mentions the church (Matthew 13:30,39-42,48-50; 24:15-31; 1 Thessalonians 1:9-10; 5:4-9; 2 Thessalonians 2:1-11; Revelation 4–18).

Granted, Scripture does say there will be Christians who live during the Tribulation period (for example, Revelation 6:9-11). But pretribulationists believe these people become Christians sometime *after* the rapture. Perhaps they become convinced of the truth of Christianity after witnessing millions of Christians supernaturally vanish off the planet at the rapture. Or perhaps they become Christians as a result of the ministry of the 144,000 Jewish Christians introduced in Revelation 7 (who themselves apparently come to faith in Christ after the rapture). It may also be that many become Christians as a result of the miraculous ministry of the two witnesses of Revelation 11, prophets who apparently have the same powers as Moses and Elijah.

It is suggested that a pretribulational rapture best explains the sudden apostasy that comes upon the world by the removal of the restrainer, who is apparently the Holy Spirit (2 Thessalonians 2:3-7). Since the Holy Spirit indwells all believers (John 14:16; 1 Corinthians 3:17), He will essentially be "removed" when the church is raptured, thus making possible the fast eruption of apostasy.

Pretribulationists argue that the rapture involves Christ coming *for* His saints in the air prior to the Tribulation, whereas at the second coming He will come *with* His saints to the earth to reign for a thousand years (Revelation 19; 20:1-6). The fact that Christ comes "with" His "holy ones" (redeemed believers) at the second coming presumes they've been previously raptured. (He cannot come *with* them until He has first come *for* them.) The rapture is a signless and imminent event, and could happen any moment.

Scripture also assures us that the church is not appointed to wrath (Romans 5:9; 1 Thessalonians 1:9,10; 5:9). This means the church cannot go through the "Great Day of Wrath" in the Tribulation period (Revelation 6:17).

It is also highly revealing that all throughout Scripture God is seen protecting His people before judgment falls (see 2 Peter 2:5-9). Enoch was transferred to heaven before the judgment of the flood. Noah and his family were in the ark before the judgment of the flood. Lot was taken out of Sodom before judgment was poured out on Sodom and Gomorrah. The firstborn among the Hebrews in Egypt were sheltered by the blood of the Paschal lamb before judgment fell. The spies were safely out of Jericho and Rahab was secured before judgment fell on Jericho. So, too, will the church be secured safely (via the rapture) before judgment falls in the Tribulation period.

Pre-Wrath Rapture

The pre-wrath view, represented by Robert Van Kampen and Marvin Rosenthal, argues that the rapture occurs toward the end of the Tribulation before the great wrath of God falls. It is argued that the Bible indicates that the church will not experience the wrath of God (2 Thessalonians 1:5-10). Since the word *wrath* does not appear in Revelation until after the sixth seal, this must mean God's wrath will not be poured out until the seventh seal (Revelation 6:12–8:1). Hence, the rapture must take place between the sixth and seventh seals.

Pretribulationists raise a number of problems with this view, not the least of which is that God's wrath is poured out on the earth prior to the seventh seal (Zephaniah 1:15,18; 1 Thessalonians 1:10; Revelation 6:17; 14:7,10; 19:2). Scripture pictures the seven seals as a sequence, all coming from the same ultimate source—God (Revelation 6; 8). This sequence features divine judgments which increase in intensity with each new seal. Both human beings and warfare are seen to be instruments of God's wrath during the first six seals. Even the unsaved who experience this wrath recognize it specifically as the "wrath of the lamb" (Revelation 6:15-16), who Himself opens each seal that causes each respective judgment (see Revelation 6:1,3,5,7,9,12; 8:1).

Progressive Dispensationalism

Progressive dispensationalism's openness to allegorism in interpreting Bible prophecy is evident in that it rejects that there is a fixed objective meaning of the biblical text. Rather, it holds that there are many meanings in a biblical text, and that we ought to seek a deeper understanding than the author's expressed meaning. This view also suggests there will be a literal fulfillment of the Abrahamic, Davidic, and new covenants in ethnic Israel, but also claims there is a present inaugural fulfillment of these covenants in the church. In other words, Christ has allegedly already inaugurated the Davidic reign in heaven, the idea being that the throne of God is the throne of David.

Classical dispensationalists respond by asserting: 1) Those who approach prophecy in such an allegorical way are inconsistent, for they approach the rest of Scripture in a literal fashion; 2) There are no objective criteria by which one can determine the alleged correct allegorical truth; 3) It goes against the precedent set by prophecies of Christ's first coming, all of which were fulfilled quite literally—including Christ being born of a virgin (Isaiah 7:14), in Bethlehem (Micah 5:2), from the line of Abraham (Genesis 15:1-6) and David (2 Samuel 7:12); 4) Israel is viewed in the New Testament as distinct from the church (see Acts 3:12; 4:8; 5:21,31,35; 21:28); 5) If words mean anything, Christ is presently seated on the heavenly throne, not David's earthly throne; and 6) Christ's present activity in heaven is as our heavenly high priest, and He will not function as Davidic ruler until the future millennial kingdom.

Prophecy

Prophecy has been called *history written in advance.* It's more accurate to say that prophecy is *God's revelation regarding history in advance,* for only God in His omniscience knows the future. In Isaiah 46:9-11, God Himself affirms: "I am God, and there is no other; I am God, and there is none like me. I make known the end from the beginning, from ancient times, what is still to come. My counsel shall stand, and I will accomplish all my purpose...I have spoken, and I will bring it to pass; I have purposed, and I will do it." Our sovereign God controls human history, and none but Him can reveal the future to us.

Prophecy, Practical Effect of on Daily Living

God doesn't just tell us the future to show off. He doesn't give us prophecy to teach us mere intellectual facts about "eschatology." It is highly revealing that many verses in the Bible that deal with prophecy follow with an exhortation to personal purity in the way we live our lives. This means that as we study Bible prophecy, it ought to change the way we live. It ought to have an effect on our behavior.

An analogy is found in ancient Jewish marriages. In biblical times, a betrothed woman would eagerly await the coming of her groom to take her away to his father's house in marriage celebration. During this time of anticipation, the bride's loyalty to her groom was tested. Likewise, as the bride of Christ (the church) awaits the coming of the messianic groom, the church is motivated to live in purity and godliness until He arrives at the rapture. Key passages related to living in purity in view of biblical prophecy include Romans 13:11-14; 2 Peter 3:10-14; and 1 John 3:2-3.

Prophecy Testifies to God's Greatness

We should ever keep in mind that Bible prophecy constantly and relentlessly points to the awesome greatness of God. This is especially evident in such passages as Isaiah 42:9; 44:6-8; 46:8-10; and Daniel 2:20-22.

Biblical prophecy certainly testifies to the fact that God transcends time. He is above the space-time universe. As an eternal being, He has always existed. He is the King eternal (1 Timothy 1:17), who alone is immortal (6:16). He is the "Alpha and Omega" (Revelation 1:8) and is the "first and the last" (Isaiah 44:6; 48:12). He exists "from eternity" (Isaiah 43:13) and "from everlasting to everlasting" (Psalm 90:2). He lives forever from eternal ages past (Psalm 41:13; 102:12,27; Isaiah 57:15). So, while events transpire on a daily basis here on planet earth, and while prophecies are fulfilled temporally, *God Himself is beyond time altogether.*

Moreover, because God transcends time—because He is above time—He can see the past, present, and future as a single intuitive

act. God's knowledge of all things is from the vantage point of eternity, so that the past, present, and future are all encompassed in one ever-present "now" to Him.

God knows all things, both actual and possible (Matthew 11:21-23). He knows all things past (Isaiah 41:22), present (Hebrews 4:13), and future (Isaiah 46:10). Because He knows all things, there can be no increase or decrease in His knowledge. Psalm 147:5 affirms that God's understanding "has no limit." His knowledge is infinite (Psalm 33:13-15; 139:11,12; 147:5; Proverbs 15:3; Isaiah 40:14; 46:10; Acts 15:18; 1 John 3:20; Hebrews 4:13). This is why we can trust God when He communicates prophecies about the future to us. *God knows all!*

Prophet

The word *prophet*—from the Hebrew word *nabi*—refers to a spokesman for God who either: 1) declares God's message regarding a contemporary situation to humankind, or 2) foretells God's actions based on divine revelation. While the predictive role is often stressed, the Bible equally emphasizes the teaching function. Both aspects require communication from God to the prophet (see 2 Samuel 7:27; Jeremiah 23:18).

See *Prophets*.

Prophetic Agnosticism

The word *agnosticism* comes from two Greek words: *a,* meaning "no" or "without," and *gnosis,* meaning "knowledge." Agnosticism literally means "no knowledge" or "without knowledge." More specifically, an agnostic is a person who claims he is unsure (having "no knowledge") about the existence of God.

As applied to biblical prophecy, there are some today who seemingly have succumbed to what might be called *prophetic agnosticism,* claiming that we are unsure (having "no knowledge") about the specifics of prophecy. For example, they might say that because there are so many views of the rapture (pretribulationism, midtribulationism, posttribulationism, the partial rapture theory, and the pre-wrath view), one cannot be sure about the timing of the rapture. Likewise, because there are different views of the millennium (premillennialism, amillennialism, and postmillennialism), one cannot be sure about the nature of the millennium.

The antidote to prophetic agnosticism is a literal approach to interpreting biblical prophecy. Just as all the prophecies relating to the first coming of Christ were literally fulfilled, so the prophecies relating to the second coming of Christ will be literally fulfilled. A literal approach naturally leads to premillennialism and pretribulationism.

Prophetic Fulfillment

It is a fact that the prophecies that have already been fulfilled in Scripture—such as the Old Testament messianic prophecies that refer to the first coming of Jesus Christ—have been fulfilled quite literally. From the book of Genesis to the book of Malachi, the Old Testament abounds with anticipations of the coming Messiah. Numerous predictions fulfilled to the "crossing of the t" and the "dotting of the i" in the New Testament relate to His birth, life, ministry, death, resurrection, and glory. Among the literally fulfilled prophecies are that the Messiah would be born of a virgin (Isaiah 7:14), from the line of Abraham (Genesis 12:2), from the line of David (2 Samuel 7:12-16), in the city of Bethlehem (Micah 5:2), would be betrayed for 30 shekels (Zechariah 11:12), be pierced for our sins (Zechariah 12:10) by being crucified between thieves (Isaiah 53:12), and would resurrect from the dead (Psalm 16:10; 22:22). Jesus literally fulfilled these and many more messianic prophecies in the Old Testament.

All this gives us confidence to expect that those prophetic utterances that are not yet fulfilled—or not yet completely fulfilled—will also end up being fulfilled literally. The fulfillment of past prophecies establishes an unbroken pattern of literal fulfillment. With this kind of precedent established, we can expect that the future, unfulfilled prophecies will also be literally fulfilled.

Prophetic Postponement

The term "prophetic postponement" refers to the delay of the messianic program of redemption for the nation of Israel. Between the first and second comings of Jesus Christ, national Israel is subject to a judicial hardening (see Matthew 13:13-15; Mark 4:11-12; Luke 8:10; John 12:40; Acts 28:26-27; Romans 11:8-10). The prophetic postponement served to interrupt Israel's restoration as stipulated under the new covenant (Jeremiah 31:31-37). This postponement is illustrated in the interruption between the first sixty-nine weeks of Daniel and the seventieth week, which is the future seven-year Tribulation period (Daniel 9:26-27). However, at the end of the Tribulation period, Israel will confess her sins and call out to her Messiah for deliverance at Armageddon, and there will be a national conversion and restoration, which will be fully realized in the 1,000-year millennial kingdom (see Romans 9–11).

Prophets

Prophets are *spokesmen for God.* The Hebrew word for prophet, *nabi,* refers to a person taken over by the power of God and who hence spoke forth God's words to the people. Often their words were directed at specific situations or problems that needed to be dealt with. In other cases, they would speak of the future. They would typically preface their words with, "Thus saith the Lord," thereby indicating that their words were not their own but came from God.

These prophets were called into service directly by God, some even before birth (Jeremiah 1:5; Luke 1:13-16). They came from all walks of life, even farmers (Amos 7:14). Whatever their background, the prophets were messengers of the Lord (Isaiah 44:26) who served God and shepherded God's people (Amos 3:7; Zechariah 11:4,7; Jeremiah 17:16).

Messages of judgment or comfort. Some prophets carried out their work prior to Israel going into captivity. Because of Israel's sin and complacency, these prophets warned that a time of judgment was coming. God would not permit the sins of His people to continue (see, for example, Amos 9:1-10). Though the prophets called the people to repentance, the people became hardened in their sin, and judgment therefore inevitably came.

During the time the Israelites were in captivity, and the people started to perceive the clear message that God had them there on purpose (because of their sins), some of the people became despondent because they realized they had brought this on themselves. At this time, the prophets spoke soothing words of comfort, and promised them that God still had a plan for their future, and would one day deliver them from their suffering (see Isaiah 6:13; 28:5; 29:5; 31:5).

Different styles. Prophets received messages from God in various ways, including visions, dreams, and even hearing God's voice. Likewise, the means that the prophets used in delivering their messages varied in that sometimes it involved a simple proclamation of the message in a sanctuary, at other times speaking face-to-face with an individual, and at other times acting out a message (see Jeremiah 19). Isaiah even went barefoot and naked for three years in pointing to the shame of his people (Isaiah 20:2-3). Regardless of the means in which the message was delivered, the people were expected to hear and obey.

Major and minor prophets. The prophetic books are divided into two categories—the Major Prophets and the Minor Prophets. The Major Prophets were Isaiah, Jeremiah, Ezekiel, and Daniel. The Minor Prophets were Hosea, Joel, Amos, Obadiah, Jonah, Micah, Nahum, Habakkuk, Zephaniah, Haggai, Zechariah, and Malachi. Interestingly, the book of Isaiah is longer than all the Minor Prophets combined.

Prophets, Mistakes?

Is it legitimate to claim that even the biblical prophets made mistakes? By no means! Some have tried to argue that Jonah made mistaken prophecies. Jonah proclaimed that in 40 days Nineveh would be overthrown by God who would bring calamity on them. What Jonah predicted about Nineveh's destruction did not come to pass.

However, Jonah told the Ninevites exactly what God told him to say (see Jonah 3:1). It is important to recognize that there was apparently a "repentance clause" built into Jonah's prophecy to the Ninevites. The Ninevites understood Jonah's prophecy to mean that Nineveh would be toppled in 40 days *unless they repented* (Jonah 3:4-9). Based on how the Ninevites responded to Jonah's prophecy, God withdrew the threatened punishment—thus making it clear that even He Himself viewed the prophecy as hinging on how the Ninevites responded.

This is related to something God said in the book of Jeremiah: "If at any time I announce that a nation or kingdom is to be uprooted, torn down and destroyed, and if that nation I warned repents of its evil, then I will relent and not inflict on it the disaster I had planned" (Jeremiah 18:7-8). This principle is clearly illustrated for us in the case of Nineveh. It is noteworthy that God is often seen showing mercy where repentance is evident (Exodus 32:14; 2 Samuel 24:6; Amos 7:3,7).

The biblical prophets were always 100 percent accurate. In fact, if a prophet was shown to be less than 100 percent accurate, he was to be stoned to death as a false prophet (Deuteronomy 13; 18:20-22).

Psalms, Eschatology of

There is a great deal in terms of personal eschatology found in the book of Psalms. For example, we are told that the psalmist believed he would be directly in the presence of God upon the moment of death, finding pleasure and fullness of joy in His presence (Psalm 16:10-11). Of course, the implication is that if ecstatic joy is found in the presence of God, then utter dismay is found in the eternal absence of His presence (in hell).

We also note David's assurance of going to heaven upon the moment of death. In the classic Psalm 23, David reflected: "Surely goodness and love will follow me all the days of my life, and *I will dwell in the house of the LORD forever*" (emphasis added).

Some psalms allude to our future judgment. For example, the psalmist said to the Lord, "Surely you will reward each person according to what he has done" (Psalm 62:12; see also Matthew 16:27). Believers will experience the Judgment Seat of Christ, while unbelievers will have to face Christ at the Great White Throne judgment.

There are also prophetic insights in the Psalms that relate to God's protection of Israel in the Tribulation. For example, Ezekiel 38:1-6 speaks of the northern military coalition that will one day invade Israel. This coalition includes Russia, Iran, Turkey, Libya, Egypt, and others. The Psalms reveal, however, that God is always watchful—"He who keeps Israel will neither slumber nor sleep" (Psalm 121:4 NASB)—and He will be Israel's defender (Ezekiel 39).

Regarding land promises made to Israel, Psalm 105:8-11 reminds us: "He remembers his covenant forever, the word he commanded, for a thousand generations, the covenant he made with Abraham, the oath he swore to Isaac. He confirmed it to Jacob as a decree, to Israel as an everlasting covenant: 'To you I will give the land of Canaan as the portion you will inherit.'" Clearly, then, the land promises made by God and recorded in the Bible are for the descendants of Abraham, Isaac, and Jacob—the Jews. From a biblical perspective, there is virtually no question about God's intended recipients of the land.

We also read in the Psalms about Sheol. In the Old Testament the word "hell" often translates the Hebrew word *Sheol.* Sheol can have different meanings in different contexts. Sometimes the word means "grave" (Psalm 49:15). Other times it refers simply to the place of departed people. The Old Testament often characterizes this place as being full of horror (Psalm 30:9).

Meanwhile, Psalm 102:19 reminds us that the Lord looks down "from his sanctuary on high," and "from heaven" He views the earth. We are told, "The LORD has established his throne in heaven, and his kingdom rules over all" (Psalm 103:19). This is why biblical prophecy can be trusted. All will unfold just as God said it would.

Purgatory

The Roman Catholic Church teaches that those who are perfect at death are admitted to heaven. Believers who are not perfectly cleansed and are still tainted with the guilt of venial sins, however, do not go to heaven but rather go to purgatory where they allegedly go through a process of cleansing (or "purging"). Such souls are oppressed with a sense of deprivation and suffer certain pain. How long they stay in purgatory—and how much suffering they undergo while there—depends upon their particular state of sin.

Roman Catholics also teach that a person's time in purgatory may be shortened, and his pains alleviated, by the faithful prayers and good works of those still alive. The sacrifice of the Mass is viewed as especially important in this regard. Catholics find support for this doctrine in 2 Maccabees 12:42-45. (Second Maccabees is an apocryphal book which Catholics—not evangelicals—consider authoritative.)

That purgatory is a false doctrine is easy to prove from the Scriptures. When Jesus died on the cross, He said "It is finished" (John 19:30). Jesus completed the work of redemption at the cross. In His high priestly prayer to the Father, Jesus said, "I have brought you glory on earth by completing the work you gave me to do" (John 17:4). Hebrews 10:14 emphatically declares, "By one sacrifice he has made perfect for ever those who are being made holy." Hence, those who believe in Christ are "made perfect" forever; no further "purging" is necessary. First John 1:7 says, "The blood of Jesus, his Son, purifies us from all sin." Romans 8:1 says, "Therefore, there is now no condemnation for those who are in Christ Jesus."

Jesus took care of "purging" our sins by His work of salvation at the cross. Hebrews 1:3 affirms, "After he had provided purification for sins, he sat down at the right hand of the Majesty in heaven." Jesus provided full purification for our sins.

Put

Put is one of the nations in the northern military coalition that will invade Israel in the end times. Scholars agree that Put, a land to the west of Egypt, is modern-day Libya. However, ancient Libya is larger than the Libya that exists today, and hence the boundaries of Put as referenced in Ezekiel 38–39 may extend beyond modern Libya, perhaps including portions of Algeria and Tunisia.

Q

Quickly, I Am Coming...

The book of Revelation begins with the words: "The revelation of Jesus Christ, which God gave him to show his servants what must *soon take place*" (Revelation 1:1, emphasis added). Then, at the end of the book, Jesus promised, "Behold, I am *coming soon.* My reward is with me, and I will give to everyone according to what he has done" (22:12, emphasis added). (Some Bible translations use the word "quickly" instead of "soon.")

Some Bible interpreters, particularly preterists, argue that because the book of Revelation refers to "things that must *soon* take place," and speaks of Jesus as "coming *soon,*" then the book must refer to events of the first century—more specifically, to the destruction of Jerusalem in A.D. 70—and not to the end times. Otherwise "soon" would not make any sense.

In the original Greek, however, the term "soon" often carries the meaning, "swiftly, speedily, at a rapid rate." An example is Luke 18:8, where this word is used to indicate that justice was to be rendered *speedily.* Hence, it is likely that in the Revelation passages, the term is intended to indicate that when the predicted events first start to occur, they will progress swiftly, or speedily, or in rapid succession. Seen in this light, there is no need for insisting that the events prophesied in the book of Revelation must refer to the first century.

It is noteworthy that key events described in the book of Revelation did not occur in A.D. 70. For example, in A.D. 70 "a third of mankind" was not killed, as predicted in Revelation 9:18. Nor has "every living thing in the sea died," as predicted in Revelation 16:3. In order to explain these texts, preterists must resort to an allegorical interpretation since they did not happen literally.

Q

R

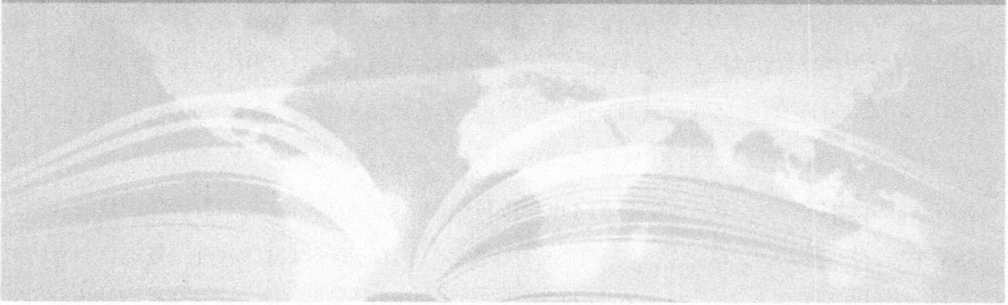

Rapture

The rapture is that glorious event in which the dead in Christ will be resurrected and living Christians will be instantly translated into their resurrection bodies—and both groups will be caught up to meet Christ in the air and taken back to heaven (John 14:1-3; 1 Corinthians 15:51-54; 1 Thessalonians 4:13-17). This means there will be one generation of Christians who will never pass through death's door. They will be alive on earth one moment; the next moment they will be instantly translated into their resurrection bodies and caught up to meet Christ in the air. What a moment that will be!

Christians love to debate end-time issues. Perhaps the hottest debate relates to when the rapture occurs. There are five primary views which I cover separately in this dictionary. 1) The partial rapture view argues that only faithful and watchful Christians will be raptured, and that unfaithful Christians will be "left behind" to suffer through the Tribulation. 2) Pretribulationism is the view that Christ will rapture the entire church *before* any part of the Tribulation begins. 3) Posttribulationism is the view that Christ will rapture the church *after* the Tribulation at the second coming of Christ. 4) Midtribulationism is the view that Christ will rapture the church in the middle of the Tribulation period.

5) The pre-wrath view argues that the rapture occurs toward the end of the Tribulation before the great wrath of God falls. It is my belief that the pretrib position—the majority view—is most consistent with the biblical testimony (Revelation 3:10; 1 Thessalonians 1:9-10; 5:4-9).

Despite the differences Christians may have on this matter, there are many agreements we can point to, and these agreements ought to serve as a basis of unity in the midst of our diversity on these issues: 1) All agree that God is sovereignly in charge of the precise timing of end-time events; 2) All agree that there *will* be a rapture; 3) All agree that there will be a physical second coming of Christ; 4) All agree there will be a future resurrection from the dead; 5) All agree there will be a future judgment; 6) All agree there will be an eternal state in which believers will live eternally with God; 7) All agree that one beneficial aspect of studying biblical prophecy is that it motivates one to holiness in life.

See *Partial Rapture View.*
See *Pretribulationism.*
See *Midtribulationism.*
See *Posttribulationism.*
See *Pre-Wrath Rapture.*

Rapture, Distinct from the Second Coming

Scripture portrays the rapture and the second coming as distinct events. For example, at the rapture the translated saints return with Christ to heaven (John 14:1-3), whereas at the second coming Christ returns to earth (Zechariah 14:4; Acts 1:11). At the rapture, there is no judgment of the nations, while at the second coming there is a judgment of the nations (Matthew 25:31-46). The rapture is an imminent event (it could happen any moment—see 1 Thessalonians 5:1-3), whereas there are many prophetic signs that precede the second coming (Luke 21:11,15). The rapture takes place before the "day of wrath" (1 Thessalonians 1:10; 5:9), while the second coming occurs after the "day of wrath." At the rapture Christ comes *for* His own (1 Thessalonians 4:17; John 14:3), whereas at the second coming Christ comes *with* His own (Revelation 19:14). At the rapture, Christ comes *for* His bride (1 Thessalonians 4:16-17), whereas at the second coming Christ comes *with* His bride (Revelation 19:6-14). Following the rapture, the Tribulation period begins, whereas following the second coming the millennial kingdom begins.

Key verses on the rapture include: John 14:1-3; Romans 8:19; 1 Corinthians 1:7-8; 15:51-53; 16:22; Philippians 3:20-21; 4:5; Colossians 3:4; 1 Thessalonians 1:10; 2:19; 4:13-18; 5:9,23; 2 Thessalonians 2:1,3; 1 Timothy 6:14; 2 Timothy 4:1,8; Titus 2:13; Hebrews 9:28; James 5:7-9; 1 Peter 1:7,13; 5:4; 1 John 2:28–3:2; Jude 21; Revelation 2:25; 3:10.

Key verses on the second coming include: Daniel 2:44-45; 7:9-14; 12:1-3; Zechariah 12:10; 14:1-15; Matthew 13:41; 24:15-31; 26:64; Mark 13:14-27; 14:62; Luke 21:25-28; Acts 1:9-11; 3:19-21; 1 Thessalonians 3:13; 2 Thessalonians 1:6-10; 2:8; 1 Peter 4:12-13; 2 Peter 3:1-14; Jude 14-15; Revelation 1:7; 19:11–20:6; 22:7,12,20.

Rebuilding of the Temple

See *Jewish Temple, Rebuilding.*

Regathering of Jews to Homeland, Necessity of

The regathering of Jews in Israel is necessary for key biblical prophecies about the Tribulation to make sense. For example, the returning of the Jews to the land prior to the Tribulation period is clearly implied in the peace covenant to be signed between the Antichrist and the leaders of Israel during the Tribulation period. This relates to the 70 weeks of Daniel.

The backdrop is that in Daniel 9 God provided a prophetic timetable for the nation of Israel. The prophetic clock began ticking when the command went out to restore and rebuild Jerusalem following its destruction by Babylon (Daniel 9:25). According to this verse,

Israel's timetable was divided into 70 groups of seven years, totaling 490 years.

The first 69 groups of seven years—or 483 years—counted the years "from the issuing of the decree to restore and rebuild Jerusalem until the Anointed One, the ruler, comes" (Daniel 9:25). The "Anointed One," of course, is Jesus Christ. "Anointed One" means Messiah. The day that Jesus rode into Jerusalem to proclaim Himself Israel's Messiah was exactly 483 years to the day after the command to restore and rebuild Jerusalem had been given.

At that point God's prophetic clock stopped. Daniel describes a gap between these 483 years and the final seven years of Israel's prophetic timetable. Several events were to take place during this "gap," according to Daniel 9:26: 1) The Messiah will be killed; 2) the city of Jerusalem and its temple will be destroyed (which occurred in A.D. 70); and 3) the Jews will encounter difficulty and hardship from that time forward.

The final "week" of seven years will begin for Israel when the Antichrist confirms a "covenant" for seven years (Daniel 9:27). When this peace pact is signed between the Antichrist and the leaders of Israel, it will signal the beginning of the Tribulation period. That signature marks the beginning of the seven-year countdown to the second coming of Christ, which follows the Tribulation period. However, such a treaty would make absolutely no sense if the Jews had not returned to their land and Israel were not a viable political entity. The point is, then, that Israel *must* be regathered to the land before the beginning of the Tribulation period. This is what makes the year 1948 so significant from a prophetic standpoint.

Reign with Christ

Scripture reveals that Christians will one day reign with Christ. For example, in 2 Timothy 2:12 the apostle Paul instructs, "If we endure, we will also reign with him." Those who endure through trials will one day rule with Christ in His future eternal kingdom (see Revelation 1:6; 5:10; 20:4,6).

There is an interesting parallel between Jesus Christ and Christians here. After all, Christ Himself endured and will one day reign (1 Corinthians 15:25). In the same way—though to a much lesser degree, and under the Lordship of Christ—believers must endure and will one day reign with Him (Revelation 3:21).

The idea of reigning with Christ is compatible with what we learn elsewhere in the book of Revelation. For example, Revelation 5:10 reveals that believers have been made "a kingdom and priests to serve our God, and they will reign on the earth." Likewise, Revelation 20:6 reveals, "Blessed and holy is the one who shares in the first resurrection! Over such the second death has no power, but they will be priests of God and of Christ, and they will reign with him for a thousand years" (ESV). What this means is that when Christ establishes His millennial kingdom, following the second coming, the church will have already been resurrected (prior to the seven-year Tribulation, at the rapture), and will reign with Christ over that kingdom for its full duration.

Then, in Revelation 22:5 we are told: "Night will be no more. They will need no light of lamp or sun, for the Lord God will be their light, and they will reign forever and ever" (ESV). So, even beyond the millennial kingdom, this privilege of reigning with Christ continues.

Reincarnation

Today approximately 30 million Americans (one in four) believe in reincarnation. The word *reincarnation* literally means to "come again in the flesh." The process of reincarnation—continual rebirths in human bodies—allegedly continues until the soul has reached a state of perfection and merges back with its source (God or the "Universal Soul").

One's lot in life, according to those who believe in reincarnation, is based on the law of karma. This law says that if bad things happen in one's life, this is an outworking of bad karma. If good things happen in one's life, this is an outworking of good karma.

"Karma" refers to the "debt" a soul accumulates because of good or bad actions committed during one's life (or past lives). If one accumulates good karma by performing good actions, he or she will be reincarnated in a desirable state. If one accumulates bad karma, he or she will be reincarnated in a less desirable state.

Scripture clearly debunks the notion of reincarnation. Hebrews 9:27 tells us that "man is destined to die once, and after that to face judgment." Each human being lives once as a mortal on earth, dies once, and then faces judgment. He does not have a second chance by reincarnating into another body (see also Philippians 1:21-23). Second Corinthians 5:8 indicates that at death the Christian immediately goes into the presence of the Lord, not into another body. Luke 16:19-31 indicates that unbelievers at death go to a place of suffering, not into another body.

We must also remember that Jesus taught that people decide their eternal destiny in a single lifetime (Matthew 25:46). This is precisely why the apostle Paul emphasized that "now is the day of salvation" (2 Corinthians 6:2).

Religious System, False

In Revelation 17 we find a discussion of religious Babylon, with verses 1-7 providing a description of it, and verses 8-18 providing an interpretation of the description. We find much symbolic language here. The passage indicates that Babylon is a great prostitute (or whore) whose religious unfaithfulness influences the people of many nations. This "great prostitute" (blasphemous religion) is said to sit on (thus controlling) a scarlet beast (who is the Antichrist).

We also read of "seven mountains on which the woman is seated" (Revelation 17:9 ESV). Apparently, the seven mountains symbolize the seven kingdoms and their kings of verse 10. Mountains often symbolize kingdoms in Scripture (Psalm 30:7; Jeremiah 51:25; Daniel 2:44-45).

These seven kingdoms refer to the seven great world empires—Egypt, Assyria, Babylon, Medo-Persia, Greece, Rome, and that of the Antichrist. The biblical text tells us that five of these kingdoms have fallen, one still exists, and one is yet to come (Revelation 17:10). What this means is that at the time of John's writing, the Egyptian, Assyrian, Babylonian, Medo-Persian and Greek empires had fallen. Rome, however, still existed, and the Antichrist's kingdom was yet to come. False paganized religion affected *all* these empires.

Based on clues in Revelation 17, this apostate religious system will be worldwide in its impact (see verse 15). It will also be utterly unfaithful to the truth (and hence be a "harlot"—verses 1,5,15-16), will exercise powerful political clout (verses 12-13), will seem outwardly glorious while being inwardly corrupt (implied in verse 4), and will persecute true believers during the Tribulation period (see verse 6).

It is instructive to compare Revelation 17 with other key verses that relate to this end-times false religious system. To begin, assuming the truth of pretribulationism, it would make sense that since the rapture of the church occurs before the Tribulation period (Romans 5:9; 1 Thessalonians 1:9-10; 5:9; Revelation 3:10), all so-called "Christians" who are left behind will be apostates, and may form the core of this end-times false religious system (see 2 Thessalonians 2:8-12). We should also keep in mind that the spirit of antichrist is already at work (1 John 4:3), seeking to bring about apostasy and unbelief among liberal Christians and others. Because of the massive apostasy already evident in churches in our own day, it is possible the stage is being set for this end-times false religious system.

It will be the role of the False Prophet to lead (indeed, *force*) these apostates into acceptance and worship of the Antichrist (see 1 Timothy 4:1-4; 2 Timothy 3:1-5; 4:1-4; 2 Peter 2:1; 1 John 2:18-19; Jude 4; Revelation 17:1-6). Indeed, Scripture reveals that this False Prophet will seek to require "everyone, small and great, rich and poor, free and slave, to receive a mark on his right hand or on his forehead, so that no one could buy or sell unless he had the mark, which is the name of the beast or the number of his name" (Revelation 13:16-17). This "squeeze play" will effectively force human beings to make a choice: Either worship the Antichrist or starve (with no ability to buy or sell).

Eventually, the false world religion will be violently overthrown. As Revelation 17:16 puts it, this religion will be made "desolate and naked," and her "flesh" will be devoured and burned "with fire" (ESV).

Repentance

The Greek word for repentance, *metanoe,* means "to change one's mind." The word was often used among the ancients of a religious or ethical change in the way a person thinks and acts. It carries the idea of changing one's way of life as a result of a change in the way one thinks, particularly in regard to the issues of sin and righteousness (see Matthew 4:17; Luke 1:16; 24:47; Acts 3:19; 9:35; 11:21; 14:15; 15:19; 26:18-21; 1 Thessalonians 1:9; 1 Peter 2:25). In some cases, the "changing of mind" had to do not with sin but with the identity of Jesus, as is apparently the case in Acts 2:38 with reference to the Jews who had rejected Jesus as the divine Messiah.

Repentance is a heavy emphasis in the book of Revelation, especially in Jesus' words to the seven churches of Asia Minor (Revelation 2–3). For example, Jesus instructed the church at Ephesus: "Remember therefore from where you have fallen; repent, and do the works you did at first..." (Revelation 2:5 ESV; see also 2:16,21,22; 3:3,19).

Following the infliction of the sixth trumpet judgment, Revelation 9:20 tells us that "the rest of mankind, who were not killed by these plagues, did not repent of the works of their hands nor give up worshiping demons and idols of gold and silver and bronze and stone and wood, which cannot see or hear or walk, nor did they repent of their murders or their sorceries or their sexual immorality or their thefts" (Revelation 9:20-21 ESV).

Still later, following the infliction of the fourth bowl judgment, we read that human beings "were scorched by the fierce heat, and they cursed the name of God who had power over these plagues. They did not repent and give him glory" (Revelation 16:9 ESV). Likewise, following the fifth bowl judgment, we read that people "cursed the God of heaven for their pain and sores. They did not repent of their deeds" (verse 11 ESV).

There will be many hardened hearts during the Tribulation period.

Replacement Theology

When Israel finally took possession of the land of milk and honey, it was in direct fulfillment of God's promise to the nation. As we read in Joshua 21:43-45:

> So the LORD gave Israel all the land he had sworn to give their forefathers, and they took possession of it and settled there. The LORD gave them rest on every side, just as he had sworn to their forefathers. Not one of their enemies withstood them; the LORD handed all their enemies over to them. Not one of all the LORD's good promises to the house of Israel failed; every one was fulfilled.

R

Today, proponents of "replacement theology" argue that because God is said to have given the Israelites the land in Joshua 21:43-45, God's obligation regarding the land promises to Israel are completely fulfilled and there are no future promises yet to be fulfilled on the matter. After all, the text tells us that "not one of all the LORD's good promises to the house of Israel failed; every one was fulfilled." Such individuals thus believe the modern state of Israel has no legitimate biblical basis. They claim it is not a fulfillment of biblical prophecy. All of God's land promises to Israel were fulfilled in the past.

There are several pertinent points that can be made in response to this claim. First, Joshua 21:43-45 is absolutely correct regarding God fulfilling His part in giving the Israelites the promised land. Israel, however, failed to take full possession of what was promised to the nation by God, and they failed to dispossess all the Canaanites, despite the fact that the gift of land had been made. It was there for the taking. God had faithfully done for Israel what He promised. Israel, by contrast, was not completely faithful. The Lord had not failed to keep His promise even though Israel had failed by faith to conquer all the land.

The idea that there are no further land promises to be fulfilled for Israel is proven to be false in view of the fact that many prophecies written far *after* the time of Joshua speak of Israel possessing the land *in the future* (see Isaiah 60:18,21; Jeremiah 23:6; 24:5-6; 30:18; 31:31-34; 32:37-40; 33:6-9; Ezekiel 28:25-26; 34:11-12; 36:24-26; 37; 39:28; Micah 2:12; 4:6-7; Amos 9:14-15; Zephaniah 3:19-20; Zechariah 8:7-8; 13:8-9). In fact, every Old Testament prophet except Jonah speaks of a permanent return to the land of Israel by the Jews. One can also observe that though Israel possessed the land at the time of Joshua, it was later dispossessed, whereas the Abrahamic covenant promised Israel that she would possess the land *forever* (Genesis 17:8).

Also against replacement theology is the fact that the church and Israel are still seen to be distinct in the New Testament. For example, we are instructed in 1 Corinthians 10:32, "Do not cause anyone to stumble, whether Jews, Greeks [Gentiles] or the church of God" (insert added). Moreover, Israel and the church are seen as distinct throughout the book of Acts, with the word "Israel" being used 20 times and the word "church" 19 times.

Let us also remember that the prophecies that have already been fulfilled in Scripture (such as the Old Testament messianic prophecies that refer to the first coming of Jesus Christ) have been fulfilled quite literally. From the book of Genesis to the book of Malachi, the Old Testament abounds with anticipations of the coming Messiah. Numerous predictions fulfilled to the "crossing of the t" and the "dotting of the i" in the New Testament relate to His birth, life, ministry, death, resurrection, and glory (for example, Isaiah 7:14; Micah 5:2; Zechariah 12:10). The prophecies that have been fulfilled completely have been fulfilled *literally,* and this gives us strong confidence to expect that the prophecies not yet fulfilled will also end up being fulfilled literally. Hence, the land promises to Israel will be fulfilled literally.

Eventually, Israel will finally (wonderfully) come to recognize Jesus as the divine Messiah and come into full possession of the promised land. The fullness of this possession will be in the future millennial kingdom. At present, however, Israel's regathering to the land is only partial and Israel is yet in unbelief. This partial regathering in unbelief is setting the stage for Israel to eventually go through the Tribulation period—the "time of trouble for Jacob" (Jeremiah 30:7)—during which time a remnant of Israel will be saved (see Romans 9–11). Israel will then come into full possession of her promised land in the millennial kingdom.

Restrainer

See *Hinderer.*

Resurrection, Evidence for

The resurrection of Jesus Christ is perhaps the best-attested miracle from ancient times. The evidence is massive and it is convincing:

1. The circumstances at the tomb reveal a missing body. Keep in mind that after Jesus' body was placed in a solid rock tomb, an extremely large stone was rolled by means of levers against the entrance. This stone would have weighed in the neighborhood of two tons (4,000 pounds). It is not a stone that would have been easily moved by human beings.

   Roman guards were then stationed at the tomb. These strictly disciplined men were highly motivated to succeed in all they were assigned by the Roman government. Fear of cruel punishment produced flawless attention to duty, especially in the night watches. These Roman guards would have affixed on the tomb the Roman seal, a stamp representing Roman power and authority.

All this makes the situation at the tomb following Christ's resurrection highly significant. The Roman seal was broken, which meant automatic crucifixion upside down for the person responsible. Furthermore, the large stone was moved a good distance from the entrance, as if it had been picked up and carried away. The Roman guards had also fled. The penalty in Rome for a guard leaving his position was death. We can therefore assume that they must have had a substantial reason for fleeing!

2. The biblical account has Jesus appearing first to a woman, Mary Magdalene (John 20:1), a fact that is a highly significant indicator of the authenticity and reliability of the resurrection account. If the resurrection story were a fabrication, made up by the disciples, no one in a first-century Jewish culture would have invented it this way. In Jewish law, a woman's testimony was unacceptable except in a very few circumstances. A fabricator would have been much more likely to portray Peter or the other male disciples at the tomb. Our biblical text, however, tells us that the Lord appeared first to Mary because, in fact, that was the way it actually happened.

   Following this, Mary promptly told the disciples the glorious news. That evening, the disciples had gathered in a room with the doors shut for fear of the Jewish religious authorities (John 20:19). This fear was well founded, for after Jesus had been arrested, Annas the high priest specifically asked Jesus about the disciples (18:19). Jesus had also previously warned the disciples in the upper room, "If they persecuted me, they will persecute you also" (15:20).

These facts no doubt lingered in their minds after Jesus was brutally crucified.

Their gloom soon turned to joy. The risen Christ appeared in their midst and said to them, "Peace be with you" (John 20:19). This phrase was a common Hebrew greeting (1 Samuel 25:6). On this occasion, however, there was added significance to Jesus' words. After their conduct on Good Friday (they all scattered like a bunch of spineless cowards after Jesus' arrest), the disciples may well have expected a rebuke from Jesus. Instead, He displayed compassion by pronouncing peace upon them.

Jesus immediately showed the disciples His hands and His side (John 20:20). The risen Lord wanted them to see that it was truly He. The wounds showed that He did not have *another* body, but the same body. He was dead, but now He is alive forevermore.

3. By all accounts, the disciples came away from the crucifixion frightened and full of doubt, and yet, following Jesus' resurrection appearance to the disciples, their lives were virtually transformed. How have these early followers turned almost instantly into fearless faith-warriors and testifiers who braved opposition, cynicism, ridicule, hardship, prison, and death on three continents, as they preached the resurrection of Jesus from the dead?

   As Jews, these followers would have been predisposed to believe that no one would resurrect from the dead before the general resurrection at the end of time. It was not in their mind-set to expect a physical resurrection of Jesus. The only thing that could account for their sudden incredible transformation into powerful witnesses for Jesus was the resurrection. This is the only thing that can explain why they were even willing to die for their beliefs.

   So that the point is not lost, one must keep in mind that

when Jesus died, His followers went into hiding. They thought it was all over. Despite their awareness that Jesus had predicted His own resurrection, their feeling was that Jesus and His whole program was over and done with. And yet, quite suddenly—seemingly overnight—these same individuals were going everywhere, boldly proclaiming that Jesus was alive. Many of these witnesses ended up being tortured and even martyred for proclaiming Christ, but they wouldn't back down. They were willing to die because they knew the truth: Jesus was risen, and Jesus' resurrection guarantees our own resurrection.

The apostles defended their belief in Jesus and His resurrection before the Jewish Sanhedrin and the high priest, an intimidating audience to say the least. The high priest said to them, "We gave you strict orders not to teach in this name. Yet you have filled Jerusalem with your teaching and are determined to make us guilty of this man's blood" (Acts 5:28). Peter and the other apostles replied: "We must obey God rather than men! The God of our fathers raised Jesus from the dead—whom you had killed by hanging him on a tree. God exalted him to his own right hand as Prince and Savior that he might give repentance and forgiveness of sins to Israel" (Acts 5:29-31).

4. The many thousands of Jews who became unflinching followers of Jesus necessarily had to abandon many of their long-held sacred beliefs and practices—including the idea that animal sacrifices were necessary for salvation, the idea that the law had to be kept for salvation, and worship on the Sabbath alone—that they formerly cherished. The only thing that can explain this radical change—this disenfranchising of themselves from the religion into which they had been indoctrinated for centuries—is the physical resurrection of Christ.
5. Only the resurrection of Jesus Christ could explain the

conversion of hardcore skeptics in New Testament times. The apostle Paul is an example. Saul, as he was also known, delighted in breathing out "murderous threats against the Lord's disciples" (Acts 9:1). We are told that he "went to the high priest and asked him for letters to the synagogues in Damascus, so that if he found any there who belonged to the Way, whether men or women, he might take them as prisoners to Jerusalem" (verses 1-2). Clearly, Saul was not open to following Jesus Christ, for he hated the disciples of Jesus Christ. Yet, as the rest of Acts 9 reveals, Saul had an encounter with the living, resurrected Jesus, and not only became His follower, but became the most explosive preacher and promoter of Jesus to have ever appeared on planet earth. Only the existence of a truly resurrected and living Christ could explain such a radical conversion of a hardcore skeptic like Paul.

Another example is James, the half-brother of Jesus. James was not initially a believer in Jesus. He was a skeptic. Yet, he not only became a follower of Jesus, but became the prominent leader of the church in Jerusalem. The Jewish historian Josephus tells us that James ended up being stoned to death because of his belief in Jesus. What brought about the radical change in the heart of this skeptic? It was the resurrection of Jesus (John 7:1-5; Acts 1:14; 1 Corinthians 15:7).

Yet another example is doubting Thomas. Thomas, who had not been with the other disciples when Jesus appeared to them, refused to take the word of the other disciples about Jesus' resurrection from the dead. He said, "Unless I see the nail marks in his hands and put my finger where the nails were, and put my hand into his side, I will not believe it" (John 20:25). Doubting Thomas soon became believing Thomas, for the resurrected Lord appeared to him and invited him to touch His wounds (verses 26-27).

Thomas' response to Jesus was, "My Lord and my God!" (verse 28).

6. Only the resurrection of Jesus could explain the growth and survival of the Christian church. Vast numbers of people—Jews and Gentiles—became believers in Jesus, and remained believers in Jesus, despite the fact that the Roman sword was against the throat of Christianity. Many of these people died for their testimony and commitment to Jesus. The only thing that could explain such widespread commitment is the reality of a resurrected Jesus who promised eternal life to those who followed Him.

7. There were too many appearances over too many days to too many people for the resurrection to be easily dismissed. Acts 1:3 says, "He showed himself to these men and gave many convincing proofs that he was alive. He appeared to them over a period of forty days and spoke about the kingdom of God." Moreover, "He appeared to more than five hundred of the brothers at the same time, most of whom are still living, though some have fallen asleep" (1 Corinthians 15:6). Paul mentions that many of these were "still living" because if Paul had uttered any falsehood, there were plenty of people who could have stepped forward to call Paul a liar. They did not do this, however, because the appearance of Christ was well attested.

8. The apostle Paul in 1 Corinthians 15:1-4 speaks of Christ's resurrection as part of a public confession that had been handed down for years. First Corinthians was written around A.D. 55, a mere 20 years after Christ's resurrection. But biblical scholars believe the confession in 1 Corinthians 15:1-4 was formulated within a few years of Jesus' death and resurrection. Some scholars trace the confession back to within two years of the actual resurrection.

Here is a very important point: The resurrection of Jesus Christ serves as the guarantee for our own future resurrections from the dead. At the rapture, we will be saved from the very presence of sin: "We shall be like Him, for we shall see him as he is" (1 John 3:2). Christ "will transform our lowly body to be like his glorious body, by the power that enables him even to subject all things to himself" (Philippians 3:21 ESV).

Resurrection, First and Second

The Scriptures indicate that there are two types of resurrection. The first is appropriately called the "first resurrection" (Revelation 20:5), also called the "resurrection of life" (John 5:29 NASB), the "resurrection of the righteous" (Luke 14:14), and the "better resurrection" (Hebrews 11:35). The second resurrection is the last resurrection (Revelation 20:5; see also verses 6,11-15), appropriately called the "resurrection of judgement" (John 5:29 NASB; see also Daniel 12:2; Acts 24:15). The first resurrection is the resurrection of Christians, while the second resurrection is the resurrection of the wicked.

To clarify, the term "the first resurrection" refers to *all* the resurrections of the righteous (see John 5:29; Luke 14:14), even though they are widely separated in time. There is one resurrection of the righteous at the rapture (*before* the Tribulation—1 Thessalonians 4:13-17); another *during* the Tribulation (the two witnesses—Revelation 11:3,11); another *at the end* of the Tribulation (the martyred dead—Revelation 20:4-5); and still another at the end of the 1000-year millennial kingdom. They all are "first" in the sense of being before the second (final) resurrection of the wicked dead. Accordingly, the term "first resurrection" applies to all the resurrections of the saints regardless of when they occur, including the resurrection of Christ Himself (the "firstfruits"—see 1 Corinthians 15:23).

The "second" resurrection, or last resurrection, is an awful spectacle. All the unsaved of all time will be resurrected at the end of Christ's millennial kingdom, judged at the Great White Throne judgment, and then cast alive into the lake of fire (Revelation 20:11-15). They will be given resurrection bodies that will last forever, but bodies that are subject to pain and suffering. They will exist forever in the lake of fire.

Resurrection unto Damnation

Jesus Himself speaks of a resurrection unto damnation in John 5:28-29: "Do not marvel at this; for an hour is coming in which all who are in the tombs will hear His voice, and will come forth; those who did the good deeds to a resurrection of life, and those who committed the evil deeds to the resurrection of judgment" (NASB).

This resurrection unto damnation will take place after the millennial kingdom, and those so resurrected will then take part in the Great White Throne judgment, which is the judgment of the wicked dead. This is referenced in Revelation 20:11-13: "Then I saw a great white throne and him who was seated on it...And I saw the dead, great and small, standing before the throne...The dead were judged according to what they had done as recorded in the books. The sea gave up the dead that were in it, and death and Hades gave up the dead that were in them, and each person was judged according to what he had done."

Following their judgment, they will be cast alive into the lake of fire (Revelation 20:15). The wicked will be given resurrected bodies that will last forever, but bodies that are subject to pain and suffering, and they will spend eternity in the lake of fire. Their experience will involve weeping and gnashing of teeth (Matthew 13:41-42), condemnation (Matthew 12:36-37), destruction (Philippians 1:28), eternal punishment (Matthew 25:46), separation from God's presence (2 Thessalonians 1:8-9), and trouble and distress (Romans 2:9).

Return, Christ's

See *Second Coming.*

Revelation

There are two primary ways God has revealed Himself—through general revelation and special revelation. Both are critically important.

General Revelation. General revelation refers to revelation that is available to all persons of all times. An example of this would be God's revelation of Himself in the world of nature (Psalm 19).

By observing nature, we can detect something of God's existence, and discern something of His divine power and glory. We might say that the whole world is God's "kindergarten" to teach us the ABCs of the reality of God.

Of course, there are limitations to how much we can learn from general revelation. For example, general revelation does not tell us anything about God's cure for humanity's sin problem. It doesn't tell us about the gospel message. It doesn't tell us anything about the prophetic future. These kinds of things require special revelation. But general revelation does give us enough information about God's existence that if we reject it and refuse to turn to God, then God is justified in bringing condemnation against us (Romans 1:20).

Special Revelation. Special revelation refers to God's specific and clear revelation via His mighty acts in history, the person and work of Jesus Christ, and His message spoken through Old Testament prophets and New Testament apostles. Let's take a brief look at each of these.

God's revelation in history. If there really is a personal God who created humankind, then we would naturally expect that He would reveal Himself among us in the outworking of human history. And indeed, God has manifested Himself historically.

God is the living God, and He has communicated knowledge of Himself through the ebb and flow of historical experience. The Bible is first and foremost a record of God's interactions with Abraham, Isaac, Jacob, the twelve tribes of Israel, the apostle Paul, Peter, John, and many others in biblical times.

The greatest revelatory act of God in the Old Testament was the deliverance of Israel from bondage in Egypt. God, through Moses, inflicted ten plagues on the Egyptians—plagues that showed His awesome power (Exodus 7–12). God's demonstration of power was all the more impressive because the Egyptians believed their many false gods could protect them from such plagues.

It is important to note that the historical miracles and events wrought by God were always accompanied by spoken words. A miracle or event was never left to speak for itself. Nor were people left to infer whatever conclusions they wanted to draw from the event. God made sure that when a significant event occurred, there was a prophet on hand to interpret it.

For example, Moses was present to record everything related to the Exodus. Jeremiah and Ezekiel were on hand to record all that happened during Israel's time of exile. Isaiah was present to preserve a record of the Israelites' return from exile. And the apostles testified about everything related to the life and death of Jesus. God has revealed Himself and He always made sure that His actions were adequately recorded!

God's ultimate revelation in Jesus Christ. The only way for God to be able to fully do and say all that He wanted was to actually leave His eternal residence and enter the arena of humanity. This He did in the person of Jesus Christ. Jesus was Immanuel—"God with us" (Matthew 1:23). He was God's ultimate "special" revelation.

Why was it so necessary for Jesus to come as God's fullest revelation? Because God is a Spirit. And because He is a Spirit, He is invisible. With our normal senses, we can't perceive Him, other than what we can detect in general revelation.

Not only that, man is also spiritually blind and deaf. Since the fall of man in the Garden of Eden, man has lacked true spiritual perception (1 Corinthians 2:14). So humankind was in need of special revelation from God in the worst sort of way.

Jesus—as eternal God—took on human flesh so He could be God's fullest revelation to man (Hebrews 1:2-3). Jesus was a revelation of God not just in His person (as God) but in His life and teachings as well. By observing the things Jesus did and the things Jesus said, we learn a great deal about God. For example:

- God's awesome power was revealed in Jesus (John 3:2).
- God's incredible wisdom was revealed in Jesus (1 Corinthians 1:24).
- God's boundless love was revealed and demonstrated by Jesus (1 John 3:16).
- God's unfathomable grace was revealed in Jesus (2 Thessalonians 1:12).

These verses serve as the backdrop as to why Jesus told a group of Pharisees, "When a man believes in me, he does not believe in me only, but in the one who sent me" (John 12:44). Jesus likewise told His disciple Philip that "anyone who has seen me has seen the Father" (John 14:9). Jesus was the ultimate revelation of God!

God's revelation in the Bible. Another key means of special revelation is the Bible. In this one book, God has provided everything He wants us to know about Him and how we can have a relationship with Him.

God is the one who caused the Bible to be written. Through it He speaks to us today just as He spoke to people in ancient times when those words were first given. The Bible is to be received as God's words to us and revered and obeyed as such. As we submit to the Bible's authority, we place ourselves under the authority of the living God.

Significance for prophecy. An important part of God's special revelation to humankind is prophecy. A prophet is one who speaks for God, and in the biblical sense had two primary roles: 1) to teach God's message in regard to a contemporary situation being faced by the people of God; and 2) the conveyance of a message regarding the future. Both require special revelation from God.

Revelation, Book of

The book of Revelation is the only apocalyptic book in the New Testament. The author is the apostle John, who had been imprisoned on the isle of Patmos, in the Aegean Sea, for the crime of sharing Jesus Christ with everyone he came into contact with (Revelation 1:9). It was on this island that John received the "revelation." The book was apparently written around A.D. 95.

The recipients of the book of Revelation were undergoing severe persecution, with some of them even being killed (see Revelation 2:13). Things were about to get even worse. John wrote this book to give his readers a strong hope that would help them patiently endure in the midst of suffering. At the time, it seemed as if evil was prevailing at every level. However, Revelation indicates that evil will one day come to an end. At the second coming, Christ will overthrow wicked governments, cast the wicked into a place of horrible suffering, and bring about an eternal state where Satan will be forever banished. There will be no further sin, sorrow, or death, and fellowship with God will be perpetual and uninterrupted.

An outline of the book of Revelation may be found in Revelation 1:19: "Write, therefore, what you have seen, what is now and what will take place later." The phrase "what you have seen" is a reference to Revelation 1, where we find a description of Jesus in His present glory, and an introduction to the book of Revelation. The things "that are" relate to the present circumstances of the seven churches of Asia Minor recorded in Revelation 2 and 3. The things "that will take place later" refer to futuristic prophecy of the Tribulation period, second coming, millennial kingdom, and eternal state described in Revelation 4–22.

This book promises that God's people will enjoy His presence forever in a "new heaven and a new earth" (Revelation 21:1). Jesus promises, "I am coming soon" (22:20). Such a wonderful promise helps suffering believers see "the big picture" regarding the future so they can patiently endure in the present.

See *Futurist View of Revelation.*
See *Idealist View of Revelation.*
See *Historicist View of Revelation.*
See *Preterism.*
See *Eclectic View of Revelation.*

Revised Dispensationalism

Revised dispensationalism holds there is only one new covenant (Jeremiah 31:31), which, while having a later literal fulfillment in national Israel, has a present application to the church. Even though revised dispensationalists see distinctives between Israel and the church, both are viewed as collectively composing one overall people of God who share in the spiritual redemption wrought by Christ.

This is in contrast to traditional dispensationalism, which holds that there are two new covenants: one for Israel (yet to be fulfilled) and one for the church (presently being fulfilled). As well, Israel and the church are viewed as two separate peoples with different destinies: one in heaven (the church) and the other on earth (Israel).

Rewards

All believers will one day stand before the judgment seat of Christ (Romans 14:8-10; 1 Corinthians 3:1-10; 2 Corinthians 5:10). At that time each believer's life will be examined in regard to deeds done while in the body. Personal motives and intents of the heart will also be weighed.

Scripture indicates that some believers at the judgment may have a sense of deprivation and suffer some degree of forfeiture and shame. Certain rewards may be forfeited that otherwise might have been received, and this will involve a sense of loss. The fact is, Christians differ radically in holiness of conduct and faithfulness in service. God in His justice and holiness takes all this into account. For this reason, 2 John 8 warns us, "Watch out that you do not lose what you have worked for, but that you may be rewarded fully." In 1 John 2:28 John wrote about the possibility of a believer actually being ashamed at Christ's coming.

What kinds of rewards will believers receive (or forfeit) at the judgment seat of Christ? Scripture often speaks of them in terms of crowns that we wear. In fact, there are a number of different crowns that symbolize the various spheres of achievement and award in the Christian life.

The *crown of life* is given to those who persevere under trial, and especially to those who suffer to the point of death (James 1:12; Revelation 2:10). The *crown of glory* is given to those who faithfully and sacrificially minister God's Word to the flock (1 Peter 5:4). The *crown incorruptible* is given to those who win the race of temperance and self-control (1 Corinthians 9:25). The *crown of righteousness* is given to those who long for the second coming of Christ (2 Timothy 4:8).

See *Crowns*.

See *Judgment Seat of Christ*.

River of Life

The "river of the water of life" has intrigued Bible interpreters since the first century. In Revelation 22:1-2, we read, "Then the angel showed me the river of the water of life, as clear as crystal, flowing from the throne of God and of the Lamb down the middle of the great street of the city. On each side of the river stood the tree of life, bearing twelve crops of fruit, yielding its fruit every month."

Perhaps one of the best explanations is that this pure river of life, though it may be a real and material river, is nevertheless symbolic of the abundance of spiritual life that will characterize those who are living in the eternal city. The stream seems to symbolize the perpetual outflow of spiritual blessing from the throne of God to all the redeemed of all ages, now basking in the full glow of eternal life. What spiritual blessedness there will be in the eternal state.

Roman Empire, Future

The idea of a revived Roman Empire of the end times is based on a prophecy found in Daniel 7. In this chapter, Daniel makes reference to four beasts. These "beasts" represent kingdoms that play an important role in biblical prophecy.

The first, Daniel says, was "like a lion, and it had the wings of an eagle," but "its wings were torn off" (verse 4). This imagery apparently represents Babylon, its lion-like quality indicating power and strength.

Daniel continued in verse 5 by referring to "another beast, a second one, like a bear" (ESV). An animal of great strength (see 1 Samuel 17:34; Amos 5:19; Hosea 13:8). This kingdom is Medo-Persia, and was well-known for its strength and fierceness in battle.

The third beast was "like a leopard, with four wings of a bird on its back. And the beast had four heads, and dominion was given to it" (Daniel 7:6 ESV). This imagery represents Greece under Alexander the Great, and the "four heads" are the four generals who divided the kingdom following Alexander's death.

The fourth beast was a *mongrel* beast composed of parts of a lion, bear, and leopard, and was more terrifying and powerful than the three preceding beasts:

> Behold, a fourth beast, terrifying and dreadful and exceedingly strong. It had great iron teeth; it devoured and broke in pieces and stamped what was left with its feet. It was different from all the beasts that were before it, and it had ten horns. I considered the horns, and behold, there came up among them another horn, a little one, before which three of the first horns were plucked up by the roots. And behold, in this horn were eyes like the eyes of a man, and a mouth speaking great things.

This wild imagery refers to the Roman Empire. Rome already

existed in ancient days, but it fell apart in the fifth century A.D. It will be revived, however, in the end times, apparently comprised of ten nations ruled by ten kings (ten horns). An eleventh horn—a little horn (the Antichrist)—emerges from within this ten-nation confederacy. He apparently starts out in an insignificant way, but grows powerful enough to uproot (overtake) three of the existing horns (or rulers). He eventually comes into power and dominance over this revived empire.

It is noteworthy that Rome has never consisted of a ten-nation confederacy with ten co-rulers. If it hasn't happened yet, this means this prophecy must deal with the future.

Related to this, in Daniel 2 we read of a prophetic dream that Nebuchadnezzar had. In this dream, this end-times Roman Empire was pictured as a mixture of iron and clay (see verses 41-43). Daniel, the great dream-interpreter, saw this as meaning that just as iron is strong, so this latter-day Roman Empire would be strong. But just as iron and clay do not naturally mix with each other, so this latter-day Roman Empire would have some divisions. They would not be completely integrated with each other.

There are many modern biblical interpreters who see the European Union as a primary prospect for the ultimate fulfillment of this prophecy. It is noted that a common monetary currency is the first step in what will eventually be a common and unified political entity. Perhaps the stage is being set for the fulfillment of Daniel 2 and 7.

Rosh

There has been tremendous debate regarding the proper meaning of the term *Rosh* in Ezekiel 38:2 and 39:1. This common Hebrew word literally means "head," "top," "summit," or "chief." The problem for Bible interpreters is that in Ezekiel 38–39, the term can be taken as either a proper noun or an adjective.

Many English translations take the term as an adjective and translate the word as "chief." An example is the New International Version, which reads, "Son of man, set your face against Gog, of the land of Magog, the *chief* prince of Meshech and Tubal..." (38:2, emphasis added). Other translations take the term as a proper noun, referring to a geographical place. The New American Standard Bible, taking the term as proper noun, reads: "Son of man, set your face toward Gog of the land of Magog, the prince *of Rosh,* Meshech and Tubal..." (38:2, emphasis added).

The evidence favors taking the term as a noun. Indeed, the translation of the term as an adjective ("chief prince") can be traced to the Latin Vulgate, translated by Jerome, following the lead of an earlier Jewish translator, Aquila. The translation of Rosh as an adjective was based not on grammatical considerations, but on the fact that these early translators could not find a geographical territory named Rosh elsewhere in Scripture.

By contrast, taking Rosh as a proper noun—a geographical area—has solid exegetical support. This is the most natural way of rendering the Hebrew. In fact, no example of Hebrew grammar has ever been cited that would support taking Rosh as an adjective. On linguistic and historical grounds, the case for taking Rosh as a proper noun (geographical territory) rather than as an adjective is substantial and persuasive.

If we are correct in taking the term as a geographical place, then the question becomes, *Where is* this geographical place? This, too, has been an issue of substantial debate. It is the consensus of many that it refers to modern Russia, though some argue against this conclusion.

Some critics of the idea that Rosh is Russia build a straw man argument and argue something like this: "Simply because an ancient Hebrew word sounds similar to a modern English word doesn't mean that Rosh is Russia—that's ridiculous." Frankly, if the view that Rosh is Russia were based solely on the similarity of sound between the two, I would agree with the above scholars. As will become clear below, however, the evidence goes much deeper than this. In what follows,

I will summarize the more substantive reasons for taking the term as referring to Russia:

1. First, there are highly respected Hebrew scholars who have taken the term as referring to Russia. This should not be taken lightly. A notable example is Wilhelm Gesenius, whose original Latin version of his lexicon titled *Thesaurus Linguae Hebraeae et Chaldaeae Veteris Testamenti* contains nearly a page of notes dealing with the word Rosh and with the Rosh people mentioned in Ezekiel 38–39.
2. There is considerable historical evidence that a place known as Rosh—sometimes using alternate spellings such as Rus, Ros, and Rox—was very familiar in the ancient world, and was located in the territory now occupied by modern Russia.
3. Related to this, the Septuagint, the Greek translation of the Hebrew Old Testament that predates the time of Christ, translates "Rosh" as "Ros." It is noteworthy that the Septuagint is not much more than three centuries removed from Ezekiel's time. Moreover, there is evidence of a people named Rosh/Rashu in the ninth through seventh centuries B.C. in Assyrian sources that predate the book of Ezekiel. Hence, quite early, we find evidence of a "Ros" people that was geographically located in today's Russia.
4. Rosh also appears as a place name in Egyptian inscriptions as Rash, dating as early as 2600 B.C. One inscription that dates to 1500 B.C. refers to a land called Reshu that was located to the north of Egypt (as is the case with modern Russia). Rosh (or its equivalent) is found in a variety of other ancient documents as well.
5. Placing Rosh in the area today known as Russia has long been a tradition in the Christian church, as early as A.D. 438.
6. Finally, in Ezekiel 39:2 Rosh is said to be "from the

remotest parts of the north" (NASB). The term "north" is to be understood in relation to Israel. If one draws a line from Israel and goes straight north, one ends up in Russia.

Russia

See *Rosh.*

S

Sacrifices

See *Millennial Temple and Sacrifices.*

Salvation, God's Plan of

Before the world began—indeed, in eternity past—the triune God fully settled the issue of salvation. Scripture reveals that the Lamb of God "was slain from the creation of the world" (Revelation 13:8). God promised eternal life to His people "before the beginning of time" (Titus 1:2). God has "saved us and called us to a holy life—not because of anything we have done but because of his own purpose and grace. This grace was given us in Christ Jesus before the beginning of time" (2 Timothy 1:9). Therefore, to the sheep of His pasture, Christ says, "Come, you who are blessed by my Father; take your inheritance, the kingdom prepared for you since the creation of the world" (Matthew 25:34).

Because God's plan of salvation is an eternal plan, it is clear that human salvation was not an afterthought on God's part. Nor was it the only possible way out of a "hopeless dilemma" for God. God planned everything from the very beginning. In view of this, we must conclude that God in His omniscience (all-knowingness) was not shocked or surprised when Satan, and then humankind, fell. God's glorious plan—which encompasses even the Fall—is from eternity past to eternity future.

Even before the beginning of time, God the Most High concerned Himself with our eternal benefit. Before the earth and the stellar universe were brought into being at God's command (Genesis 1), even then He had thoughts of you and me. The thoughtful Christian can only respond with awe as he contemplates what God has done for him.

Scripture indicates that each person of the Trinity has an important role to play in the outworking of God's eternal plan of salvation. In theological circles, God's plan of salvation for humanity is related to His "decree." God's decree may be defined as His eternal purpose, according to the counsel of His own sovereign will, whereby, for His own glory, He has foreordained whatsoever comes to pass.

There are literally hundreds of passages in Scripture related to the outworking of God's sovereign plan. A look at just a few of these shows that what He has planned will, in fact, be accomplished down to the smallest detail: "For the LORD Almighty has purposed, and who can thwart him? His hand is stretched out, and who can turn it back?" (Isaiah 14:27); "I make known the end from the beginning, from ancient times, what is still to come. I say: My purpose will stand, and I will do all that I please" (46:10).

God's people in biblical times recognized the sure and certain nature of God's sovereign plan. Job said, "I know that you can do all things; no plan of yours can be thwarted" (Job 42:2). We read in Proverbs: "Many are the plans in a man's heart, but it is the LORD's purpose that prevails" (Proverbs 19:21). David affirmed, "All the days ordained for me were written in your book before one of them came to be" (Psalm 139:16).

A careful reading of Scripture shows that it was the Father who planned and ordained salvation (John 3:16; Isaiah 53:6,10). The apostle Paul told the Ephesian Christians that they had been chosen in Christ by the Father before the foundation of the world (Ephesians 1:4). Paul likewise wrote to the Roman Christians about the Father's foreknowledge, predestination, and sovereign calling of certain individuals before time even began (Romans 8:29-30). Peter, writing to saints scattered throughout Asia Minor, described them as elect of God the Father (1 Peter 1:2). Within the eternal plan of salvation, it was the Father's unique role to elect and call certain individuals to salvation.

The Son's task in the eternal plan included playing a key role in the creation of the universe (John 1:3; Colossians 1:16; Hebrews 1:2), making possible preincarnate appearances to the patriarchs in Old Testament times as the "angel of the LORD" (Genesis 16:7; 22:11), coming to earth as God's ultimate revelation (John 1:18; Hebrews 1:1-2), dying on the cross as a substitutionary sacrifice for human sin (John 3:16), resurrecting from the dead (1 Peter 1:3; 3:21), and being the Mediator between the Father and humankind (1 Timothy 2:5). The eternal plan also called for the second coming of the Son in glory to consummate human redemption (Revelation 19–22).

The Holy Spirit also played a key role in the outworking of the plan of salvation. The Holy Spirit undertook the ministry of inspiring Scripture (2 Peter 1:21), regenerating believers (Titus 3:5), indwelling believers (1 Corinthians 6:19), baptizing believers (1 Corinthians 12:13), sealing believers (Ephesians 4:30), and bestowing spiritual gifts upon believers (1 Corinthians 12:11).

All that the triune God determined *before* time was carried out in time. For this reason, God's plan of salvation is called His "eternal purpose" (Ephesians 3:11), and God is praised as the "King of the ages" (1 Timothy 1:17).

Sardis

Sardis is a city that hosted one of the seven churches of Asia Minor mentioned in Revelation 2–3 (see Revelation 3:1-6). The city is about thirty miles southeast of Thyatira, and was located at the foot of a mountain called Tmolus, on the river Pactolus. It was at one time the capital city of Lydia. In fact, the city was located on an important trade route that ran through Lydia.

Sardis featured pagan worship, as both the Roman Caesar and Artemis, goddess of fertility, were worshiped there. Within the confines of the city was a magnificent world-famous Temple of Artemis.

The primary business of this industrial city was harvesting wool, dying it, and making garments from it. The city also had a strong jewelry business.

Jesus had stern words for this church: "You have the reputation of being alive, but you are dead" (Revelation 3:1). For the most part, there was no spiritual vitality there, even though there were a few genuine believers left (see verse 4; compare with Matthew 23:27). This church had become utterly complacent, and essentially needed a spiritual resurrection from the dead, so it could again become a living, vibrant church. Jesus instructed the church to repent, or judgment would fall (verse 3).

Satan

Satan, formerly known as Lucifer, is a fallen angel who is aligned against God and His purposes, and he heads up a vast company of fallen angels, called demons, who are also aligned against God and His purposes. Though he possesses creaturely limitations—he is not omnipresent, omnipotent, or omniscient like God is—Satan is nevertheless pictured in Scripture as being extremely powerful and influential in the world. He is called the "ruler of this world" (John 12:31 NASB) and "the god of this world" (2 Corinthians 4:4). He is called the "prince of the power of the air" (Ephesians 2:2 NASB). He is also said to deceive the whole world (Revelation 12:9: 20:3). He is portrayed as having power in the governmental realm (Matthew 4:8-9; 2 Corinthians 4:4), the physical realm (Luke 13:11,16; Acts 10:38), the angelic realm (Jude 9; Ephesians 6:11,12), and the ecclesiastical (church) realm (Revelation 2:9; 3:9).

We learn much about Satan and his work by the various names and titles used of him:

- Satan is called the *accuser of the brethren* (Revelation 12:10). The Greek of this verse indicates that accusing God's people is a continuous, ongoing work of Satan. He never lets up. He brings charges against believers before God (Zechariah 3:1; Romans 8:33), and he accuses believers to their own conscience.
- Satan is called our *adversary* (1 Peter 5:8). This words indicates that Satan opposes us and stands against us in every way he can.
- Satan is called *Beelzebub* (Matthew 12:24). This word literally means "lord of the flies," carrying the idea, "lord of filth." The devil corrupts everything he touches.
- Satan is called the *devil* (Matthew 4:1). This word carries the idea of "adversary" as well as "slanderer." The devil was and is the adversary of Christ; he is the adversary of all who follow Christ. Satan slanders God to man (Genesis 3:1-7), and man to God (Job 1:9; 2:4).
- Satan is called our *enemy* (Matthew 13:39). This word comes from a root meaning "hatred." It characterizes Satan's attitude in an absolute sense. He hates both God and His children.
- Satan is called the *evil one* (1 John 5:19). He opposes all that is good and is the promoter of all that is evil. Indeed, he is the very embodiment of evil.
- Satan is called the *father of lies* (John 8:44). The word "father" is used here metaphorically of the originator of a family or company of persons animated by a deceitful character. Satan was the first and greatest liar.
- Satan is called a *murderer* (John 8:44). This word literally means "man killer" (see 1 John 3:12,15). Hatred is

the motive that leads one to commit murder. Satan hates both God and His children, so he has a genuine motive for murder.

- Satan is called the *god of this age* (2 Corinthians 4:4). This does not mean that Satan is deity. It simply means that this is an evil age, and Satan is its "god" in the sense that he is the head of it.
- Satan is called the *prince of the power of the air* (Ephesians 2:2). It would seem that the "air" in this context is that sphere in which the inhabitants of this world live. This sphere represents the very seat of Satan's authority.
- Satan is called the *prince of this world* (John 12:31; 14:30; 16:11). The key word here is "world." This word refers not to the physical earth but to an anti-God system that Satan has promoted which conforms to his ideals, aims, and methods.
- Satan is called a *roaring lion* (1 Peter 5:8,9). This graphic simile depicts Satan's strength and destructiveness.
- Satan is called the *tempter* (Matthew 4:3). His constant purpose is to incite man to sin. He whispers the most plausible excuses and striking advantages of sinning against God.
- Satan is called a *serpent* (Genesis 3:1; Revelation 12:9). This word symbolizes the origin of sin in the Garden of Eden, as well as the hatefulness and deadly effect of sin. The serpent is characterized by treachery, deceitfulness, venom, and murderous proclivities.

Many scholars believe Ezekiel 28 and Isaiah 14 provide insights regarding how Lucifer fell and became Satan. The being described in Ezekiel 28 is portrayed as having the nature of a cherub (verse 14), as being initially blameless and sinless (verse 15), as being on the Holy Mount of God (verses 13-14), as being cast out of the mountain of God and thrown to the earth (verse 16), and is said to have been full of wisdom, perfect in beauty, and having the seal of perfection (verse 12). Since such things cannot be said of a mere human being, many believe this is a reference to Lucifer.

Our text tells us that he was created in a state of perfection (Ezekiel 28:12,15), and he remained perfect in his ways until iniquity was found in him (verse 15). What was this iniquity? We read in verse 17, "Your heart became proud on account of your beauty, and you corrupted your wisdom because of your splendor." Lucifer apparently became so impressed with his own beauty, intelligence, power, and position that he began to desire for himself the honor and glory that belong to God alone. The sin that corrupted Lucifer was self-generated pride. This seems to be confirmed in Isaiah 14:12-17, which describes the five boastful "I wills..." of Lucifer.

God rightfully judged this mighty angelic being: "I threw you to the earth" (Ezekiel 28:17). As a result of his heinous sin, Lucifer was banished from living in heaven (Isaiah 14:12). He became corrupt, and his name changed from Lucifer ("morning star") to Satan ("adversary"). His power became completely perverted (14:12,16,17). And his destiny, following the second coming of Christ, is to be bound in the bottomless pit during the thousand-year millennial kingdom over which Christ will rule (Revelation 20:3), and eventually be thrown into the lake of fire (Matthew 25:41).

Scoffers

Christians are warned in 2 Peter 3:3-4 of the unbelief that will predominate on the earth in proximity to the second coming of Jesus Christ. We are told that "scoffers will come in the last days with scoffing, following their own sinful desires" (verse 3 ESV). They will scoff by saying, "Where is the promise of his coming? For ever since the fathers fell asleep, all things are continuing as they were from the beginning of creation" (verse 4 ESV; see John 14:1-3; Acts 1:11; 1 Corinthians 15:23; 2 Corinthians 1:14; Philippians 1:6; 1 Thessalonians 3:13; 4:14-18;

2 Thessalonians 1:10; 2:1; 1 Timothy 6:14; 2 Timothy 4:8; Titus 2:13; Hebrews 9:28; James 5:7). Jude 18 likewise affirms, "In the last time there will be scoffers, following their own ungodly passions" (ESV). Christians will be increasingly mocked and ridiculed for their beliefs! Such is already occurring among a new more-vitriolic breed of atheists, agnostics, and skeptics.

Sea of Glass

In Revelation 4:6, we read of the heavenly throne room: "Before the throne there was as it were a sea of glass, like crystal…" (ESV). The floor of the heavenly throne room, with the appearance of being a sea of glass, like crystal, is wondrous and awe-inspiring. It involves the attempt to use human language to describe the indescribable. What a sight the divine habitat must be. The crystal pavement must appear much like a glistening sea.

This brings to mind a verse from the Old Testament. In Exodus 24:10 we read that Moses and some others "saw the God of Israel. Under his feet was something like a pavement made of sapphire, clear as the sky itself" (see also Ezekiel 1:22). Sapphire was associated with diamonds and other precious stones in the Old Testament (Exodus 28:18).

Seal Judgments

Human suffering will steadily escalate during the Tribulation period. The first set of judgments to be unleashed on earth are the seal judgments, and these involve bloodshed and war, famine, death, economic upheaval, a great (and deadly) earthquake, and cosmic disturbances (Revelation 6). Following this are the trumpet judgments, which involve hail and fire mixed with blood, the sea turning to blood, water turning bitter, further cosmic disturbances, affliction by demonic scorpions, and the death of a third of humankind (Revelation 8:6–9:21). Finally are the bowl judgments, which involve horribly painful sores on human beings, more bodies of water turning to blood, the death of all sea creatures, people being scorched by the sun, total darkness engulfing the land, a devastating earthquake, and much more (Revelation 16).

It is interesting to observe that in Jesus' Olivet discourse, He speaks of things that will occur during the Tribulation period, and more than a few scholars have noticed the parallel that seems to exist between these events and the seal judgments. Jesus speaks of the rise of false Christs (Matthew 24:4-5), just as the first seal speaks of the rise of Antichrist (Revelation 6:1-2). Jesus speaks of wars and rumors of wars (Matthew 24:6), just as the second seal is said to involve warfare in which nations rise up against each other (Revelation 6:3-4). Jesus speaks of famines (Matthew 24:7), just as the third seal involves famine (Revelation 6:5-6). Jesus speaks of earthquakes (Matthew 24:7), just as the sixth seal involves an earthquake (Revelation 6:12-14).

Second Advent

See *Second Coming.*

Second Coming

S

The second coming is that event when Jesus Christ—the King of kings and Lord of lords—will return to the earth in glory at the end of the present age and set up His kingdom. The very same Jesus who ascended into heaven will come again at the second coming (Acts 1:9-11).

The second coming will involve a visible, physical, bodily coming of the glorified Jesus. One key Greek word used to describe the second coming of Christ in the New Testament is *apokalupsis.* This word carries the basic meaning of "revelation," "visible disclosure," "unveiling," and "removing the cover" from something that is hidden. The word is used of Christ's second coming in 1 Peter 4:13: "To the degree that you share the sufferings of Christ, keep on rejoicing, so that also at the revelation of His glory you may rejoice with exultation" (NASB).

Another Greek word used of Christ's second coming in the New Testament is *epiphaneia,* which carries the basic meaning of "to appear," or "to shine forth." In Titus 2:13 Paul speaks of "looking for the blessed hope and the appearing of the glory of our great God and Savior, Christ Jesus" (NASB). In 1 Timothy 6:14 Paul urges Timothy to "keep the commandment without stain or reproach until the appearing of our Lord Jesus Christ" (NASB).

The second coming will be a universal experience in the sense that "every eye" will witness the event. Revelation 1:7 says, "Behold, He is coming with the clouds, and every eye will see Him, even those who pierced him; and all the tribes of the earth will mourn over Him" (NASB). Moreover, at the time of the second coming, there will be magnificent signs in the heavens (Matthew 24:29-30). Christ will come as the King of kings and Lord of lords, and there will be many crowns on His head—crowns that represent absolute sovereignty. His eyes will be like blazing fire (Revelation 19:11-16).

See *Parousia.*

Second Death

See *Death, First and Second.*

S

Second Resurrection

See *Resurrection, First and Second.*

Selfishness

In 2 Timothy 3, the apostle Paul informs young Timothy of the conditions that will exist in the "last days." Among these conditions is that "people will be lovers of self, lovers of money, proud, arrogant, abusive, disobedient to their parents, ungrateful, [and] unholy" (verse 2 ESV). The Greek word for "lovers of self" (*philautoi*) carries the idea of "self-centered," or "narcissistic." The structure of 2 Timothy 3:2 indicates that all the other vices listed (lovers of money, proud, arrogant, abusive, disobedient to parents, ungrateful, unholy) are an outgrowth or result of being a "lover of self." Virtue will truly be lacking among many in the end times!

Sensationalism Inappropriate

First Peter 4:7-10 is jam-packed with wisdom for how we ought to live in view of biblical prophecy:

> The end of all things is near; therefore, be of sound judgment and sober spirit for the purpose of prayer. Above all, keep fervent in your love for one another, because love covers a multitude of sins. Be hospitable to one another without complaint. As each one has received a special gift, employ it in serving one another as good stewards of the manifold grace of God (NASB).

Many people tend to become sensationalistic and alarmist about end-time prophecies. But God here tells us to be sober-minded and to maintain sound judgment. The best way to be sober-minded and maintain sound judgment is to regularly feed our minds upon the Word of God. Keeping our minds stayed upon the Scriptures will keep us on-track in our thinking and in our life choices in the light of biblical prophecy.

Seven Churches of Revelation

In the book of Revelation, the apostle John says he saw "seven golden lampstands," and "among the lampstands was someone like a son of man, dressed in a robe reaching down to his feet and with a golden sash around his chest" (Revelation 1:12-13). Jesus Himself was in the midst of the seven lampstands—that is, He "walks among the seven golden lampstands" (2:1).

Jesus reveals that "the seven lampstands are the seven churches" (verse 20) that are discussed in Revelation 2–3: the churches of Ephesus,

Smyrna, Pergamum, Thyatira, Sardis, Philadelphia, and Laodicea. The churches are no doubt symbolized as lampstands because they are intended to be the bearer of God's light in this dark world (compare with Matthew 5:16). As Jesus reveals in Revelation 2–3, however, they do not always succeed and are often in need of correction. Still, Jesus commends the churches if they have done something worthy of commendation. Jesus promises a reward for those who "overcome" and correct the shortcomings He mentions.

See *Ephesus.*
See *Smyrna.*
See *Pergamum.*
See *Thyatira.*
See *Sardis.*
See *Philadelphia.*
See *Laodicea.*

Seven Mountains

In Revelation 17 we find a discussion of religious Babylon, with verses 1-7 providing a description of it, and verses 8-18 providing an interpretation of the description. There is much symbolic language here. The passage indicates that Babylon is a great prostitute (or whore) whose religious unfaithfulness influences the people of many nations. This "great prostitute" (blasphemous religion) is said to sit on (thus controlling) a scarlet beast (who is the Antichrist). It is in this context that we come upon a reference to "seven mountains on which the woman is seated."

Biblical scholars have debated what is meant by these "seven mountains." Some point out that Rome has long been known as the legendary city on seven hills. It is suggested, then, that this religious system will be centered in Rome headed by Antichrist in the end times.

Other biblical scholars suggest that perhaps the seven mountains symbolize the seven kingdoms and their kings mentioned in Revelation

17:10. After all, mountains often symbolize kingdoms in Scripture (Psalm 30:7; Jeremiah 51:25; Daniel 2:44-45).

These seven kingdoms are the seven great world empires—Egypt, Assyria, Babylon, Medo-Persia, Greece, Rome, and that of the Antichrist. The biblical text tells us that five of these kingdoms have fallen, one still exists, and one is yet to come (Revelation 17:10). What this means is that at the time of John's writing, the Egyptian, Assyrian, Babylonian, Medo-Persian and Greek empires had fallen. Rome, however, still existed, and the Antichrist's kingdom was yet to come. False paganized religion affected all these empires.

Seven Spirits of God

In Revelation 1:4 we read about the "seven spirits before his throne." Revelation 3:1 makes reference to the words of Jesus, or the "words of him who holds the seven spirits of God and the seven stars." Then, in Revelation 4:5 we read that "before the throne were burning seven torches of fire, which are the seven spirits of God" (ESV). Finally, in Revelation 5:6 we read of the Lamb having "seven horns and with seven eyes, which are the seven spirits of God sent out into all the earth" (ESV). What are the "seven spirits of God"?

Scholars have offered several suggestions. Some have suggested that perhaps the seven spirits are seven angels that are before the throne of God in heaven. Others suggest that the seven spirits are specifically the seven angels mentioned in conjunction with the seven churches of Revelation 2–3. Still others understand the seven spirits to be a metaphorical reference to the Holy Spirit in His fullness (seven being a number of completeness or fullness). If this is correct, a possible cross reference is Isaiah 11:2, which speaks of the sevenfold ministry of the Holy Spirit as related to the divine Messiah: "The Spirit of the LORD shall rest upon him—the Spirit of wisdom and understanding, the Spirit of counsel and of power, the Spirit of knowledge and of the fear of the LORD."

Seventy Sevens

See *Daniel and the Seventy Weeks.*

Seventy Weeks

See *Daniel and the Seventy Weeks.*

Sheep and Goats, Judgment of the Nations

See *Judgment of the Nations.*

Sheol

In the Old Testament the word "hell" often translates the Hebrew word *Sheol* which can have different meanings in different contexts. Sometimes the word means "grave" (Psalm 49:15). Other times it refers to an underground region (Numbers 16:30,33; Amos 9:2), said to be shadowy and gloomy, where disembodied souls have a conscious but dull and inactive existence (see 2 Samuel 22:6; Ecclesiastes 9:10). The Old Testament often characterizes this place as being full of horror (Psalm 30:9), weeping (Isaiah 38:3), and punishment (Job 24:19). It was believed that both the righteous and the unrighteous went to this place at death (see Genesis 37:35; Psalm 9:17; Isaiah 38:10).

Hades is the New Testament counterpart to Sheol, and came to refer to the state or place of the dead (see Matthew 11:23; Acts 2:27,31; Revelation 1:18). In the Septuagint—the Greek translation of the Hebrew Old Testament that predates the time of Christ—*Sheol* is actually translated as "Hades."

Signs of the Times

As a preface, it is critical to understand that no one can know the day or the hour of specific end-time events. Matthew 24:36 tells us, "Concerning that day and hour no one knows, not even the angels of heaven, nor the Son, but the Father only" (ESV). Likewise, Acts 1:7

instructs us, "It is not for you to know times or dates that the Father has set by his own authority." Having said this, however, the Lord Jesus did indicate that we can know the general time of His coming in the parable of the fig tree (see Matthew 24:33).

The term "signs of the times" describes specific characteristics and/or conditions that will exist in the end times, such that when they are witnessed by those on earth, it can be deduced that one is in the end times. For example, in the Olivet discourse, Jesus Himself warned: "See that no one leads you astray. For many will come in my name, saying, 'I am the Christ,' and they will lead many astray. And you will hear of wars and rumors of wars...Nation will rise against nation, and kingdom against kingdom, and there will be famines and earthquakes in various places...Many will fall away and betray one another and hate one another. And many false prophets will arise and lead many astray. And because lawlessness will be increased, the love of many will grow cold..." (Matthew 24:4-14).

We also read in 2 Timothy 3:1-5 that "in the last days there will come times of difficulty. For people will be lovers of self, lovers of money, proud, arrogant, abusive, disobedient to their parents, ungrateful, unholy, heartless, unappeasable, slanderous, without self-control, brutal, not loving good, treacherous, reckless, swollen with conceit, lovers of pleasure rather than lovers of God, having the appearance of godliness, but denying its power."

We are likewise informed in 1 Timothy 4:1 that "the Spirit expressly says that in later times some will depart from the faith by devoting themselves to deceitful spirits and teachings of demons" (ESV). We see this in the kingdom of the cults.

All of these, then, are "signs of the times" that clue us in to the reality that we are living in the end times.

See *Fig Tree, Parable.*

Sinai Covenant

God's covenant with Israel at Mount Sinai, following Israel's sojourn through the wilderness after being delivered from Egypt, constituted the formal basis of the redemptive relationship between God and the Israelites (Exodus 19:3-25). This covenant was couched in terms of ancient Hittite suzerainty treaties made between a king and his subjects. In such treaties, there would always be a preamble naming the author of the treaty, a historical introduction depicting the relationship between the respective parties, a list of required stipulations explaining the responsibilities of each of the parties, a promise of either blessing or judgment invoked depending on faithfulness or unfaithfulness to the treaty, a solemn oath, and a religious ratification of the treaty. In such treaties, the motivation for obedience to the stipulations was the undeserved favor of the king making the treaty. Out of gratitude, the people were to obey the stipulations.

Such parallels between ancient treaties and God's covenant with Israel show that God communicated to His people in ways they were familiar with. Key parallels between such treaties and the Sinai Covenant are that God gave stipulations to the people explaining their responsibilities (the law, Exodus 20:1-17), and gave a promise of blessing for obeying the law, and a promise of judgment for disobeying the law (see Exodus 19:8; 24:3,7). Sadly, Israel was often disobedient to God's covenant (Exodus 32:1-31; Jeremiah 31:32).

Sleep, Death

Death is often described in the Bible as "sleep," for the body takes on the appearance of sleep. The soul, however, does not sleep. It is fully conscious. The believer's soul in the afterlife is fully awake and active in the presence of God (Revelation 6:9-11; see also 2 Corinthians 5:8; Philippians 1:21-23). The unbeliever's soul is fully conscious in a place of great suffering (Luke 16:19-31).

Smyrna

Smyrna is a city that hosted one of the seven churches mentioned in Revelation 2–3 (see Revelation 2:8-11). Smyrna was located about 35 miles north of Ephesus and was a seaport city, which made it a prosperous commercial center. Because of its business successes, the city became large and wealthy. The city was a center of science and medicine.

It was not easy to live as a Christian in Smyrna, for a large population of Jews as well as a Roman imperial cult was located there. The Roman imperial cult, in particular, brought severe persecution upon the church. Christ admonished the Christians there to be "faithful until death" and they would receive a "crown of life" (Revelation 2:10 NASB). In the second century, the pastor of the church in Smyrna, Polycarp (a pupil of the apostle John), was burned alive for refusing to worship Caesar. This city holds the distinct honor, along with the church in Philadelphia, of not being rebuked by Christ in Revelation 2–3.

Son of Man

Jesus often referred to Himself as the "Son of Man" (for example, Matthew 8:20; 20:18; 24:30). Some have suggested that this term seems to point to Jesus' humanity more than His deity. If He was really the divine Messiah, why did He use the self-description, "Son of Man"?

It is critical to recognize that even if the phrase "Son of Man" is a reference to Jesus' humanity, it is not a denial of His deity. By becoming man, Jesus did not cease being God. The incarnation of Christ did not involve the subtraction of deity, but the addition of humanity. Jesus clearly claimed to be God on many occasions (Matthew 16:16-17; John 8:58; 10:30). But in addition to being divine, He was also human (Philippians 2:6-8). He had two natures conjoined in one person.

Furthermore, Jesus was not denying His deity by referring to Himself as the Son of Man. In fact, the term "Son of Man" is used in contexts of Christ's deity. The Bible says that only God can forgive sins (Isaiah 43:25; Mark 2:7). But as the "Son of Man," Jesus had the power to forgive sins (Mark 2:10). Likewise, Christ will return to earth as the

"Son of Man" in clouds of glory to reign on earth (Matthew 26:63-64). "Son of Man" is clearly a messianic term (see Daniel 7:13).

What is more, when Jesus was asked by the high priest whether He was the "Son of God" (Matthew 26:63), He responded affirmatively, declaring that He was the "Son of Man" who would come in power and great glory (verse 64). This indicated that Jesus Himself used the phrase "Son of Man" in contexts of His deity.

Son of Man, Sign of

In Jesus' Olivet discourse, Jesus speaks about the future Tribulation period: "Immediately after the tribulation of those days the sun will be darkened, and the moon will not give its light, and the stars will fall from heaven, and the powers of the heavens will be shaken. And then the sign of the Son of Man will appear in the sky, and then all the tribes of the earth will mourn, and they will see the Son of Man coming on the clouds of the sky with power and great glory" (Matthew 24:29-30 NASB).

There has been considerable debate among Christian expositors about what specifically the "sign of the Son of Man" will be. Some have suggested that the sign of the cross will be planted in the sky for all to see. Others have suggested that it refers to the lightning that "comes from the east and shines as far as the west" (Matthew 24:27 ESV). Others suggest that perhaps it is the glory of Christ that will be greatly manifest at the second coming. Still others choose not to define the sign, affirming that the main thing is that Christ Himself will be visibly coming. It may be that the Son of Man Himself is the sign (see Daniel 7:13; Acts 1:11; Revelation 19:11–21).

Sorceries

Following the infliction of the sixth trumpet judgment, Revelation 9:20-21 tells us that "the rest of mankind, who were not killed by these plagues, did not repent of the works of their hands nor give up worshiping demons and idols of gold and silver and bronze and stone and wood, which cannot see or hear or walk, nor did they repent of their murders or their sorceries or their sexual immorality or their thefts."

The term "sorceries" here carries the idea of magical arts and the use of potions (see Galatians 5:20; Revelation 18:23; 21:8; 22:15). The Greek word for sorceries, *pharmakeiōn,* is the basis for the English word "pharmacy." This makes sense, for ancient occultists often utilized drugs to bring about altered states of consciousness which are allegedly helpful for spirit contact, séances, and other occultic arts.

Stage-Setting

"Stage-setting" refers to the idea that even though a particular prophecy may not be coming to fulfillment in our present day, the stage is nevertheless being set for the fulfillment of the prophecy in the future. For example, the Ezekiel invasion into Israel—involving Russia, Iran, Turkey, Libya, and other Muslims nations—is not now being fulfilled, but it does appear that the stage is presently being set for this future invasion. After all, these various nations are presently making military alliances with each other, and many are openly claiming they want to destroy Israel.

Stars

See *Cosmic Disturbances.*

Sun

See *Cosmic Disturbances.*

Super-Sign

God's prophetic plan for the future hinges largely on Israel. Many prophecy interpreters believe that the reconstitution of Israel as a nation is a "super-sign" for the end times (see Ezekiel 36–37; Romans 9–11). They say this because so many of the biblical prophecies of the end times relate in some way to Israel, and hence Israel *must* exist in order for these prophecies to come to pass. Put another way, many of these other prophecies do not have meaning *until* and *unless* Israel is a nation. Hence, the year 1948 is extremely significant from a prophetic standpoint, for it was that year that Israel became a nation again.

T

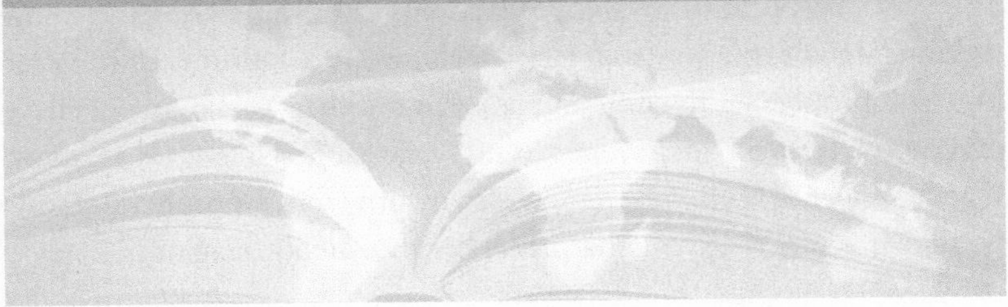

Tartarus

The word *tartarus* (translated "hell") refers to a place of confinement for a certain group of angels who apparently committed an especially heinous sin against God. In classical mythology the term was used to refer to a subterranean abyss to house rebellious gods and spirits. The Greeks thought of Tartarus as a place of punishment lower than Hades.

The sin of these fallen angels may relate to Genesis 6:2-4, where we read of "sons of God" (perhaps fallen angels—Job 1:6; 2:1) engaging in sexual relations with human women. Jude 6 may refer to this same confinement.

Scripture reveals that there is yet another group of angels that are presently confined in the bottomless pit (Luke 8:31; Revelation 9:2). These spirits are apparently so depraved that God disallowed their freedom to roam the earth. According to Revelation 9, however, these depraved fallen angels will be released during the future Tribulation period and afflict any who do not have God's seal on their forehead (verses 3-11).

Temple, Jewish

There were three different temples in Israel's history. David had sought to build the first temple for God, though it was not to happen, for David was a warrior, and this served to disqualify him. It was through his son Solomon that this temple was eventually built (1 Kings 6–7; 2 Chronicles 3–4).

The temple was built in Jerusalem, was rectangular in shape, running east and west, and measured about 87 by 30 feet. It was 43 feet high. The walls of the temple were made of cedar wood, and carved into the wood were cherubim angels, flowers, and palm trees. The walls were overlaid with gold. The floor was made of cypress.

Hiram, the King of Tyre, aided Solomon in the building of the Jerusalem temple. He supplied trees, carpenters, and expert craftsmen for this project (2 Chronicles 2:3). Solomon raised up an Israelite labor force of 30,000 men to assist Hiram in Lebanon's forests (1 Kings 5:13). Solomon also had 70,000 men to carry burdens, and 80,000 gathering stone in the mountains (1 Kings 5:15).

Like the tabernacle, Solomon's temple had a holy place and a Holy of Holies. In the holy place (the main outer room) was the golden incense altar, the table of showbread, and five pairs of lampstands, as well as utensils used for sacrifice. Double doors led into the Holy of Holies, in which was found the Ark of the Covenant. The Ark was between two wooden cherubim angels, each standing ten feet tall. God manifest Himself in the Holy of Holies in a cloud of glory (1 Kings 8:10-11).

This temple—the heart and center of Jewish worship for the kingdom of Judah—was eventually destroyed by Nebuchadnezzar and the Babylonians in 587 B.C.

Following the Babylonian exile, many Jews returned to Jerusalem and constructed a smaller, leaner version of Solomon's temple. King Cyrus of Persia had allowed them to return, along with the Temple vessels Nebuchadnezzar had looted, and gave them permission to rebuild this temple.

The returned exiles started out well in 538 B.C., but soon ran out of steam. The prophets Haggai and Zechariah had to work hard to encourage them, and finally, the second temple was completed in 515 B.C.

However, it was not nearly as magnificent as Solomon's temple (see Ezra 3:12). It had little of its former glory and was a dim reflection of the original. This temple was without the Ark of the Covenant, which had never been recovered, and had only one seven-branched lampstand (Solomon's ten lampstands were never recovered). This temple lasted about 500 years.

Israel's third temple in Jerusalem was built by King Herod the Great. Herod believed this ambitious building program, which he began in 19 B.C., would be a great way to earn favor with the Jews of his time (that is, his subjects), as well as impress the Roman authorities.

Completed in A.D. 64, it was much larger and more resplendent (with more gold) than Solomon's temple. It was an enormous, cream-colored temple that shone exceedingly bright during the day. It measured 490 yards (north to south) by 325 yards (east to west).

This magnificent temple was destroyed in A.D. 70 along with the rest of Jerusalem by Titus and his Roman warriors, a mere six years after the project was completed. How ironic that those Herod sought to impress in Rome were the instigators of the temple's destruction.

Scripture reveals that yet another temple will be built during the future seven-year Tribulation period. There will also be a millennial temple.

See *Jewish Temple, Rebuilding.*

See *Millennial Temple and Sacrifices.*

Ten-Horned Beast

See *Roman Empire, Future.*

Ten-Nation Confederacy

See *Roman Empire, Future.*

Test the Spirits

Many false prophets have come under the influence of demonic spirits and have communicated to followers false prophecies regarding the future. This is common in the kingdom of the cults. It is for this reason that Scripture urges Christians, "Do not believe every spirit, but test the spirits to see whether they are from God, because many false prophets have gone out into the world" (1 John 4:1). A Christian can "test the spirits" by measuring the teachings of the false prophet against the Word of God, which was inspired by the Holy Spirit (2 Timothy 3:16; see also Acts 17:11).

Thessalonians, 1 and 2

The church of Thessalonica was founded around A.D. 50. Thessalonica was a capital of the Roman province of Macedonia in northern Greece. It was a very prosperous port.

Paul had visited Thessalonica for just a short time. He would have stayed longer, but Jewish resistance shortened his stay. The Jews did not like it when Paul won converts to Christianity from among their own. Hence, for Paul's own safety, the Christians in Thessalonica sent him to Berea (Acts 17:1-10).

Understandably, Paul, with a pastor's heart, very much wanted to know the situation of the young church in Thessalonica. Within a year he sent his young associate Timothy to Thessalonica to ascertain the status of the church. Timothy then delivered his report. Soon after, in early A.D. 51, Paul wrote these babes in Christ a letter in order to answer some of the questions they had about spiritual matters.

When Paul was with them, he taught them the key doctrine that Jesus would one day come again. But what about Christians who died *before* Christ came? What became of them? Apparently some of the Thessalonian Christians were very concerned about this, and hence Paul wrote 1 Thessalonians to comfort them in this regard. Paul assured them that the dead in Christ will indeed rise from the dead (1 Thessalonians 4:13-17), and hence there is no need to worry. Paul urged his readers to be constantly ready for the return of Christ.

Paul probably wrote 2 Thessalonians from Corinth during the

summer of A.D. 51. Several months had passed since he had written 1 Thessalonians, and now he wrote 2 Thessalonians to further explain and clarify God's program of events relating to the day of the Lord, and to encourage the brethren to correct the disorders remaining among them.

More specifically, some of the Thessalonian brethren were apparently concerned that Christ had already returned, for some phony epistles had surfaced teaching this idea. Paul responded by teaching that there were certain noticeable events that would precede Christ's second coming, including the emergence of the Antichrist and various social upheavals (2 Thessalonians 2:1-12).

Paul also found it necessary to deal with what should be the proper attitude as one awaits the second coming. On the one hand, Paul clearly taught that believers should be constantly ready for Christ's coming. On the other hand, those people who were so caught up in prophetic excitement that they stopped working and lived off of others were to be rebuked (2 Thessalonians 3:6-13). Balance is necessary.

Throne of David

Based upon the Davidic covenant (2 Samuel 7:11-16; 1 Chronicles 17:10-14), a key element of Israel's final restoration is the reestablishment of the Davidic throne. Related to this, one might recall that when the angel Gabriel appeared to Mary and informed her that she would give birth to the Messiah, the angel spoke in terms of the Davidic covenant. Gabriel specifically informed Mary that Jesus would reign on the throne of His father David. Jesus, who in His humanity was a direct descendant of David (Matthew 1:1), will rule from David's throne during the future 1,000-year millennial kingdom in which there will be perfect righteousness and peace (2 Samuel 7:16; Psalm 89:3-4,28-37). This kingdom will be inaugurated immediately following the second coming of Christ (Revelation 19).

Three words were used by Gabriel in Luke 1:32-33 to describe this future rule of Christ: "throne," "house," and "kingdom." ("The Lord God will give him the *throne* of his father David, and he will reign over the *house* of Jacob forever; his *kingdom* will never end" [emphasis added]). It is significant that each of these words is found in the covenant that God made with David—a covenant in which God promised that someone from David's line would rule forever (2 Samuel 7:16).

Gabriel's words must have brought these Old Testament promises to mind for Mary, who was a devout young Jew. Indeed, Gabriel's message constituted an announcement as clear as was possible to make it that Mary's son would fulfill the promise given to David that one of David's sons would sit on David's throne and rule over David's kingdom. Jesus would come not only to be the *Savior* but also to be the *Sovereign.*

Amillennialists claim that the throne of David promise is not to be taken literally. They spiritualize the promise by saying that it refers to Christ's present spiritual reign over the church. The problem with such a view is that precedent has already been set regarding how to interpret biblical prophecy. All the prophecies in the Old Testament pertaining to the first coming of Christ were fulfilled literally. In just the same way, all the prophecies relating to the second coming of Christ will be fulfilled literally, including Christ reigning on the throne of David (see Isaiah 2:1-4; 9:6-7; 11:1-10; 16:5; 24:23; 32:1-2; 40:1-11; 42:3-4; 52:7-15; Daniel 2:44; 7:27; Micah 4:1-8; 5:2-5; Zechariah 9:9; 14:16-17).

Throne of God

God's throne is the place of His sovereign rule. As Psalm 103:19 puts it, "The LORD has established his throne in the heavens, and his kingdom rules over all" (see also Psalm 9:7; 11:4; 45:6; 93:2). The throne room is described in majestic terms in the book of Revelation:

> Behold, a throne stood in heaven, with one seated on the throne. And he who sat there had the appearance of jasper and carnelian, and around the throne was a rainbow that

> had the appearance of an emerald. Around the throne were twenty-four thrones, and seated on the thrones were twenty-four elders, clothed in white garments, with golden crowns on their heads. From the throne came flashes of lightning, and rumblings and peals of thunder, and before the throne were burning seven torches of fire, which are the seven spirits of God, and before the throne there was as it were a sea of glass, like crystal. And around the throne, on each side of the throne, are four living creatures, full of eyes in front and behind...(Revelation 4:2-6 ESV).

The book of Revelation also reveals that believers will be "before the throne of God, and serve him day and night...and he who sits on the throne will shelter them with his presence" (Revelation 7:15). This is a scene of great intimacy between our sovereign God and His followers.

In chapter 19, the book of Revelation portrays believers in the eternal state as offering worship and praise before the throne of God and Christ. What a wonder it will be.

Thyatira

T

Thyatira was a city that hosted one of the seven churches of Asia Minor mentioned in Revelation 2–3 (see Revelation 2:18-28). This city was located about halfway between Pergamum and Sardis, and had for centuries been under Roman rule. This city hosted a large military detachment whose essential role was to guard Pergamum, 40 miles to the northwest.

The city was a thriving manufacturing and commercial center during New Testament times. The primary industries were wool and dye. Lydia, a seller of cloth dyed purple, was from this city (Acts 16:14). Other trades prominent in the city were pottery and brass-working.

Though Christ commended the church for its love, faith, service, and endurance (Revelation 2:19), He also chastised the church for tolerating the woman Jezebel, a false prophetess who led people in the church into sexual immorality. Jesus promised judgment unless there was immediate repentance (verses 21-23).

Time of Jacob's Trouble

See *Jacob's Trouble, Time of.*

Times of the Gentiles

See *Gentiles, Times of the.*

Transfiguration

When Christ became flesh (John 1:14), the glorious presence of God was fully embodied in Him, for He is the true Shekinah. Indeed, the same Shekinah glory that Moses beheld in the tabernacle (Exodus 40:34-38) and that the priest saw in the temple (1 Kings 8:10-11) was revealed in the person of Jesus Christ on the Mount of Transfiguration.

In the transfiguration, which occurred prior to Jesus' crucifixion, Jesus "pulled back the veil" and allowed His intrinsic glory to shine forth in all of its splendor. According to the three Synoptic Gospels (Matthew, Mark, and Luke), while Jesus was praying, He was "transfigured" before the disciples (Matthew 17:2), and "the appearance of his face changed" (Luke 9:29). "His face shone like the sun," and his clothing was also changed so that they "became as white as the light" (Matthew 17:2), or "as bright as a flash of lightning" (Luke 9:29). His clothing was "dazzling white, whiter than anyone in the world could bleach them" (Mark 9:3). If this magnificent transformation took place at night, as Luke's account suggests (9:32,37), the scene unfolding before the disciples must have been all the more awesome, beyond the capacity of words to describe.

The word "transfigured" (Matthew 17:2) is rich with meaning. The verb, which comes from the Greek word *metamorphoo,* does not refer to a superficial change of outward appearance. Rather, it denotes a transformation of Christ's essential form, proceeding from within. We derive the English word *metamorphosis* from this Greek word. It carries the meaning, "to be changed into another form." The disciples saw Him, at that moment, as He will be when He returns visibly in power and glory at the second coming to establish His kingdom on earth (see Acts 15:14-18; 1 Corinthians 15:20-28; Revelation 1:14-15; 19:15; 20:4-6). The disciples witnessed the outshining of the essential glory that belongs to God alone, and that essential glory belongs to Jesus Christ.

At the transfiguration, the one who had hidden His glory beneath the form of a servant (Philippians 2:6-8) allowed His intrinsic glory to break through the veil of His flesh and shine out until His very clothing kindled to the dazzling brightness of the light. What a magnificent sight it must have been!

Tree of Life

The tree of life is first seen in the Garden of Eden—a tree that bestows continuing life (see Genesis 2:9,17; 3:1-24). Once Adam and Eve sinned against God, death entered the universe, and Cherubim angels were placed by God to guard the tree of life, so that Adam and Eve could no longer partake of it while in a state of sin.

We encounter the tree of life again in the future eternal city of heaven known as the New Jerusalem. Indeed, two fascinating components of the eternal city are the *river of the water of life* and the *tree of life.* According to Revelation 22:2, the New Jerusalem will have "on either side of the river, the tree of life with its twelve kinds of fruit, yielding its fruit each month. The leaves of the tree were for the healing of the nations."

The Greek word for "healing" in Revelation 22:2 is *therapeia,* from which the English word therapeutic is derived, almost directly transliterated from the Greek. Rather than specifically meaning "healing," it should be understood as "health-giving." In other words, the leaves of the tree apparently promote the enjoyment of life and a sense of well-being in the New Jerusalem, and are not for correcting ills which do not exist. There will be only perpetual health in the eternal state.

Tribulation, The

The word *tribulation* literally means "to press" (as grapes), "to press together," "to press hard upon," and refers to times of oppression, affliction, and distress. The Greek word (*thlipsis*) is translated variously as "tribulation," "affliction," "anguish," "persecution," "trouble," and "burden." The word has been used in relation to: 1) Those "hard pressed" by the calamities of war (Matthew 24:21); 2) a woman giving birth to a child (John 16:21); 3) the afflictions of Christ (Colossians 1:24); 4) those "pressed" by poverty and lack (Philippians 4:14); 5) great anxiety and burden of heart (2 Corinthians 2:4); and 5) a period in the end times that will have unparalleled tribulation (Revelation 7:14).

General tribulation is to be distinguished from this period known as the Tribulation in the end times. All Christians may expect a certain amount of general tribulation in their lives. Jesus Himself said to the disciples, "In the world you will have tribulation" (John 16:33). Paul and Barnabas also warned that "through many tribulations we must enter the kingdom of God" (Acts 14:22 NASB).

Such general tribulation is to be distinguished from the Tribulation period of the end times, based on the following facts: 1) Scripture refers to a definite period of time at the end of the age (Matthew 24:29-35); 2) It will be of such severity that no period in history past or future will equal it (Matthew 24:21); 3) It will be shortened for the elect's sake (Matthew 24:22), as no flesh could survive it; 4) It is called the time of Jacob's trouble, for it is a judgment on Messiah-rejecting Israel (Jeremiah 30:7; Daniel 12:1-4); 5) The nations will also be judged for their sin and rejection of Christ during the Tribulation (Isaiah 26:21; Revelation 6:15-17); 6) This Tribulation period is seven years in length

(Daniel 9:24,27); 7) It will be so bad that people will want to hide and even die (Revelation 6:16).

Pretribulationist scholars have often noted that a central problem for posttribulationists is that they must get the church through the Tribulation relatively unscathed. But the only way they can do this is to ignore the plain teachings of the book of Revelation on this subject. After all, this period is characterized by wrath (Zephaniah 1:15,18), judgment (Revelation 14:7), indignation (Isaiah 26:20-21), trial (Revelation 3:10), trouble (Jeremiah 30:7), destruction (Joel 1:15), darkness (Amos 5:18), desolation (Daniel 9:27), overturning (Isaiah 24:1-4), and punishment (Isaiah 24:20-21). Simply put, no passage can be found to alleviate to any degree whatsoever the severity of this time that shall come upon the earth.

Scripture reveals that this Tribulation will come upon the whole world. Revelation 3:10 describes this period as "the hour of trial that is coming on the whole world, to try those who dwell [not merely 'some' who dwell] on the earth" (insert added). Isaiah likewise speaks of this Tribulation: "Behold, the LORD will empty the earth and make it desolate, and he will twist its surface and scatter its inhabitants" (Isaiah 24:1 ESV). Verse 17 continues along the same lines: "Terror and the pit and the snare are upon you, O inhabitant of the earth" (ESV). Obviously, it seems impossible that the church could avoid experiencing tribulation if she indeed goes through the Tribulation period.

Regarding the actual source of the Tribulation, Scripture reveals that this is a time of both divine wrath and satanic wrath—especially divine wrath. We are told that the Tribulation is a "day of the wrath of the LORD" (Zephaniah 1:18 ESV). The earth will experience "the wrath of the Lamb" (Revelation 6:16-17). "The LORD will empty the earth" (Isaiah 24:1), and "the LORD is coming out from his place to punish the inhabitants of the earth for their iniquity" (Isaiah 26:21 ESV). Satan's wrath is evident in Revelation 12:4,13,17.

The actual purpose of the Tribulation is several-fold. First, the Tribulation will bring to conclusion "the times of the Gentiles" (Luke 21:24).

Second, the Tribulation will bring judgment against the Christ-rejecting nations of the world. Third, the Tribulation will prepare for the restoration and the regathering of Israel in the millennial reign of Christ following the second coming. Thus, the purpose of the Tribulation has nothing to do with purging the church or the discipline of believers.

In view of all the above, we can conclude that there are a number of supportive evidences regarding why the church will not go through the Tribulation. For example: 1) The nature of the Tribulation relates to Israel and Gentiles, not the church. 2) No Old Testament passage on the Tribulation mentions the church. 3) No New Testament passage on the Tribulation mentions the church. 4) The church is not appointed to wrath. It is promised salvation from the wrath to come (1 Thessalonians 1:10; 5:9). 5) The church is promised deliverance from the actual period of Tribulation (Revelation 3:10). 6) It is characteristic of God to deliver believers before divine wrath and judgment (for example, Noah and Lot). 7) Pretribulationism does not confuse terms like *believers* (general) with terms like *church* (specific). So the presence of "believers" in the Tribulation does not prove the church is in the Tribulation. These people become believers *during* the Tribulation. 8) Pretribulationism distinguishes between general tribulation and the Tribulation period. 9) Pretribulationism is the only view that uses a consistently literal interpretation of all Old Testament and New Testament passages on the Tribulation. 10) If the church is raptured at the end of the Tribulation, as posttribulationists hold, there will be no mortals left on earth to populate the millennial kingdom in their mortal bodies (see Matthew 25:31-46). 11) At the rapture, the church goes to the Father's house (John 14:3), not back to earth again as posttribulationists hold. 12) Because the first 69 weeks of Daniel were subject to literal fulfillment, the final (seventieth) week will have a similar fulfillment. All 70 weeks of Daniel are totally in reference to Israel and her relation to Gentile powers and the rejection of Israel's Messiah. (There is no reference to the church.)

A Qualification. We should note a minor difference of opinion that some Christians hold on this issue. There are some Christians who call the entire seven-year period the Great Tribulation. However, Scripture indicates that it is the last three-and-one-half years—the second half of the Tribulation—that is properly called the Great Tribulation. After all, the abomination of desolation takes place in the middle of the Tribulation period (Matthew 24:15). It is *after* this event that we are told that "there will be *great tribulation,* such as has not been from the beginning of the world until now, no, and never will be" (verse 21 ESV emphasis added).

Tribulation Saints

Scripture reveals that even though the church will be raptured prior to the Tribulation period (1 Thessalonians 1:10; 4:13-17; 5:9; Revelation 3:10), nevertheless many believers will live during the Tribulation period (see Matthew 25:31-46). Perhaps they become convinced of the truth of Christianity after witnessing millions of Christians supernaturally vanish off the planet at the rapture. (Many Bibles and Christian books will be "left behind" to explain the event.) Or perhaps they become Christians as a result of the ministry of the 144,000 Jewish evangelists introduced in Revelation 7 (who themselves apparently come to faith in Christ after the rapture). It may also be that many become Christians as a result of the miraculous ministry of the two witnesses of Revelation 11, prophets who apparently have the same kinds of powers as Moses and Elijah. The book of Revelation indicates that many people will respond to the gospel of the kingdom during the Tribulation (Revelation 7:9-10).

Trumpet Judgments

Human suffering will steadily escalate throughout the Tribulation period. First are the seal judgments, involving bloodshed, famine, death, economic upheaval, a great earthquake, and cosmic disturbances (Revelation 6). Then come the trumpet judgments, involving hail and fire mixed with blood, the sea turning to blood, water turning bitter, further cosmic disturbances, affliction by demonic scorpions, and the death of a third of humankind (Revelation 8:6–9:21). Then come the increasingly-worse bowl judgments, involving horribly painful sores on human beings, more bodies of water turning to blood, the death of all sea creatures, people being scorched by the sun, rivers drying up, total darkness engulfing the land, a devastating earthquake, widespread destruction, and much more (Revelation 16). Such is the judgment of God on a Christ-rejecting world.

Tubal

Tubal is typically mentioned in association with Meshech as one of the nations that will participate in the end times invasion into Israel (see Ezekiel 38:1-6). Interestingly, in years past popular treatments on Bible prophecy have interpreted Meshech and Tubal (Ezekiel 38:2) to be Moscow and Tobolsk, based primarily on the similarity of the pronunciation of the terms. This is the way C.I. Scofield took it in his popular Scofield Study Bible. In fact, he indicated that all agree on this identification.

Biblically, Meshech and Tubal were the sixth and fifth sons of Japheth, the son of Noah (Genesis 10:2). All things considered, it would seem that Meshech and Tubal—often mentioned together in Scripture—refer to the geographical territory to the south of the Black and Caspian Seas of Ezekiel's day, which is today modern Turkey, though there may be some overlap with some neighboring countries.

It is noteworthy that Meshech and Tubal are identified with the Mushki and Tabal of the Assyrians, and the Moschi and Tibareni of the Greeks. Historically, these groups inhabited the territory that is now in the modern nation of Turkey. This is confirmed by the ancient historian Herodotus.

Twenty-Four Elders

See *Elders, 24.*

Twinkling of an Eye

In 1 Corinthians 15:51-52, the apostle Paul speaks about the rapture: "Behold! I tell you a mystery. We shall not all sleep, but we shall all be changed, in a moment, in the twinkling of an eye, at the last trumpet. For the trumpet will sound, and the dead will be raised imperishable, and we shall be changed" (ESV). The phrase "twinkling of an eye" is Paul's way of demonstrating how brief the "moment" of the rapture will be. The fluttering of an eyelid, the blinking of an eye, is exceedingly fast. Hence, the bodily transformation that living believers will experience at the rapture will be near-instantaneous. One moment they are on earth in mortal bodies, the next moment they meet Christ in the clouds, instantly transformed into their glorified resurrection bodies.

Two Witnesses

During the Tribulation period, God will raise up two mighty witnesses who will testify to the true God with astounding power. In fact, the power of these witnesses bring to mind Elijah (1 Kings 17; Malachi 4:5) and Moses (Exodus 7–11). It is significant that in the Old Testament two witnesses were required to confirm testimony (see Deuteronomy 17:6; 19:15; Matthew 18:16; John 8:17; Hebrews 10:28). In Revelation 11:3-6 we read God's prophetic promise:

> I will grant authority to my two witnesses, and they will prophesy for 1,260 days, clothed in sackcloth. These are the two olive trees and the two lampstands that stand before the Lord of the earth. And if anyone would harm them, fire pours from their mouth and consumes their foes. If anyone would harm them, this is how he is doomed to be killed. They have the power to shut the sky, that no rain may fall during the days of their prophesying, and they have power over the waters to turn them into blood and to strike the earth with every kind of plague, as often as they desire (ESV).

These witnesses will wear clothing made of goat or camel hair, garments that symbolically express mourning—more specifically, mourning over the wretched condition and lack of repentance in the world. The reference to olive trees and lampstands is intended to symbolize the light of spiritual revival. Those who stand against these two witnesses will encounter a fiery response!

Many expositors believe the two witnesses will actually be Moses and Elijah. Among their reasons: 1) The Tribulation is a period in which God deals with the Jews—just like He did in the first 69 weeks of Daniel. Moses and Elijah are unquestionably the two most influential figures in Jewish history. It would thus make good sense that they be on the scene during the Tribulation period. 2) Moses and Elijah appeared on the Mount of Transfiguration with Jesus. This shows their centrality. Hence, it would be appropriate for them to be on the scene during the future Tribulation. 3) The miracles portrayed in Revelation 11 are very similar to those previously performed by Moses and Elijah in Old Testament times. While these reasons are valid, one cannot be dogmatic, and it is entirely possible that the two witnesses will be two entirely new prophets of God.

The time frame of these two witnesses—1,260 days—measures out to precisely three-and-a-half years. It is not clear from Revelation 11 whether this is the first three-and-a-half years of the Tribulation, or the last three-and-a-half years.

It may be best to conclude that the two witnesses do their miraculous work during the first three-and-a-half years, for the Antichrist's execution of them seems to fit best with other events that will transpire in the middle of the Tribulation (such as the Antichrist's exaltation of himself to godhood). Moreover, the resurrection of the two witnesses—after being dead for three days—would make a bigger impact on the world in the middle of the Tribulation than at the end, just prior to the second coming of Christ.

The martyrdom of the two witnesses is described in detail in Revelation 11:8-12:

> When they have finished their testimony, the beast that rises from the bottomless pit will make war on them and conquer them and kill them, and their dead bodies will lie in the street of the great city that symbolically is called Sodom and Egypt, where their Lord was crucified. For three and a half days some from the peoples and tribes and languages and nations will gaze at their dead bodies and refuse to let them be placed in a tomb, and those who dwell on the earth will rejoice over them and make merry and exchange presents, because these two prophets had been a torment to those who dwell on the earth. But after the three and a half days a breath of life from God entered them, and they stood up on their feet, and great fear fell on those who saw them. Then they heard a loud voice from heaven saying to them, "Come up here!" And they went up to heaven in a cloud, and their enemies watched them.

This resurrection will serve as a mighty testimony to the power of God during the Tribulation. How awesome a day this will be.

Typology

A type may be defined as a figure or representation of something to come. More specifically, it is an Old Testament institution, event, person, object, or ceremony which has reality and purpose in biblical history, but which also by divine design foreshadows something yet to be revealed. Types are therefore prophetic in nature, and many of the types we find in the Old Testament speak prophetically of Christ in some way. Bible expositors say there are about fifty important types of Christ—which constitute about half of the recognized total in the entire field of typology.

It is important to distinguish types and prophecies in their respective forms. A *type* prefigures something that is coming in the future, while a *prophecy* verbally delineates the future. One is expressed in events, persons, and acts; the other is couched in words and statements.

Two extremes are to be avoided in the study of typology. There are some interpreters who read too many "types" into the Old Testament. Directly opposite to this group are those who see all alleged types as a case of forced exegesis. Both of these extremes are unbalanced and should be avoided.

Legitimate types in the Old Testament are types not because man has said so but because God is sovereign in the revelatory process.. The reason some Old Testament persons or things foreshadow someone or something in the New Testament is that God planned it that way.

There are many examples of typology that are worthy of note. David is a type of Christ in that he was both a shepherd and a king. As a shepherd, he led and cared for his sheep. As a king, he ruled in power and sovereignty over his people.

Joseph is also a type of Christ, for both Joseph and Christ were born by a special intervention of God (Genesis 30:22-24; Luke 1:35); both were objects of special love by their fathers (Genesis 37:3; Matthew 3:17; John 3:35); both were hated by brethren (Genesis 37:4; John 15:24-25); both were robbed of their robes (Genesis 37:23; Matthew 27:35); both were conspired against (Genesis 37:18,24; Matthew 26:3-4; 27:35-37); both were sold for silver (Genesis 37:28; Matthew 26:14-15); both were condemned though innocent (Genesis 39:11-20; Isaiah 53:9; Matthew 27:19,24); and both were raised from humiliation to glory by the power of God (Genesis 45:16-18; Philippians 2:9-11).

These and dozens of other examples demonstrate that the Old Testament is rich in types pointing to the future person and work of Jesus Christ. In the revelatory process, God in His sovereignty so arranged the outworking of history so that certain individuals, things, events, ceremonies, and institutions foreshadow Christ in some way.

U

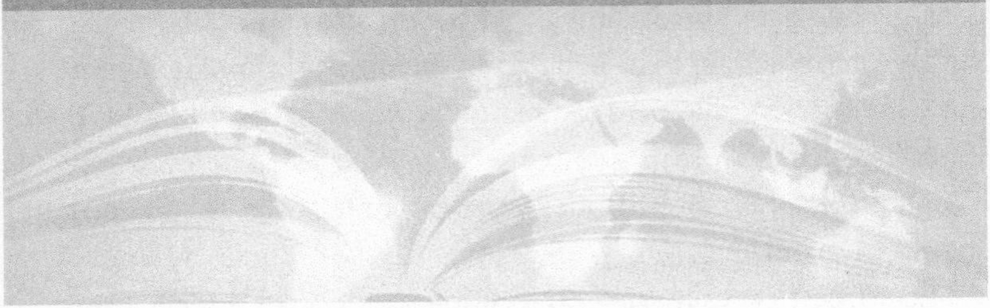

Ultradispensationalism

E.W. Bullinger (1837–1913), a noted Greek scholar of the late nineteenth century, was the father of the ultradispensational movement which placed the origin of the Christian church after Acts 28, contending that the earliest believers were a Jewish church (in an earlier dispensation) in which baptism and the Lord's Supper were practiced. All references to water baptism or the Lord's Supper during those early years, prior to Acts 28, allegedly do not apply to our present dispensation. The true church—the mystery body of Christ (Ephesians 3:3-5)—allegedly did not appear until Paul's prison epistles (such as Ephesians and Colossians), which Bullinger contends have no reference to water baptism or communion.

Bullinger's argumentation is weak. For example, the argument that there are no references to water baptism in any epistle written after the time of Acts 28 is an argument from silence. *Omission does not mean exclusion.* Just because some ordinance is not mentioned in some books does not mean it was not in effect. Even the resurrection of Christ is not mentioned in some books (for example, James, Philemon, 2 John, 3 John, and Jude), but this does not mean that the author of those books did not believe it.

Moreover, many argue that the apostle Paul refers to water baptism in Colossians 2:12, since he refers to baptism as "burial" with Christ which depicts immersion, a mode of water baptism expressed in the New Testament (compare with Romans 6:1-4 and Matthew 3:16-17). Likewise, Ephesians 4:4-5 refers to "one body and one Spirit" (which would be Spirit baptism) and "one Lord, one faith" *before* it mentions "one baptism." (Mention of these items in this order would be the logical sequence for water baptism to be referred to last.)

Further, Bullinger's argument collapses if it can be shown that the church as the "body" of Christ occurs earlier than Acts 28, and some indeed believe there is good evidence that it existed earlier. They point out: 1) The church as Christ's body resulted from the baptism of the Holy Spirit (1 Corinthians 12:13). This baptism of the Holy Spirit first occurred only "days" after Jesus' ascension (Acts 1:5), which was the day of Pentecost (Acts 2). 2) Jesus told Saul that he was persecuting His body in Acts 9:4 where Jesus said: "Saul, Saul, why do you persecute me?" Paul later conceded, "I am the least of the apostles and do not even deserve to be called an apostle, because I persecuted *the church of God*" (1 Corinthians 15:9, emphasis added).

Finally, ultradispensationalism misses the point of Acts 10, where Peter was called to witness to Gentiles, who were baptized into the body of Christ. Also, in Acts 15 the apostles—who are part of the foundation of the church (Ephesians 2:20)—issued a declaration that Gentiles were fellow heirs of the gospel along with the Jews, and this is precisely what the "mystery" of the body of Christ is (see Ephesians 3:6 and Colossians 1:27). The mystery of the body of Christ, then, clearly existed at least as early as Acts 10, which Peter clearly relates to what happened on the day of Pentecost in Acts 2 (compare with Acts 11:15).

United States in Prophecy

See *America in Biblical Prophecy.*

Universalism

Universalism states that sooner or later, all people will be saved. This position holds that the concepts of eternal hell and punishment are inconsistent with a loving God.

The older form of universalism, originating in the second century, taught that salvation would come after a temporary period of punishment. The newer form of universalism declares that all men are now saved, though all do not realize it. Therefore the job of the preacher and the missionary is to tell people they are already saved. Certain passages—John 12:32, Philippians 2:11, and 1 Timothy 2:4—are typically twisted out of context in support of universalism. Such passages, interpreted properly, do not support universalism:

- John 12:32 says that Christ's work on the cross makes possible the salvation of both Jews and Gentiles. Notice, however, that the Lord—in the same passage—warned of judgment of those who reject Christ (verse 48).
- Philippians 2:10-11 assures us that someday all people will acknowledge that Jesus is Lord, but not necessarily as Savior. (Even those in hell will have to acknowledge Christ's lordship.)
- First Timothy 2:4 expresses God's desire that all be saved, but does not promise that all will be. This divine desire is only realized in those who exercise faith in Christ.

The Scriptures consistently categorize people into one of two classes: saved/unsaved, also called believers/unbelievers; and portray the final destiny of every person as being one of two realities: heaven or hell.

- In Matthew 13:30 Jesus in a parable said, "Let both [tares and wheat] grow together until the harvest. At that time I will tell the harvesters: First collect the weeds and tie them in bundles to be burned; then gather the wheat and bring it into my barn" (insert added). Here unbelievers and believers are spoken of as *tares* and *wheat*. Two classes!

- In Matthew 13:49 Jesus said, "This is how it will be at the end of the age. The angels will come and separate the wicked from the righteous." Again, two classes are mentioned—unbelievers and believers spoken of as the *wicked* and the *righteous.*
- In Matthew 25:32 Jesus said that following His second coming, "All the nations will be gathered before him, and he will separate the people one from another as a shepherd separates the sheep from the goats." Here believers and unbelievers are differentiated by the terms *sheep* and *goats.* The sheep will enter into God's kingdom (verse 34) and inherit eternal life (verse 46), while the goats go into eternal punishment (verse 46).

Clearly, then, the Scriptures speak of two classes of people (the saved and the unsaved) and two possible destinies (heaven for the saved, hell for the unsaved). And each respective person ends up in one of these places based upon whether or not he or she has placed saving faith in Christ during his or her time on earth (John 3:16-17; Acts 16:31).

Unthankful

In 2 Timothy 3, the apostle Paul informs young Timothy of the conditions that will prevail in the "last days." Among these conditions is that "people will be lovers of self, lovers of money, proud, arrogant, abusive, disobedient to their parents, ungrateful, [and] unholy" (verse 2). The word translated *ungrateful* here (ESV) is rendered "unthankful" in the King James Version. There is an obvious close relationship that exists among these various vices. Virtue will truly be lacking among many in the end times.

V

Valley of Dry Bones

In Ezekiel 36, God promised Israel, "I will multiply the number of people upon you, even the whole house of Israel. The towns will be inhabited and the ruins rebuilt" (Ezekiel 36:10). God promised, "I will take you out of the nations; I will gather you from all the countries and bring you back into your own land" (36:24). Israel would again be prosperous, for God "will increase the fruit of the trees and the crops of the field, so that you will no longer suffer disgrace among the nations because of famine" (36:30).

Then, in the vision of dry bones in Ezekiel 37, the Lord is miraculously portrayed as bringing the bones back together into a skeleton, and the skeleton becomes wrapped in muscles and tendons and flesh, and God then breathes life into the body. There is no doubt that this chapter in Ezekiel is speaking about Israel, for we read: "Son of man, these bones are the whole house of Israel" (verse 11). Hence, this chapter portrays Israel as becoming a living, breathing nation, brought back from the dead, as it were.

It is in view of this that 1948 is a year to remember. As a backdrop, in A.D. 70, Titus and his Roman warriors trampled on and destroyed

Jerusalem, definitively and quite thoroughly ending Israel as a political entity (see Luke 21:20). Since then, the Jews have been dispersed worldwide for many centuries. In the year 1940, no one could have guessed that within a decade Israel would be a nation again. And yet, it happened. Israel achieved statehood in 1948. Then, in 1967, Israel captured Jerusalem and the West Bank during the Six-Day War, which was precipitated by an Arab invasion. Jews have been returning to their homeland ever since.

What is interesting to observe is that Christian writers living back in the sixteenth and seventeenth centuries were already writing about Jews coming back to the land, centuries before 1948! They wrote in this manner because they believed God's prophecies in Ezekiel would literally come to pass.

Views of Revelation

There are four primary interpretive approaches to studying the book of Revelation:

1. The *preterist* approach holds that the prophecies of Revelation were fulfilled in the first century A.D.—more specifically, in A.D. 70 when Titus and his Roman warriors overran Jerusalem and destroyed the Jewish temple.
2. The *historicist* view holds that the book of Revelation supplies a prophetic overview of the entire panoramic sweep of church history, from the first century to the second coming of Christ.
3. The *futurist* view holds that most of the events described in the book of Revelation will take place in the end times, just prior to the second coming of Jesus Christ.
4. The *idealist* view holds that the book of Revelation is primarily a symbolic description of the ongoing battle between God and the devil, between good and evil. Seen in this light, the book of Revelation gives strength to believers as they suffer through persecution and various injustices.

While these are the four primary views regarding how the book of Revelation should be interpreted, there is also the *eclectic* view, which is a mixed view that combines the features of these four views. The eclectic view says that there is both a present and a future fulfillment of the prophecies contained in the book of Revelation.

Vision

Prophets and apostles received messages from God in various ways, including visions, dreams, and even hearing God's voice (Hebrews 1:1; see also Luke 24:23; Acts 26:19; 2 Corinthians 12:1). Visions are especially characteristic of apocalyptic literature, such as the book of Daniel and the book of Revelation. The term *vision* comes from the Latin word *visio,* which means "to see." Through visions, God's prophets and apostles were enabled to see things normally hidden from human eyes. Such visions often involved a supernatural appearance from God that conveyed some form of revelation. Visions are typically delivered in the first person, as the visionary describes his experience, often by saying "I saw..." Such visions might relate to seeing God on His throne (for example, Isaiah 6:1-5), or some other heavenly reality (see the book of Revelation), or an earthly reality of something present or yet to come (1 Kings 22:17), or something else.

For example, Ezekiel had a vision of dry bones in which God revealed to him that Israel would be restored and reborn as a nation (see Ezekiel 37). In this vision, God illustrated to Ezekiel how he would bring Israel "back from the dead," as it were, and make her a living entity again. Clearly, visions can be a very graphic form of divine revelation.

Voice of the Archangel

We find a description of the rapture in 1 Thessalonians 4:13-17. Verses 16 and 17 tell us that "the Lord himself will descend from heaven with a cry of command, with the voice of an archangel, and with the sound of the trumpet of God. And the dead in Christ will rise first. Then we who are alive, who are left, will be caught up together with them in the clouds to meet the Lord in the air, and so we will always be with the Lord."

There has been some debate among Bible expositors as to what is meant by the phrase, "with the voice of an archangel." Some have suggested that perhaps Jesus will issue the shout with an archangel-like voice. However, it seems more natural to the text to interpret this shout as actually coming from the voice of the archangel himself.

Certainly we know that at the second coming, the Lord Jesus shall be "revealed from heaven *with His mighty angels*" (2 Thessalonians 1:7 ESV, emphasis added). If the angels accompany Christ at the second coming, then surely this includes the archangel Michael. And if the angels accompany Jesus at the second coming, there is no reason to assume that they won't accompany Him at the rapture as well. This especially makes sense in view of the teaching elsewhere that the angels are heavily involved in end-time events (see Revelation 5:11; 7:1-2,11; 8:2,4,6,13; 9:14-15; 10:10; 12:7,9; 14:10; 15:1,6-8; 16:1; 17:1; 21:9,12).

W

War of the Great Day of God

Revelation 16:14 makes reference to the "battle on the great day of God Almighty." This is another way of referring to the campaign of Armageddon, mentioned in verse 16.

The word Armageddon literally means "Mount of Megiddo," and refers to a location about 60 miles north of Jerusalem. This is the location of Barak's battle with the Canaanites (Judges 4) and Gideon's battle with the Midianites (Judges 7). This will be the site for the final horrific battles of humankind just prior to the second coming (Revelation 16:16).

See *Armageddon.*

Weapons, Literal or Figurative

One of the highly debated aspects of the future end-times invasion of a northern military coalition into Israel relates to the fact that the invading force is described as having "horses and horsemen, all of them splendidly attired, a great company with buckler and shield, all of them wielding swords" (Ezekiel 38:4 NASB), and "all of them with shield and helmet" (verse 5 NASB). This seems to be a description of ancient warfare. The question is, then, why are ancient weapons mentioned if this is a prophecy of a yet-future invasion into Israel?

There are two primary interpretive options for understanding this passage: 1) First, it is always possible (albeit strange) that this passage might be literally fulfilled, with armies riding horses and carrying swords. 2) It is possible that Ezekiel was merely using terms familiar to his own day in order to describe modern techno-warfare of which he had virtually no chance of understanding or describing. Both views are considered below.

A literal interpretation. It is always possible (though it would be strange) that this passage might be literally fulfilled, with armies riding horses and carrying swords. There are four possible scenarios that might make sense:

1. One possible scenario is that this largely Muslim invasion into Israel—all but one of the invading nations listed in Ezekiel 38:1-6 is presently Muslim-dominated—might purposely mimic the prophet Muhammad. Recall that Muhammad—the "prophet of the sword"—led an invading force of over 10,000 men on horseback with swords into Mecca in order to overtake the holy city and bring it into submission. Allah in the Quran virtually commands that infidels be dealt with (Sura 2:216; 9:5; 47:4). So, perhaps a Muslim invasion into Israel will seek to fulfill this injunction from Allah in the style and glory of Muhammad. This would be in keeping with the desire of Muslims worldwide to emulate the behavior of Muhammad (Sura 33:21), which emulation is the primary reason for the existence of Muslim tradition—the Hadith (which contains massive records of Muhammad's behavior under various circumstances).

2. Perhaps a more likely scenario is that Israel—a nuclear power—at some point becomes aware of an impending invasion from the Russians and Muslim nations (Ezekiel

38:1-6) through its intelligence agency, the Mossad, one of the best in the world. Israel might therefore detonate one or more nuclear weapons in the atmosphere of these countries, thereby causing an electromagnetic pulse (EMP) that completely fries all electronic components in these countries—including computers, phones, radios, all kinds of communication devices, cars, trucks, tanks, jets, helicopters, guidance systems, radar, and the like. The effects of an EMP attack would be catastrophic:

- Nuclear experts affirm that a single nuclear weapon, delivered by a ballistic missile to an altitude of a few hundred miles over a country, would cause catastrophic damage and/or disruption to all things electrical—including the infrastructures for handling electric power, sensors and protective systems of all kinds, computers, cell phones, telecommunications, radios, guidance systems, radars, cars, boats, airplanes, trains, transportation, banking and finance, emergency services, fuel and energy, and even food and water.
- It is estimated that it could take months to even a year or more to fully restore critical infrastructures after an EMP attack.
- Transportation could easily revert to nineteenth-century options (including the use of horses).
- Starvation and disease could ultimately result following a severe EMP attack.
- Military systems are just as vulnerable to disruption as civilian systems.

Here is the point: If the military hardware of these northern invading nations becomes disrupted, perhaps a "Plan B" attack will be launched using nonelectric transportation—horses! After all, if an army's *trucks* no longer work—if an army's *tanks* no longer work—if an army's *helicopters* no longer work—if an air force's *jets* no longer work—indeed, if *nothing* electronic works—and these various means of transportation will continue not to work for months and maybe even a year or more—then a military invasion on horseback suddenly becomes much more realistic.

3. Some interpreters have suggested that if ancient weapons are used in this invasion, perhaps some kind of disarmament treaty has previously been signed and enforced among the nations. Some claim that primitive weapons, such as those described in Ezekiel, would be easy to manufacture and use, thereby making possible a surprise attack. (This option seems unrealistic.)
4. Other interpreters suggest that the first three-and-a-half years of the Tribulation period may be so catastrophic—so destructive—in certain parts of the world that a reversion to ancient weaponry becomes a necessity.

A metaphorical interpretation. Another interpretive option is that the "swords" and "horses" are simply metaphorical terms chosen by Ezekiel to describe a modern invasion using transportation and weapons for which he had no words. Ezekiel may have been simply speaking in the language of his day to describe an otherwise indescribable invasion. He was communicating in a way that people of his day would have understood. After all, the mention of missiles and tanks would have been utterly meaningless to an audience in Bible times.

Regardless of which approach is used in interpreting the transportation and weapons described by Ezekiel—literal or metaphorical—the basic reality is that Russia will lead a northern military coalition against Israel in the end times (Ezekiel 38:1-6). So large will the invading force be that it will seem utterly unstoppable. But God Himself will annihilate the invaders (39).

Witnesses, Two

See *Two Witnesses.*

Woman of Revelation 12

In Revelation 12:1 we read of "a woman clothed with the sun, with the moon under her feet, and on her head a crown of twelve stars" (ESV). She was said to be "pregnant and was crying out in birth pains and the agony of giving birth" (verse 2 ESV). We are told that a dragon "stood before the woman who was about to give birth, so that when she bore her child he might devour it" (verse 4). Then we read: "She gave birth to a male child, one who is to rule all the nations with a rod of iron, but her child was caught up to God and to his throne, and the woman fled into the wilderness, where she has a place prepared by God, in which she is to be nourished for 1,260 days" (verses 5-6).

In this passage, the woman represents Israel, building on Old Testament imagery in which Israel was viewed as the wife of God (Isaiah 54:5-6; Jeremiah 3:-8; 31:32; Ezekiel 16:32; Hosea 2:16). In keeping with this, the twelve stars represent the twelve tribes of Israel, while the moon may allude to God's covenant relationship with Israel because new moons are associated with covenant worship (1 Chronicles 23:31; 2 Chronicles 2:4; 8:13).

The male child refers to Jesus Christ. The mention of the dragon seeking to devour the child likely alludes to the massacre of male children commanded by Herod (Matthew 2:13-18; Luke 4:28-29). The child was caught up to God in the sense that He ascended into heaven following His resurrection (Acts 1:9; 2:33; Hebrews 1:1-3; 12:2). The child—the divine Messiah—is destined to rule the nations (see Psalm 2:6-9).

Word of God, Title of Jesus

In John 1:1 we read, "In the beginning was the Word, and the Word was with God, and the Word was God." Jesus is clearly identified as the Word of God in this verse. Then, in Revelation 19:13, we read of Jesus at the second coming: "He is clothed in a robe dipped in blood, and the name by which he is called is The Word of God."

Among the most powerful evidences of Christ's deity is John's affirmation that Christ is the divine "Word." The Greek noun for "Word" in John 1:1 is *Logos,* a term that has been the subject of much debate down through the centuries since the time of Christ. Its importance lies in the fact that Christ the Logos is portrayed as a preexistent, eternal Being. Indeed, John even says that the Logos is God. The Logos is also said to be the Creator of the universe, for "all things were made through him, and without him was not any thing made that was made" (John 1:3 ESV).

The concept of "the Word" has a long history beginning in Old Testament times. In the Old Testament, the "Word of God" is portrayed as having an active character and was viewed as an effective agent for accomplishing God's will. For example, God is quoted in Isaiah as asserting: "So shall my word be that goes out from my mouth; it shall not return to me empty, but it shall accomplish that which I purpose, and shall succeed in the thing for which I sent it" (55:11 ESV).

Another aspect of the Jewish understanding of "the Word" is evident in the Jewish Targums—simplified paraphrases of the Old Testament Scriptures. In the Targums, we learn that the Jews, out of reverence for God, sometimes substituted the phrase *the Word of God* in place of the word *God.* The Jews were fearful of breaking the Third Commandment: "You shall not take the name of the LORD your God in vain, for the LORD will not hold him guiltless who takes his name in vain" (Exodus 20:7 ESV). So, for example, where our Bible says, "Then Moses brought the people out of the camp to meet God" (Exodus 19:17), the Targum says that Moses took the people to meet the Word of God."

Around A.D. 25, a Jewish philosopher named Philo developed a concept of the Word (or Logos) that was dualistic in nature. Philo taught that God (who is spirit) is good, but matter is evil. Because matter is evil, a holy God could not have created it. For Him to do so would have been sin. Since matter was not created by God, Philo reasoned, matter must be just as eternal as God. They must have co-existed for all eternity.

So holy is God, Philo said, that God could not even come into contact with the material universe. He would become defiled if He did. Because of this, God has always been completely separate from the physical universe. But Philo suggested that God communicated and interacted with the material universe through a "mediating principle." He called this impersonal intermediary the Logos.

When we come to John's Gospel, we find that John does not adopt either the Old Testament concept or Philo's philosophical concept when he refers to Jesus Christ as the Logos. For John, the "Word" is a divine person who has come into the world to reveal another person (the Father) to the world.

All things considered, it would seem that John chose the term *Word* (or *Logos*) because both Greeks and Jews would be somewhat familiar with the term, but he invested it with an entirely new meaning. He gave it a much higher connotation than it ever had before. Indeed, when John used Logos of Jesus Christ, he did so not with the intention of presenting Christ as a divine principle, but as a living Being who was the source of all life; not as a mere personification (as Philo had suggested in his writings), but as a person who was nothing less than God Himself: "the Word was with God, and the Word was God" (John 1:1).

John's assertion is highly significant in view of his monotheistic background. The belief in monotheism was not an optional doctrine for the Jews. It was a conviction to be clung to and defended with fierce tenacity. John's background was one that recognized with an unshakable certainty the existence of only one true God. It is against this backdrop that John unflinchingly asserted that Christ the Logos is God. It is this divine being who will come again in glory at the second coming (Revelation 19:13).

World Religion

See *Religious System, False.*

World Ruler

See *Antichrist.*
See *Four Beasts of Daniel.*

Wormwood

The term "wormwood" is found in the prophecy in Revelation 8:10-12:

> The third angel sounded, and a great star fell from heaven, burning like a torch, and it fell on a third of the rivers and on the springs of waters. The name of the star is called Wormwood; and a third of the waters became wormwood, and many men died from the waters, because they were made bitter. The fourth angel sounded, and a third of the sun and a third of the moon and a third of the stars were struck, so that a third of them would be darkened and the day would not shine for a third of it, and the night in the same way (NASB).

Many believe this "star" will, in fact, be a case of near-extinction-level "deep impact" of a large meteor or an asteroid striking planet earth. It has the appearance of a "star" because it literally bursts into flames—burning like a torch—as it plummets through earth's atmosphere. It results in turning a third of the waters bitter so that people who drink it die. It may contaminate this large volume of water by the residue from the meteor's disintegration as it races through earth's atmosphere. Or it may be that the meteor plummets into the headwaters from which some of the world's major rivers and underground water sources flow, thereby spreading the poisonous water to many people on earth.

Some scholars have speculated that it may be this "deep impact" that ultimately causes a reduction in sunlight and other celestial bodies. Following this impact, a catastrophic level of dust will be kicked up into the atmosphere, thereby blocking light (see Revelation 8:12).

What is both fascinating and sobering is that today's top scientists are saying that it is not a matter of *if* such a celestial body will strike earth, it is a matter of *when* it will happen. The mathematical probabilities render this a certainty at some point in the future. And when it happens, it will likely involve a significant celestial body striking the earth with a minimum velocity of 130,000 miles per hour. The sad reality is that this event will, in fact, happen during the Tribulation period, and the result will be truly catastrophic. Many will die!

Wrath of God

In the Bible, God's wrath is often manifested as a result of a violation of His holiness. When people engage in sin—especially idolatry—God responds in wrath. The effects of God's wrath are painful, including general affliction (Psalm 88:7), drought (Deuteronomy 11:17), leprosy (Numbers 12:10), pestilence (Ezekiel 14:19), plagues (2 Samuel 24:1), slaughter (Ezekiel 9:8), destruction (Ezekiel 5:15), being delivered to enemies (2 Chronicles 28:9), and exile (2 Kings 23:26-27; Ezekiel 19:12).

During the Tribulation period, God's wrath will be thoroughly made manifest throughout. Scripture pictures the seven seal judgments as a sequence, all displaying God's wrath, and all coming from the same ultimate source—God (Revelation 6; 8; see also Zephaniah 1:15,18; 1 Thessalonians 1:10; Revelation 6:17; 14:7,10; 19:2). This sequence features divine judgments which increase in intensity with each new seal. Both human beings and warfare are seen to be instruments of God's wrath during the first six seals. Even the unsaved who experience this wrath recognize it specifically as the "wrath of the Lamb" (Revelation 6:15-16), who Himself opens each seal that causes each respective judgment (see Revelation 6:1,3,5,7,9,12; 8:1). The wrathful judgments of God then continue in the trumpet judgments (Revelation 8:1–9:21; 11:15-19) and the bowl judgments (16:1-21). *How awful is the wrath of God!*

Wrath of the Lamb

In Revelation 6, we read about the seal judgments that are poured out on humankind. These involve bloodshed, war, famine, death, economic upheaval, a great (and deadly) earthquake, and cosmic disturbances. So bad will the judgments be that those who suffer them hide themselves "in the caves and among the rocks of the mountains. They called to the mountains and rocks, 'Fall on us and hide us from the face of him who is seated on the throne and from the wrath of the Lamb'" (verses 15-16).

This is the first time in the book of Revelation that earth's inhabitants realize that the "Lamb"—Jesus Christ—is a source of their present trouble. Inasmuch as it is the Lamb who unfolds the seal judgments (see Revelation 5), it is clear that earth dwellers are indeed suffering the wrath of the Lamb! *And how awful is that wrath!*

Z

Zechariah

The book of Zechariah was written by the prophet and priest Zechariah between 520 and 518 B.C. His name means "the Lord remembers," which is appropriate because throughout his message is a theme that God will bring blessing to the people because He remembers the covenant He made with Abraham.

Zechariah was born in Babylon in exile, and he and his father, Iddo, were among the first exiles to return to Jerusalem following the exile. Like his contemporary Haggai, Zechariah was a prophet chosen by God to motivate the Jews to finish the task of rebuilding the temple.

The problem was that when the people first returned from exile in 538 B.C., they made a good start in beginning to rebuild the temple, but now apathy had set in and the whole project had stagnated (Ezra 4:4-5). The people were too busy building their own homes to pay much attention to the temple. Zechariah was one of the prophets chosen by God to get the people on their feet again and finish the task.

The people needed encouragement because they had a defeated state of mind. While they were excited to be home again, they were also despondent over the ruination of their city. They were especially despondent over the fact that it was their own unfaithfulness that had brought this ruination. Zechariah, along with Haggai, sought to motivate the people to finish up the temple so worship could begin again.

Instead of seeking to motivate the people by rebuking them, Zechariah's approach was to demonstrate the importance of the temple (Zechariah 1–8). The rebuilding of the temple was important not only because it was the religious center of Jewish life, but also because it represented the presence of the one true God among the Israelites before a watching pagan world. For the temple *not* to be rebuilt might give the impression to pagan nations that the true God was no longer interested in Israel, and no longer paying attention to the covenants He had made with His people.

Of great relevance is the fact that there are key messianic prophecies in the book of Zechariah. For example, Zechariah prophesied that Christ would be betrayed for a mere 30 pieces of silver (11:12-13), that He would be pierced on the cross (12:10), and that He would come again in glory (14:4). As such, Zechariah is an important book for Christological studies in the Old Testament.

Zechariah also sets forth prophecies that will find fulfillment in the end times. For example, in Zechariah 12:10, we read, "I will pour out on the house of David and the inhabitants of Jerusalem a spirit of grace and pleas for mercy, so that, when they look on me, on him whom they have pierced, they shall mourn for him, as one mourns for an only child, and weep bitterly over him, as one weeps over a firstborn" (ESV). This prophecy will be fulfilled near the second coming of Christ, when Israel is in mortal danger due to Armageddon, and—finally recognizing their forefathers' (and their own) error in rejecting Jesus as the Messiah—will plead for Him to come in deliverance. This Jesus will do, and Israel will experience complete restoration in the millennial kingdom that follows.

Zechariah 14:1-5 also prophesies about one of the last battles of Armageddon, which leads up to the second coming of Christ. According to this passage, just when it appears that the nations aligned against Israel are beyond defeat, the Lord Jesus Christ personally and visibly will return at the second coming, and His feet will stand upon the Mount of Olives. It will be a glorious moment. Verse 6 goes on to prophesy about the cosmic disturbances that will accompany Christ's second coming (see also Acts 2:19-20). Verses 16-19 then speak of how God, through Christ, will live among His people during the millennial kingdom.

Zephaniah

The book of Zephaniah was written by a prophet of the same name in about 625 B.C. He was the great-great-grandson of the godly King Hezekiah. His ministry took place during the reign of King Josiah of Judah (640–609 B.C.), and his preaching may have been a factor in some of the reform that took place during Josiah's rule.

Zephaniah's message repeated familiar prophetic themes. God would judge the people for not being faithful to the covenant He had established with them. Instead of living the way He had instructed them, the people picked up the habits of the pagan cultures around them. God would not permit this to continue. Hence, judgment was imminent (Zephaniah 1:2-3; 2:2; 3:6-7). Zephaniah continually hammered home the idea that the day of the Lord was approaching (see 1:7,14-16; 3:8). He affirmed that the fire of God's judgment would have a purifying effect on the nation, melting away their sinful complacency. Yet, he also spoke of the blessing that would eventually come in the person of the Messiah (see 3:14-20).

Zephaniah also sets forth some end-time prophecies. For example, in Zephaniah 3:8, God declares, "Wait for me...for the day when I rise up to seize the prey. For my decision is to gather nations, to assemble kingdoms, to pour out upon them my indignation, all my burning anger; for in the fire of my jealousy all the earth shall be consumed" (ESV). This prophecy will be fulfilled in the future seven-year Tribulation period, culminating at Armageddon (Revelation 16:14-15). Then, following the second coming of Christ will be the judgment of the nations (Joel 3:2; Matthew 25:31-46).

Zephaniah 3:9-20 then prophesies regarding Christ's millennial kingdom, over which He will rule for 1,000 years. In this kingdom there will be pure worship (verse 9), a regathered and purified Jewish nation (verses 10-13), the divine Messiah (Christ) personally reigning (verse 15), a sense of security for all (verse 16), and Israel being restored to her land (verse 20).

Bibliography

Ankerberg, John, and Dillon Burroughs. *Middle East Meltdown.* Eugene: Harvest House, 2007.

Harrison, Everett, ed. *Baker's Dictionary of Theology.* Grand Rapids: Baker Books, 1960.

Berkhof, Louis. *Manual of Christian Doctrine.* Grand Rapids: Eerdmans, 1983.

Berkhof, Louis. *Systematic Theology.* Grand Rapids: Eerdmans, 1977.

Block, Daniel. *The Book of Ezekiel: Chapters 25–48.* Grand Rapids: Eerdmans, 1998.

Buswell, James. *A Systematic Theology of the Christian Religion.* Grand Rapids: Zondervan, 1979.

Demar, Gary. *End Times Fiction.* Nashville: Thomas Nelson, 2001.

Erickson, Millard. *Christian Theology.* Grand Rapids: Baker, 1985.

Feinberg, Charles. *The Prophecy of Ezekiel.* Eugene: Wipf and Stock, 2003.

Fruchtenbaum, Arnold. *The Footsteps of the Messiah.* San Antonio: Ariel, 2004.

Geisler, N. L. and William Nix. *General Introduction to the Bible.* Chicago: Moody, 1986.

Geisler, Norman. *Systematic Theology: Church/Last Things,* vol. 4. Minneapolis: Bethany House, 2005.

Geisler, Norman. *Systematic Theology: Introduction and Bible,* vol. 1. Minneapolis: Bethany House, 2005.

Geisler, Norman. *Systematic Theology: Sin and Salvation,* vol. 3 Minneapolis: Bethany House, 2004.

Hays, J. Daniel, J. Scott Duvall, and C. Marvin Pate. *Dictionary of Biblical Prophecy and End Times.* Grand Rapids: Zondervan, 2007.

Hitchcock, Mark. *Bible Prophecy.* Wheaton: Tyndale House, 1999.

________. Hitchcock, Mark. *Iran: The Coming Crisis.* Sisters: Multnomah, 2006.

________. Hitchcock, Mark. *Is America in Bible Prophecy?* Sisters: Multnomah, 2002.

________. Hitchcock, Mark. *The Coming Islamic Invasion of Israel.* Sisters: Multnomah, 2002.

________. Hitchcock, Mark. *The Second Coming of Babylon.* Sisters: Multnomah, 2003.

Hodge, Charles. *Systematic Theology.* Grand Rapids: Eerdmans, 1952.

Hoyt, Herman. *The End Times.* Chicago: Moody, 1969.

Ice, Thomas, and Randall Price. *Ready to Rebuild: The Imminent Plan to Rebuild the Last Days Temple.* Eugene: Harvest House, 1992.

Ice, Thomas, and Timothy Demy. *Prophecy Watch.* Eugene: Harvest House, 1998.

________. *When the Trumpet Sounds.* Eugene: Harvest House, 1995.

Ladd, George Eldon. *I Believe in the Resurrection of Jesus.* Grand Rapids: Eerdmans, 1975.

LaHaye, Tim. *The Beginning of the End.* Wheaton: Tyndale, 1991.

________. *The Coming Peace in the Middle East.* Grand Rapids: Zondervan, 1984.

LaHaye, Tim, and Jerry Jenkins. *Are We Living in the End Times?* Wheaton: Tyndale, 1999.

LaHaye, Tim and Ed Hindson, eds., *The Popular Bible Prophecy Commentary,* Eugene: Harvest House, 2006.

________. *The Popular Encyclopedia of Bible Prophecy,* Eugene: Harvest House, 2004.

LaHaye, Tim, and Thomas Ice. *Charting the End Times.* Eugene: Harvest House, 2001.

McDowell, Josh. *Evidence That Demands a Verdict.* San Bernardino: Campus Crusade for Christ, 1972.

Pentecost, J. Dwight. *Things to Come.* Grand Rapids: Zondervan, 1964.

Price, Randall. *Fast Facts on the Middle East Conflict.* Eugene: Harvest House, 2003.

________. *Unholy War.* Eugene: Harvest House, 2001.

Prophecy Study Bible, ed. Tim LaHaye. AMG, 2001.

Rhodes, Ron. *Answering the Objections of Atheists, Agnostics, and Skeptics.* Eugene: Harvest House, 2006.

________. *Christ Before the Manger: The Life and Times of the Preincarnate Christ.* Grand Rapids: Baker, 1992.

________. *Christianity According to the Bible.* Eugene: Harvest House, 2006.

Rosenberg, Joel. *Epicenter: Why Current Rumblings in the Middle East Will Change Your Future.* Wheaton: Tyndale, 2006.

Ruthven, Jon Mark. *The Prophecy That Is Shaping History: New Research on Ezekiel's Vision of the End.* Fairfax: Xulon, 2003.

Ryrie, Charles. *Basic Theology.* Wheaton: Victor, 1986.

________. *Dispensationalism Today.* Chicago: Moody, 1965.

Walvoord, John F. *End Times.* Nashville: Word, 1998.

________. *The Millennial Kingdom.* Grand Rapids: Zondervan, 1975.

________. *The Prophecy Knowledge Handbook.* Wheaton: Victor, 1990.

________. *The Return of the Lord.* Grand Rapids: Zondervan, 1979.

Walvoord, John F. *Jesus Christ Our Lord.* Chicago: Moody, 1980.

Walvoord, John F., and John E. Walvoord. *Armageddon, Oil, and the Middle East Crisis.* Grand Rapids: Zondervan, 1975.

Yamauchi, Edwin. *Foes from the Northern Frontier: Invading Hordes from the Russian Steppes.* Eugene: Wipf and Stock, 1982.

Other Books by Ron Rhodes

Almost 2,700 years ago, the prophet Ezekiel detailed a massive end-times attack against Israel. The coalition he describes is still making headlines today. Bible scholar Ron Rhodes analyzes current events in the light of biblical prophecy and empowers you to "interpret the signs of the times" (Matthew 16:3).

This up-to-date assessment of the situation in the Middle East reveals vital information about…

- financial and political ties between the group of nations north of Israel
- Muslim leaders' growing antagonism toward Israel and the United States
- Iran's development of nuclear weapons and the threat to global security
- globalization and its role in setting the stage for a cataclysmic war

You will grow in your confidence in God, for to Him, "the nations are like a drop in a bucket" (Isaiah 40:15).

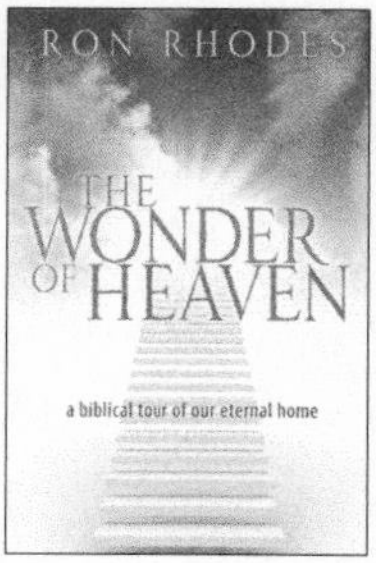

Increasing economic and cultural instability is leading many people to wonder more and more about existence beyond death. Many sources—some trustworthy, some not—are offering opinion, conjecture, and comforting words.

Noted Bible teacher Ron Rhodes, bestselling author of *Angels Among Us,* goes to the Scriptures, God's gift to help us live on earth in a way that prepares us for heaven. He tackles the important questions:

- What is the moment-of-death transition actually like?
- In what state will believers exist? Will they know loved ones?
- What will God's people do in eternity? What will it be like to live with God forever?

The Wonder of Heaven punctures the notion of a harp-strumming, do-nothing eternity. After glimpsing your home with God—and with people as God meant them to be—you, as a Christian, will be filled with an anticipation that will make your life brighter, stronger, and more effective today.

Includes some material from the book *Heaven: The Undiscovered Country*

Innovative. Comprehensive. Easy to use. *Find It Fast in the Bible* is a quick reference that lives up to its name! This time-saving guide to Scripture includes the key concept in each Scripture referenced. Readers don't have to look up ten Scriptures before they discover the one they want! They'll find it in seconds with this friendly format…

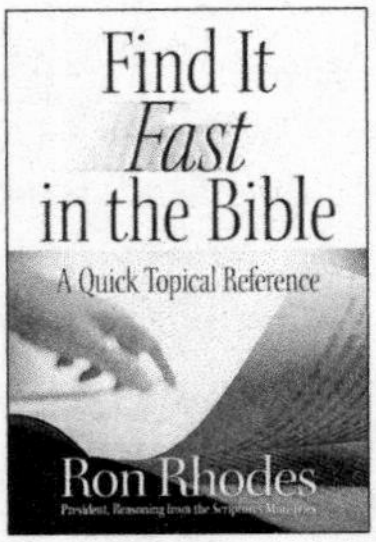

Adoption into God's Family

- By faith in Christ—*Galatians 3:26.*
- Father allows us into His family—*1 John 3:1,2.*
- Gentiles in God's family too—*Ephesians 2:19.*
- Jesus firstborn of many brothers—*Romans 8:29.*
- Jews and Gentiles heirs together—*Ephesians 3:6.*
- Lord disciplines us as His children—*Hebrews 12:6-9.*

Now sized smaller than the popular trade paper edition (more than 80,000 copies sold), this compact guide can be especially useful to the on-the-go, busy reader who doesn't want to search through exhaustive, clunky reference books.